Afro-Asian Conflicts

Changing Contours, Costs and Consequences

Afro-Asian Conflicts

Changing Contours, Costs and Consequences

Edited by

Seema Shekhawat
Debidatta Aurobinda Mahapatra

New Century Publications
New Delhi, India

NEW CENTURY PUBLICATIONS
4800/24, Bharat Ram Road,
Ansari Road, Daryaganj,
New Delhi -110 002 (India)

Tel.: 011 – 2324 7798, 4358 7398, 6539 6605
Fax: 011 – 4101 7798
E-mail: indiatax@vsnl.com
www.newcenturypublications.com

Editorial office:
34, Gujranwala Town, Part-2,
Delhi - 110 009

Tel.: 27247805, 27464774

First Published – **August 2008**

ISBN: 978-81-7708-183-1

Published by New Century Publications and printed at Salasar Imaging Systems, New Delhi

Designs: Patch Creative Unit, New Delhi

PRINTED IN INDIA

THE BOOK

The issues of conflict and peace are of immense relevance in the post-cold war scenario, which has witnessed an unprecedented rise in violent conflicts locally with global ramifications. Whether it is Asia or Africa or other continents, the conflicts have been protracted with horrendous consequences. This volume looks at some of the conflicts in Asia and Africa, commonly referred to as the third world, and their political and humanitarian dimensions. It aims at exploring causes and changing contours of these conflicts with focus on costs and consequences. By emphasizing on these twin aspects, this volume brings into forefront victimization of common people caught in conflict situations.

The subject of conflict being one of the focal areas in international politics, the book would be of interest to a vast readership globally. It would be helpful to researchers, international, governmental as well as non-governmental organizations and policy makers dealing with issues related to conflict, peace, displacement and human rights.

THE EDITORS

Seema Shekhawat (M.A. Gold Medallist) received her Ph.D. in Political Science from the University of Jammu, J&K, India. She has conducted extensive research on issues of human rights, conflict, displacement and gender. Her published works include *Conflict and Displacement in Jammu and Kashmir: The Gender Dimension* (Jammu: Saksham Books International, 2006). Currently, she is associated with Centre for African Studies, University of Mumbai, Mumbai, India.

Debidatta Aurobinda Mahapatra received his Ph.D. from the School of International Studies, Jawaharlal Nehru University (JNU), New Delhi, India. He has conducted extensive research on issues related to conflict and peace with special focus on Kashmir and Chechnya. His published works include, *India-Russia Partnership: Kashmir, Chechnya and Issues of Convergence* (New Delhi: New Century Publications, 2006). Currently, he is associated with Centre for Central Eurasian Studies, University of Mumbai, Mumbai, India.

The joint works of the editors include *Conflict in Kashmir and Chechnya: Political and Humanitarian Dimensions* (New Delhi: Lancer Books, 2007) and *Kashmir Across LOC* (New Delhi: Gyan Books, 2008). Their other published research works include reports on the *Kargil Displaced* funded by Internal Displacement and Monitoring Centre (IDMC), Geneva. They have also published extensively, individually as well as jointly, on the conflict-related issues in national as well as international journals, magazines and newspapers. Dr. Shekhawat and Dr. Mahapatra were also editors of *Across LOC,* quarterly newsletter published by University of Jammu, from January 2005 to May 2007.

PREFACE

Though conflict is a global phenomenon it appears more prominent in developing countries, especially in those which have passed through a period of transition and experienced colonisation. In fact, in some of the developing countries conflict-related expenditures claim significant portion of national budget. Asia and Africa are two of the most violent-prone continents in the world. The countries of these two continents, referred to as the third world, were mostly colonies in the past. The birth ordeals of these countries from subordinated political entities to independence have never been smooth. Many of these countries, having heterogonous societies afflicted with complex array of problems, have passed or have been passing through a period of transition from feudalistic and traditional pattern of governance to modern democratic system of governance. Many of the ongoing conflicts in these two continents, thus, have their roots in their colonial past. Their independence has not ended all the problems inherited from the colonial past or otherwise.

The issues of conflict and peace are of immense relevance in the post-cold war order. Though a third world war picture is not yet portrayed, it is true that there is an unprecedented rise in the conflicts locally with global ramifications. Whether it is Asia or Africa, the conflicts have been protracted with horrendous consequences. This volume looks at some of the conflicts in both the continents and their political and humanitarian dimensions. It aims at exploring causes and changing contours of the conflicts with focus on costs and consequences. The humanitarian costs of conflict include loss of lives, displacement, destitution, degradation of women, children and elderly, psychological disorders etc. The economic costs include not only destruction of private and public properties but also dismal prospects of development of the region for decades.

Besides two theoretical chapters and a chapter on Northern Ireland as peace model, the book has eleven chapters, each dealing with a particular conflict. There are six chapters on conflicts in Asia, i.e. Nepal, Sri Lanka, Balochistan, Kashmir, Cambodia and Philippines and five on conflicts in Africa, i.e. Kenya, Rwanda, Sierra Leone, Democratic Republic of Congo and Darfur.

It can be mentioned here that all the conflicts, which the book has undertaken for study are not same in nature and scope. Also, while some of these conflicts have almost been resolved, some are in the process of resolution and some others continue to flare up. However, the costs and consequences of all these conflicts are huge, which the book brings into focus. By emphasising on the twin aspects of costs and consequences of these conflicts, this volume aims at bringing into forefront the victimisation of civilians caught in conflict situations. In violent conflicts, it is the common people who suffer in various ways starting from loss of lives to forced displacement, from rights violation to post-settlement ordeals. The chapters focus on these inter-connected themes after providing a brief description of the conflict. The chapters also analyse attempts at peace and their sustainability.

Editing a volume covering some of the major conflicts in Asia and Africa and looking at them from the prism of the costs and consequences appears to the editors a realistic as well as a moral imperative. Our interactions with fellow academicians, researchers, students and policy makers motivated us to bring out this volume in a humble effort to make aware individuals across the globe the futility of violent conflicts. Notwithstanding a rich collection of literature spreading across various journals and books, the editors feel there is scant literature available on the conflicts and their costs in developing societies in a single volume. This edited volume, with contributions from experts who belong to the conflict areas or who have conducted extensive research there, would be a definite contribution to the literature on conflicts.

We are thankful to contributors to this volume for their keen interest in making this book see light of the day. Special thanks are due to Evelin G. Lindner of Human Dignity and Humiliation Studies and Emma Leslie of Action Asia, Pnom Penh for encouragement and for connecting us with some of the contributors. Thanks are also due to Neil Jarman, Institute for Conflict Research, Belfast. We thank our family members and friends for their encouragement and moral support. Thanks are also due to Sandeep Sury of New Century Publications, New Delhi for bringing out the book within the stipulated time period.

Editors
Mumbai

CONTRIBUTORS

Aasim Sajjad Akhtar holds a PhD in political economy from the School of Oriental and African Studies, University of London. Dr. Akhtar has been teaching at the Lahore University of Management Sciences since 2003, and was previously associated with the Sustainable Development Policy Institute (SDPI), Islamabad.

Evelin G. Lindner (Dr psychol, Dr med) is the Founding Director and President of Human Dignity and Humiliation Studies. She is associated with Columbia University Conflict Resolution Network, New York; Department of Psychology, University of Oslo, Norway and the Maison des Sciences de l'Homme, Paris.

Jean-Damascène Gasanabo, PhD in Education from the University of Geneva (2004) is Head of Support for Communication, Research and Special Projects at Geneva Call, an international humanitarian organization. He has also worked with UNESCO in Paris as Programme Specialist in Education Sector (2005-2006) and is the author of various articles reflecting on history textbooks, exclusive identities and the genocide in Rwanda.

Kennedy Agade Mkutu is a Senior Lecturer in Public Administration/International relations and security studies in Mzumbe University, Dar es saalam, Tanzania. Dr. Mkutu is also a frequent lecturer in peace-building and conflict transformation at MS-TCDC in Arusha. MS-TCDC is a Training Centre for Development Cooperation in Eastern and Southern Africa.

Manish Thapa is Executive Director of Asian Study Centre for Political and Conflict Transformation (ASPECT) and Regional Coordinator of South Asian

Regional Cooperation Academic Network, a joint project between McGill-University of Montreal Joint Research Group in International Security and ASPECT.

Mneesha Gellman is a PhD student in the Northwestern University, USA. She holds an MA in International Studies from the University of Queensland, Australia, where she was a Rotary World Peace Fellow. Mneesha worked as a consultant to the Khmer Institute of Democracy in Phnom Penh, Cambodia in 2006-2007. Her interests include insider-outsider ontologies in post-conflict reconstruction, the hegemonies of (neo) liberal peace-building, and food politics.

Neil Jarman is Director of the Institute for Conflict Research, Belfast, Northern Ireland. He was an adviser to the Secretary of State for Northern Ireland during the disputes over parades in the 1990s, and a specialist adviser to the Northern Ireland Affairs Committee for their inquiry into hate crime (2004-2005). Dr. Jarman is chair of the panel on freedom of assembly at the Office of Democratic Institutions and Human Rights, part of the Organization for Security and Co-operation in Europe, based in Warsaw, Poland.

Nirmanusan Balasundaram, a recipient of 'Ambassador for Peace' award by Universal Peace Federation, Germany (2007), is currently associated with Berghof Foundation for Conflict Studies, Sri Lanka office. He is associated with People's Action for Free and Fair Elections (PAFFREL). He is also a freelance journalist and is Vice Secretary of Sri Lanka Tamil Media Alliance.

Ofelia Durante is the Director of the Ateneo de Zamboanga University Research Center. She is also a Visiting Professor of the Graduate Schools of Ateneo de Davao, Ateneo de Zamboanga University and Notre

Dame University, Cotabato. Earlier Dr. Durante was Vice President of Notre Dame University, Mindanao, Philippines.

Shailender Shekhawat holds Masters in Business Administration and is currently working as a human rights activist.

Toh Swee-Hin is Director of the Multi-Faith Centre of Griffith University, Australia. He is also a Senior Fellow of the United Nations mandated University for Peace, Costa Rica and Convenor of the Peace Education Commission (2006-2008) of the International Peace Research Association. Prof Toh is a Laureate, UNESCO Prize in Peace Education (2000).

Virginia F. Cawagas is a Senior Fellow and Visiting Professor at the UN mandated University for Peace, Costa Rica. Dr. Cawagas is also an Adjunct Associate Professor of the School of Education and Professional Studies, Griffith University, Australia and Educational Policy Studies, University of Alberta, Canada.

Zinurine Alghali, is Programme Officer at the African Centre for the Constructive Resolution of Disputes in South Africa. He is a founding member of the Mass Communication Student Association of the University of Sierra Leone, Fourah Bay College Campus, Hope for the Vulnerable and the Youth and Child Advocacy Network and a Member of the 50/50 (Gender Parity) Group of Sierra Leone.

CONTENTS

The Book v
The Editors vi
Preface vii
Contributors x

Part I: Theoretical Framework

1. Conflicts, Costs and the Afro-Asian Context 3
Seema Shekhawat and
Debidatta Aurobinda Mahapatra

2. Futility of Armed Conflict: The Role of Dignity and Humiliation 18
Evelin G. Lindner

3. Long War and Long Peace in Northern Ireland 35
Neil Jarman

Part II: The Asian Context

4. Challenges of Ethno-Nationalism in Balochistan 63
Aasim Sajjad Akhtar

5. Maoist Insurgency in Nepal: Context, Cost and Consequences 78
Manish Thapa

6. Justice or Reconciliation?: Prospects and Problems of Peace-building in Cambodia 101
Mneesha Gellman

7. Causes and Consequences of Ethno-Political Conflict in Sri Lanka 128
Nirmanusan Balasundaram

8. Kashmir Conflict: Causes, Costs and Prospects of Peace 147
Debidatta Aurobinda Mahapatra and Shailender Shekhawat

9. Transcending Conflicts: Challenges and Hopes for Peace in the Philippines 164
Virginia F. Cawagas, Toh Swee-Hin and Ofelia Durante

Part III: The African Context

10. Rwandan Genocide: Sociological, Economic and Psychological Consequences 193
Jean-Damascène Gasanabo

11. Congo in Crisis: Violent Conflict and its Consequences 217
Seema Shekhawat

12. Kenya in Crisis: Causes and Consequences of the Post-December 2007 Election Conflict 235
Kennedy Agade Mkutu

13. Sierra Leone Conflict: Liberation or Incarceration? 252
Zinurine Alghali

14. Darfur Conflict: Costs and Politics 272
Seema Shekhawat

Index 291

Part I: Theoretical Framework

1

Conflicts, Costs and the Afro-Asian Context

Seema Shekhawat and
Debidatta Aurobinda Mahapatra

Though in the modern society conflict study assumes newer dimensions taking into account the scarcity of resources, the diversity of perceptions and the inventions of science and technology, the conflict is pervasive from the ancient times. In modern times, the patterns of conflict have changed, contestants are different and objectives vary from the past. Broadly speaking, conflicts are neither inherently good nor bad, but simply facts of life. However, when the contest for incompatible goals take a violent shape the situation becomes critical with short term and long term implications. Though the causes of conflicts may vary from case to case the costs and consequences are largely common with local, national, regional and global ramifications. This volume compiles essays on some of the violent conflicts in Asia and Africa, with the objective of studying their causes, changing contours and costs and consequences from a humanitarian perspective.

The Modern Conflicts

The term 'conflict' has been used loosely in the recent years to include various kinds of situations. Hence, it becomes important to elaborate the term conflict and its usage. Broadly, conflict is understood as the pursuit of incompatible goals by different people or groups. These competing goals can range from contradictory needs within family to competition over scarce resources between members of a community or between neighbouring countries, to opposing factions seeking political or economic control. According to Lewis A. Coser, the objective of the individuals or groups engaged in conflict is to neutralize, injure or eliminate their rivals so that they can enjoy the scarce resources, the status symbols, and power bases. [1]

When conflict becomes violent and includes weapons, the term usually used is armed conflict. Armed conflict is different from warfare. Unlike the later, the former is an undeclared war wherein, in contrast to the prescribed rules of The Hague convention of 1907, neither a formal declaration is made nor an ultimatum is given to the neutral states. Thus, armed conflict is a narrow category of the general term conflict denoting a situation where one or both sides resort to the use of force. Modern day armed conflicts are defined as 'a prolonged combat between the military forces of two or more governments or between the military forces of one government and at least one organized armed group resulting in, as a minimum, thousand battle-related deaths.' The Uppasala Conflict Data Project defines a major armed conflict as a "contested incompatibility that concerns government and/ or territory over which the use of armed force between the military forces of two parties, of which at least one is the government of a state, has resulted in at least 1000 battle-related deaths in any single year." [2] Thus, major conflicts are 'the ones in which more than a thousand people have died, involve more than two parties, and/or have the near-term potential to turn into a multi-national regional conflict.'

The modern conflicts are far too complex in nature. Most of the conflicts in the modern era are intrastate rather than interstate, meaning while earlier conflicts were waged between sovereign states the recent conflicts are fought within state boundaries. Thus, there is gradual disappearance of inter-state or international conflicts. The United Nations Development Programme (UNDP) reported conflicts within states outnumbered conflicts between states. To quote Skelsbaek and

Smith, "From the beginning of 1990 until the end of 1999, the world saw 118 armed conflicts... Few of these wars have been open clashes between two sovereign states. Most have been civil wars, many of them internationalised through the involvement of outside powers....These are long, slow conflicts, often confined to one region of a country." [3] As per estimates, since 1990, about 220,000 people died in wars between states compared to nearly 3.6 million within states. [4]

There are divergent factors that contribute to the emergence of conflict. Most of these conflicts are fuelled by racial, ethnic, religious or ideological factors. Inequality and discrimination, whether actual or perceived, is also a major factor in this context. The failure of the state to provide equal rights and opportunities for growth may generate a conflict situation. For instance, in India the past decade has witnessed rapid growth of the Maoist movement, which is violent and extremist in its ideology. Based on radical ideology, this Maoist group has made a corridor of influence starting from Nepal to Indian state of Tamil Nadu on the coast of the Bay of Bengal, engulfing many of the poor Indian states. Their popularity among poor people is driven by their assurance of a better future under a new Maoist dispensation. The state's apparent weakness to secure its borders, check lawlessness and provide justice to the poor, hence, is a major contributing factor to a violent conflict.

The resilience and strength of institutions in a state also determine the nature and scope of conflict. In a democracy, where the institutions are strong enough to counter anti-social and anti-state activities the potential for violent conflict is less. In a democracy the popular demands as well as dissatisfactions are channeled through well functioning civil society groups, media, political parties and legislative mechanisms, thus reducing the scope to express the dissatisfactions and disagreements in anti-democratic manner. Democracy does not discourage competition or conflicts; rather it encourages these natural human qualities in a commonly agreed framework of fair play and justice. In a democracy, political inclusion and effective participation guarantee that groups with competing interests can engage in a political search for solutions. Equality before law and equal protection of law are two strong principles of democracy which not only encourages healthy competition and equitable distribution of goods, but also discourages the misuse of power. The advocates of Democratic Peace argue democracies seldom go to war. Weak institutions fail to provide public goods, and this failure fosters violence.

Besides the state weakness and inequality factor, economic disparity can play a major spur in violent conflict. It is true there are other factors like religion, territorial ambitions, ethnicity etc. that can lead to conflict generation, but poverty can further aid the process of alienation from the mainstream polity, thus further fuelling the violent conflict. Research shows good political institutions, ethnic and religious homogeneity, or high military spending are insufficient to defend against large-scale violence in the absence of economic development. [5] The greed of dictators, armed groups and militias and vested interests too can contribute to violent conflict. For instance, Charles Taylor, the former president of Liberia, was estimated to have made more than $400 million per year from his country's civil war between 1992 and 1996, [6] thus providing further grounds for poverty at mass level, hence further scope for conflict. Similarly, multiple parties involved in the Democratic Republic of Congo (DRC) conflict are estimated to have made millions of dollars by exploiting the natural resources of the trouble-torn country.

Costs of Conflict

It is difficult to have exact estimation of costs of conflict. So far, there has not been any exact methodology for this purpose due to obvious reasons. Conflicts are not unilinear throughout the world as the causes and consequences differ from case to case. The geographic setting, socio-cultural milieu, and the popular aspirations and ways to respond to differing situations- all make it difficult to have exact estimation of costs of conflict. Hence, costs and consequences can not be generalized as they are specific to different situations.

Modern day conflicts have ended any distinction between combatants and civilians as targets of war. As Skelsbaek and Smith argues, "They are no longer...part of the 'collateral damage,' consigned to the margins as the perhaps regrettable and probably unintended but unfortunately inevitable causalities of military exigencies... in many wars, the civilians are the targets." Thus, the stereotype of war as fought among soldiers in the battlefield has changed and now-a-days they take place amidst the civilian populations. Non-combatants, therefore, become the victim of the conflicts not necessarily accidentally but also many times as intended targets. In many of modern armed conflicts, civilian casualty is not simply a by-product of war but the consequence of the deliberate targeting of non-combatants. [7] Consequently, there is increasing toll of civilians. As per an estimate, civilian fatalities increased from 5 per cent at the turn of the century to 15 per cent during First World War. It increased to 65 per cent by the end of Second World War and to more than 90 per cent during 1990. [8]

Another very important cost of conflict is uprooting of people from their homes. Worldwide conflicts and repression have made millions of people internally displaced, refugees and asylum seekers. These uprooted are referred to as Internally Displaced Persons (IDPs) if they remain within the territorial boundaries of their country or refugees if they cross the border. Irrespective of the fact that both the categories of uprooted people flee for the same reasons- persecution, human rights abuse, civil war etc. - and suffer the consequences, often IDPs are more vulnerable than their refugee counterparts. This is despite the fact that IDPs constitute a much larger group than refugees. As per the World Refugee Survey 2003, out of a total number of 34.8 million globally uprooted people 13.0

million were refugees and asylum seekers whereas the internally displaced were as many as 21.8 million. [9]

Displacement further leads to the predicament of the people caught in the situations of conflict. It impels the people to leave their homes and possessions along with families because of either a deliberate strategy of forced displacement of civilians or being caught up in the fighting. Even after leaving the native places, displaced remain exposed to violence and other human rights violations. Many of them may not find safe shelter. In the camps and settlements, where many uprooted are congregated, displaced live in conditions of dire poverty compounded by no steady supply of food, clean water, medical facilities etc. Many displaced also die due to epidemics and hunger. Many others suffer from physical as well as psychological problems. There are generally very little prospects of any form of income-generating activity or self-reliance. [10] Most displaced, thus, depend on occasional humanitarian assistance provided by the concerned government or the international agencies. Long-term displacement also causes loss of traditional livelihood skills, changes in socio-cultural life, disintegration of families and community structures etc.

When conflict is brought to the civilian population the group, as a whole, bears the consequences. But, there is a context of specificity as regarding the experiences of different categories. This is especially the case of those who otherwise are vulnerable within the larger group-children, elderly, women etc. Some of the other consequences of modern conflicts are the rise of child soldiers, targeting of aid workers and increasing gender specific atrocities. The impacts of violence on women and children are too far reaching. In IDP camps in northern Uganda, boys and girls play games 'only about violence, about the war, abduction, and death. Not about family life—cooking, hunting, and digging—like it used to be.' [11] The destruction of educational institutions deprives children to have educational opportunities.

Women experience the conflict doubly. On one hand, they share common experiences with the group as a major constituent of the civilian population. Due to ideologically ascribed male and female gender roles, there is also gender specificity. The gender-specific experience for most of the women may also be the result of patriarchal control, lack of exposure and mobility, lack of decision-making power, etc. They may also be rooted in the global culture of discrimination that denies women equal status with men. The sense of fear and the sense of threat to identity appear pervasive during conflict situations leading to magnifying of the cultural violence, directly impacting women. For instance, during the Kashmir conflict extremist elements in the Kashmir valley imposed restrictions on women in the name of cultural identity. The most significant was the attempt to impose veil that was traditionally never a part of Kashmiri culture. The girls above the age of 14 years were warned against studying in schools and colleges. Diktats were issued to women to quit jobs in the state police.

More alarmingly women become the victims of the sexual violence in all conflict situations. Innumerable instances of various kinds of sexual violence during the times of conflict ranging from rape to eve teasing with long term physical and psychological affects have been reported from all over the globe. Besides the armed groups party to the conflict those who are supposed to protect the common people caught between the guns i.e. peace keepers too many a times do not shy away from taking advantage of the situation. The United Nations peace keepers have been time and again accused of committing the heinous crimes ranging from rape to exploiting the local resources for making money. [12] There are many universal declarations which aim at protecting human rights of women during the conflict situations. The worth mentioning are the Vienna Declaration and Programme of Action (1993) adopted by the World Conference on Human Rights and the Convention on the Elimination of All Forms of Discrimination against Women (1979). Such an international campaign notwithstanding, women continue to be one of the worst sufferers during the conflict situations.

The modern day armed conflicts last much longer, ranging from a few months to a few decades. Beyond the direct toll of deaths they also have long-term grave socio-economic implications for the civilians. The conflict situations have the effect, sometimes deliberate and sometimes incidental, of rendering normal life problematic and making survival difficult. All the developmental activities come to a halt. More severely, it destroys the existing infrastructure comprising society, homes, health, and educational and work systems. It also deprives the civilians of their material and emotional needs by disrupting the social networks. There also develop an environment of uncertainty and fear in which the gross human rights violations become a norm. Besides, the civilians suffer during conflict situations in many other ways. Many times combatants often live or seek shelter in villages and sometimes use innocent civilians as human shields. In some cases, non-combatants may be forced to provide logistic support to armed groups and consequently may become targets. There may also be attempts by the combatants to restrict the access of civilians to food and other forms of life-saving assistance.

Armed conflicts also affect important sources of livelihood. Besides, the conflict environment prevents people from maximally utilizing the available resources. Due to the situation of violence and fear, private industries do not invest in conflict-regions. Another very important cost of violence is related to wastage of human talent. Most of the displaced people living on the relief provided by the concerned government or NGOs are too far from engagement in any productive activity. The fear of violence forces people to think only about survival and not progress. The progressive bent of mind that plays a crucial role in the progress of a society appears diminishing in conflict-prone region. Conflict also severely reduces prospects of growth by discouraging investment and destroying human and physical capital. It diverts much needed fund for welfare to nonproductive purposes, thus causing deterioration in the quality of life. In developing countries, violent conflict may undermine the principles of democracy and help growth of authoritarianism and dictatorship.

The economic costs of the violent conflict can be direct or indirect. While the direct costs involves actual experience related to violence directly, the indirect costs are related to both short term and long term loss of opportunities as well resources. Similarly, the costs can be seen in both tangible and intangible terms. While tangible cost can be estimated or quantified in material terms, the intangible costs can not be quantified as these are related to more invisible aspects of society such as community relations, capacity to development, socio-cultural impact on women, children, etc. The intangible costs of conflict bear heavily on the long term growth of state and society. Though it depends on the degree of violence and its spread, nonetheless in almost every case of violent conflict, the societal relations get ruptured with negative impacts like disruption of communal harmony. Conflicts, especially the internal ones, thus have the potential to polarize societies on the basis of religion, caste, race, language, thus generating further violence and extremism. As pointed out by Ashutosh Vershany, who studied communal conflicts in India, the inter-community harmony reduces the scope of conflict, but its absence may further heighten the conflict. [13]

The post-conflict situation does not witness positive atmosphere for development as the economies remain shattered for many years due to the factor of 'war overhang.' As per an estimate, if, during peacetime, the average military spending of a developing country amounts to 2.8 per cent of its GDP, this increases to around five per cent during civil war, and remains elevated to 4.5 per cent during the first post-conflict decade. [14] Besides economic slow down, the dangers related to violent practices during conflict situations affect the post-conflict life. For example, though in Kashmir the violence has come down, deaths of common people and their live stocks due to mining planted long years back still continues. Landmines also create an extra burden, as land remains inaccessible and unproductive. [15]

There are various conventions on international humanitarian and human rights law setting out the rights of civilians and the obligations of combatants during conflict. Major instruments in international humanitarian law are the four Geneva Conventions (1949) and the two Additional Protocols (1977). The major human rights treaties include the Convention on the Prevention and Punishment of the Crime of Genocide (1948), the International Convention on the Elimination of All Forms of Racial Discrimination (1965), the International Covenant on Civil and Political Rights (1966), the International Covenant on Economic, Social and Cultural Rights (1966), the Convention against Torture and Other Cruel, Inhuman or Degrading Treatment or Punishment (1984), the Convention on the Rights of the Child (1989).

The major instruments of refugee law are the Convention on the Status of Refugees (1951) and its Protocol (1967). Other relevant instruments are the Convention for the Protection of Cultural Property in the Event of Armed Conflict (1954) and its Protocol (1999), the Convention on Conventional Weapons (1980) and its four Additional Protocols, the Convention on the Safety of United Nations and Associated Personnel (1994), the Convention on the Prohibition of the Use, Stockpiling, Production and Transfer of Anti-Personnel Mines and on their Destruction (1997) and the Statute of the International Criminal Court (1998). However, the failure of parties in armed conflict to comply with the law on the one hand, and the lack of effective enforcement mechanisms on the other, has led to a situation in which civilians continue to suffer disproportionately all over the globe.

The Afro-Asian Context

Though conflict is a world wide phenomenon, it is more prominent in developing countries or those countries in transition and which have recently passed through the phase of decolonization. In fact, significant proportions of national budgets in most of the developing countries are spent on conflict-related things. The Carnegie Commission report *Preventing Deadly Conflict* in 1997 [16] estimated that in 1995 developing countries spent over US$ 150 billion on defence. This expenditure has long-term implications for the economy of the state concerned.

The overall number of armed conflicts around the globe declined between 1999 and 2002, and has held steady at around 30 active conflicts each year since 2002. [17] Asia and Africa are the most violent-prone continents in the world. Given the wide variation in contexts, both African and Asian countries experience armed conflicts in different forms and at distinct rates but with also a wide range of similarities in terms of causes as well as consequences. The countries of these two continents, referred to as the third world, were mostly colonies in the 20th Century. These developing countries have been passing through a period of transition, and their emergence from subordinated political entities to independence has not witnessed a smooth process, which appears to continue. The origin of most of the conflicts in these two continents can be partly or even largely traced to colonial legacy. Both the continents are characterized by an array of political practices, cultural traditions, economic performance, ethnic groups, religions, and languages besides being resident to some of the poorest countries of the world.

The continent of Africa has been marred by more than 20 major crisis situations since 1960. Rwanda, Somalia, Angola, Sudan, Liberia, DRC, Burundi, etc. are some of the countries that have witnessed armed conflict with serious implications. Compared to peaceful countries, African countries in conflict have, on an average: 50 per cent more infant deaths, 15 per cent more undernourished people, life expectancy reduced by five years, 20 per cent more adult illiteracy, 2.5 times fewer doctors per patient and 12.4 per cent less food per person. [18] According to a study conducted by IANSA, Oxfam, and Safe World, Africa has lost around US$ 300 billion since 1990 due to armed conflict in Algeria, Angola, Burundi, Central African Republic, Chad, DRC, Republic of Congo, Côte d'Ivoire, Djibouti, Eritrea, Ethiopia, Ghana, Guinea, Guinea-Bissau, Liberia, Niger, Nigeria, Rwanda, Senegal, Sierra Leone, South Africa, Sudan and Uganda. The study estimates that this amount of money, if properly utilized, could have solved the problems of HIV and AIDS in Africa, or addressed its education, water and sanitation issues, and prevented diseases like tuberculosis and malaria. The study also pointed that Africa loses around US$ 18 billion per year due to wars, civil wars, and insurgencies. [19] The real costs that weigh far beyond the economic consequences for obvious reasons would be much higher.

Like Africa, Asia has also witnessed violent conflicts. Many Asian countries witnessed violent conflicts since their independence. Some of the notable among them are between and in India and Pakistan, Afghanistan, Sri Lanka, Cambodia, Myanmar, and the Philippines. Some of these armed conflicts have lasted decades and proven extremely resistant to efforts at resolution, including those in Sri Lanka, Myanmar and the Philippines. Armed conflict in Asia has been predominantly intra-state in nature since the 1990s. The majority of intrastate conflicts in Asia are of low-intensity. The conflicts in Asia are comparatively confined to specific geographical limitations rather than engulfing the whole country or the region. The conflicts are mostly localized, and those involve issues of border, ethnic identity or disparity in resources or a mixture of all these factors. For instance, in Kashmir the conflict is related not only to the territorial controversy between India and Pakistan, but also to the ethnic and religious composition of the state and its linkages to politics of both the countries. On the other hand, in the Philippines in Southeast Asia conflict is largely confined to the southern provinces, especially to Mindanao and the surrounding areas and in Sri Lanka it has been confined to the north and east of the country, mainly involving two ethnic communities-the Singhalese and the Tamil. [20]

The common realization shows that violent means in the form of armed conflicts cannot bring lasting solutions and lasting peace. For instance, the Allied propaganda billed the Great War in Europe as the 'war to end all wars.' Although the Allies won the war, the resulting 'peace' Treaty of Versailles only set the stage for the even bloodier Second World War. The great apostles of truth and non-violence, Mahatma Gandhi in Asia and Nelson Mandela in Africa have shown how peaceful means can address conflict situations successfully. Though peace activities have been initiated in conflict areas, there appears to be more hurdles in realizing peace than waging in violence. However, it may be pessimistic not to give due importance for conflict resolution through peaceful means. As the Northern Ireland case shows, the violent conflict ended after the historic Good Friday agreement. The peace agreement in a sense put the onus on the all the stakeholders to see the conflict ends in a mutual agreed framework. In this context, it also needs emphasis though peace is generally understood as absence of hostilities or violent conflict, the term denotes not only absence of violence but also positive growth of human personality and development.

Notes

1. Lewis A. Coser, *The Functions of Social Conflict* (New York: Free Press, 1956). The similar viewpoints are expressed by writers such as, G. Dessler, *Organisation Theory: Integrating Structure and Behaviour* (Englewood Cliffs: Prentice Hall, 1980); C. W. Moore, *The Mediation Process: Practical Strategies for Resolving Conflict* (San Francisco: Jossey Bass, 1986); D.G. Pruitt and J.Z. Rubin, *Social Conflict: Escalation, Stalemate, and Settlement* (New York: Random House, 1986).

2. *SIPRI Yearbook 2002* (Oxford: Oxford University Press, 2003), Appendix 1B, p. 77.
3. Inger Skjelsbaek and Dan Smith, *Gender, Peace and Conflict* (New Delhi: Sage Publications, 2001), p. 3.
4. "Deepening Democracy in a Fragmented World," *Human Development Report 2002* (New York: Oxford University Press, 2002).
5. "Breaking the Conflict Trap: Civil War and Development Policy," *A World Bank Policy Research Report* (Washington, D.C.: World Bank, 2003).
6. M. Berdal and D. Malone, eds., *Greed and Grievance: Economic Agendas in Civil Wars* (Boulder: Lynne Rienner, 2000).
7. http://www.un.int/canada/html/s1999957.htm. (A.O. 20 August 2004).
8. http://www.unicef.org/graca/patterns.htm. (A.O. 12 August 2004).
9. http://www.refugees.org/downloads/wrs03/SSKeyStatistics.pdf. (A. O. 22 August 2004).
10. Karen Jacobsen, "Livelihoods in Conflict: The Pursuit of Livelihoods by Refugees and the Impact on the Human Security of Host Communities," *International Migration Review*, vol. 40, no. 5, pp. 96-99.
11. "Uganda: Traditions Eroded by Years of War," *IRIN*, 21 May 2007.
12. For details see Chiyuki Aoi, Cedric de Coning and Ramesh Thakur, eds., *Unintended Consequences of Peace Keeping Operations* (United Nations University Press, 2007).
13. See Ashutosh Varshney, *Ethnic Conflict and Civic Life: Hindus and Muslims in India* (New Haven and London: Yale University press 2002).
14. "Africa's Missing Billions, International Arms Flows and the Cost of Conflict," Briefing Paper 107, IANSA, Oxfam and Saferworld, October 2007, p. 18.
15. Seema Shekhawat and Debidatta Aurobinda Mahapatra, "Kargil Displaced of Akhnoor in Jammu and Kashmir: Enduring Ordeal and Bleak Future," IDMC, Geneva, 2006.
16. *Preventing Deadly Conflict,* Carnegie Commission (New York: Carnegie Corporation, 1997).
17. "Uppsala Conflict Data Program."

http://www.pcr.uu.se/research/UCDP. (A. O. 20 April 2008).

18. Figures cited in n. 14, p. 6.
19. Ibid.
20. For an Overview of the Asian conflicts see "Armed Violence in Asia and the Pacific: An Overview of the Causes, Costs and Consequences," Briefing Paper, UNDP, May 2008.

2

Futility of Armed Conflict: The Role of Dignity and Humiliation

Evelin G. Lindner

This chapter argues that a new concept of Realpolitik is currently emerging and it has to be developed more succinctly. Old Realpolitik was defined by fear, collective fear of attack from outgroups, informed by the so-called security dilemma (a term used in international relations theory). In this context, armed conflict was accepted, both practically and normatively. The human and material cost of armed conflict was regarded as necessary price to pay for victory. To proceed with a provocative question: Is it true that armed conflict is futile? Proud war veterans would violently contest that using arms in conflicts is futile. Historic victories in war are usually celebrated, and the price of material and humanitarian loss and suffering considered worth paying. Even suicide bombers view explosive suicide and homicide as noble rather than futile. In other words, even violent self-destruction as a means to achieving goals appears utile rather than futile to those who choose this path.

Many believe that violent struggle is unavoidable, that it is part and parcel of the natural order of things, both in the animal kingdom and among humans, just as unavoidable as natural laws. 'The strongest wins, and in order to win, violence is indispensable' is a sentence that many subscribe to. 'Might is right' is the short version of this popular philosophy. And violence will only increase—this is the forecast—since conflicts over scarce resources, for example water, or fertile soil, will only become more pressing in an overpopulating world. Disputing this interpretation of the human condition is regarded by many as blue-eyed idealism that only misguided dreamers can entertain.

This chapter supports contemporary realism within a larger historical context. The chapter draws on a transdisciplinary description of human history to explain why we face this contest of opinions about the futility versus utility of armed conflicts, and why armed conflict indeed is futile in our present-day interdependent world. The argument in this chapter is that a new concept of Realpolitik [1] is emerging at the present point in human history, a concept that needs to be shaped and developed more purposefully and proactively. This new concept is part of the currently unfolding larger normative paradigm shift toward a more efficient implementation of human rights. In the context of a strong security dilemma as in the case of Old Realpolitik, armed conflict is almost inevitable —this is why it is called a dilemma—and thus it came to be regarded as 'normal.' And undeniably, 'might' most often turned out to be 'right' throughout the past millennia. No wonder that armed conflict, including its cost, was accepted, both practically and normatively.

In the context of a strong security dilemma no statistics of the cost of war and violent conflict, even the most disastrous ones, can persuade policy makers to abandon war and violent conflict. For the adherents of the old concept of Realpolitik mere statistics of cost have little significance for decision-making. They will find no flaw with the fact that the world's military expenditure in 2006 reached a new high of US$ 1204 billion, while the annual cost of meeting the Millennium Development Goals by 2015 would amount to little more than 10 per cent of these funds. In contrast, the new concept of Realpolitik takes into account that the reality of our world is in the process of changing. Today, we no longer live in several villages, pitted against each other in mutual fear of attack, but in what emerges as one single global village.

More so, the new normative system that currently gains mainstream acceptance in a globalizing world, namely human rights, replace the old definition of security, which is 'keeping enemies out, and underlings down,' with a new definition. The new definition reads: 'integrating all humankind in a world of equal dignity for all.' In the new context, armed conflict is no longer utile and therefore no longer acceptable. And the more this historically completely novel fact is being understood and grasped, an increasing number of people cease to accept armed conflict, be it practically or normatively. In the new context, armed conflict represents a recipe for collective suicide—and not victory. Armed conflict no longer serves anybody's self-interest (except the interest of those who thrive on martyrdom and do not hesitate to mete out death to the rest).

In the new context, the old fear of attack is replaced with humiliation as defining negative emotion, namely feelings of humiliation felt by individuals in response to failing respect for equal dignity. If the transition to the new world is handled well by the international community and humankind at large, it entails hope, if not, it can seriously undermine any chances for building a sustainable future for humanity. Two facts in particular threaten peace, locally and globally, at the current point in historic times. First, feelings of humiliation represent 'the nuclear bomb of the emotions' (a term that the author has coined)—meaning that feelings of humiliation are so strong that they easily push people into violent cycles of humiliation. Second, in the new context such cycles are ubiquitously destructive if carried out with arms. Therefore, the transition toward the new normative universe of human rights, including new definitions of Realpolitik, is endangered by 'clashes of humiliation,' clashes that have to be avoided. There is an urgent need to help making the transition more constructive. Part of this effort is explaining why taking up arms against alleged 'enemies' is no longer feasible in a fledging global village. The only niche left for arms—at least a certain type of arms—are democratically legitimised police forces that guard the inner peace of the global village (these forces have still to be created—United Nations peace keeping troops represent only a rudimentary inception).

Humiliation should not be seen as an historic emotional process, but as a historical-cultural-social-emotional construct that changes over time. The currently living generations find themselves in a crucial historical transition shifting from an older world grounded in ranked honour—an honour world (with the experience of honour-humiliation)—to a vision of a future world of equal dignity (and a quite distinct experience of dignity-humiliation). In traditional hierarchical societies, elites were socialized into translating feelings of humiliation into an urge to fight back in a duel-like fashion. They defended their honour against humiliation with the sword (in duels, or in duel-like wars, with historically increasingly lethal weapons), while underlings (women and lowly men) were expected to humbly, subserviently, and obediently accept being subjugated without invoking or expressing any feelings of humiliation. In this context, rulers were not held responsible for caring for the well-being of their subjects. Rulers fought their wars over honour and land, and the suffering of their subjects went unmentioned. When people perished, through human-made or natural disaster, and when they were traumatized, this meant little.

This conceptualisation of the world began to hold sway about ten thousand years ago, when hierarchical societal systems emerged as more complex agricultural societies evolved. [2] Until recently, such hierarchical societal systems were regarded as thoroughly legitimate, even as divinely ordained. This world was guided by the old Realpolitik. Today, in many places, people still subscribe to such concepts. Yet, this state-of-affairs is in the process of changing. The fact that the phenomenon of humiliation is gaining significance is part of this large-scale paradigm shift. It gains significance within society at large and therefore also as a topic to be studied, not just by researchers, but in a transdisciplinary fashion, by all social sciences. This chapter lays out the changing role of humiliation during the past ten thousand years, and its significance in current times of paradigmatic transition. This historic analysis illuminates why it is not the net cost of armed conflict that drives decision making, but the larger context within which such cost is gauged.

Old Realpolitik: Self-interest Defined by Borders and Honour

William Ury, anthropologist and director of the Harvard University Project on Preventing War, conceptualises human history by drawing together anthropology, game theory and conflict studies. [3] He differentiates three major types of society: (a) simple hunter-gatherers, who dominated human history until circa ten thousand years ago, (b) complex agriculturists, who lasted throughout the past ten thousand years and (c) the currently emerging knowledge society. This categorisation follows a Weberian ideal-type approach. [4]

The defining element of the hunter-gatherer way of life was that their wherewithal—wild food—represented an expandable pie of resources that offered a rather benign frame of life because it allowed for win-win solutions. Conflicts were addressed, not through force and domination, but through negotiation in open networks. The hunter-gatherer way of life defined human history for ninety percent of its total duration, until approximately ten thousand years ago, when deep change occurred: Homo sapiens developed agriculture. The exact factors and sequence in the causal chain that led to the emergence of agriculture are hotly debated. What is clear is that agriculture represents a way of life that is defined by the fixity of the pie of resources—land is either mine or yours—a fixity that forces all participants into a rather malign win-lose definitorial frame. Hence, complex agriculturalists lived in a world of coercion and closed hierarchical pyramids of power instead of open networks.

Apart from anthropology, also international relations theory sheds light on human life during the past ten thousand years. Agriculturalists lived in communities that were pitted against each other in what international relations theory calls the security dilemma. John Herz introduced the term in 1950 to explain why states wage war against each other without intending to. The security dilemma is defined by fear, fear of attack. It has the nature of a dilemma because it aggravates fear instead of mitigating it. Its inherent tendency is to trigger arms races: 'I have to amass power, because I am scared. When I amass weapons, you get scared. You amass weapons, I get more scared.'

In a world of honourable domination/submission, everybody accepts that it is divinely ordained or represents nature's order that higher beings hold down lesser beings. Even the most atrocious schemes, when seen as 'honourable' strategies, are regarded as beneficial for the victims and society at large. Victims have no right to invoke the notion of humiliation as a form of violation, for them being humiliated has to be equivalent to being rightfully humbled, of being 'justly' shown their 'due lowly place.' Only their masters, when their privileged position is questioned, can appeal to humiliation as an infringement on their honour, and redeem it, for example, by going to duel. For many thousands of years this system was identified with 'civilization,' while equality meant 'barbarism.' In a book on early civilizations, we read, 'If egalitarianism was known, it was as a feature of some of the despised, barbarian societies that existed beyond the borders of the civilized world.' [5]

Slavery, bondage, serfdom, feudalism, lords, vassals, Apartheid, Coverture—terms abound that describe the various degrees to which a person could lose the relative sovereignty a hunter-gatherer enjoyed prior to ten thousand years ago, and the different ways in which a person could be subordinated, stripped of her equality in dignity, and turned into the property of a master.

Systems of domination/submission were developed to various degrees of sophistication and thoroughness during the history of the past millennia. Examples range from

Mesopotamia, Pharaonic Egypt, old China, to more recent colonial empires. German Prussia, for instance, developed the honour code to a high point of a combination of discipline and honourable rank; [6] historic France developed etiquette at its royal court, a refined way of honouring rank; [7] in Rwanda, ubuhake signified a clientilist kind of strong interdependence between a patron, who was mostly Tutsi, with clients who could be Hutu (means 'servant') or lower-ranked Tutsi. This rather malign set up is in the process of being undone by the *ingathering* of the human tribe (ingathering is the appropriate anthropological term for the coming together of humankind as part of globalization). The advent of globalization and human rights entails the benign promise to liberate humankind from a host of malign framings, dilemmas and biases.

New Realpolitik: Self-interest Identical with Common Interest

Human rights, in contrast to honourable domination/submission, could be described as an adaptation to new circumstances, namely to currently ever-increasing global interdependence. In the emerging global knowledge society, the security dilemma gets increasingly weaker as defining principle. As soon as there is only One World, only One 'global village'—no longer many 'villages' pitted against each other—new moral adaptations are called for. And indeed, human-rights ideals are gaining mainstream visibility, while honour strategies lose their taste of 'heroism,' and begin to smack of abuse. What was once legitimate rank, transmutes into illegitimate rankism. [8] According to Ury, a knowledge society resembles the hunter-gatherer model because the pie of resources—knowledge—can be expanded infinitely (there are always new ideas to be developed), thus re-opening the door for win-win solutions. Rigid hierarchical structures become obsolete and the more benign open networks typical of early hunter-gatherers re-emerge. Negotiation and contract replace command lines, and coexistence, embedded in values of equal dignity for everybody, replaces the ranking of people in higher and lesser beings.

The first sentence in Article 1 of the Universal Declaration of Human Rights reads, 'All human beings are born free and equal in dignity and rights.' In other words, human rights ideals oppose hierarchical rankings of human worthiness that were once regarded as 'normal' (and are still 'normal' in many parts of the world). Practices of routine humiliation of underlings, which once were legitimate virtually everywhere around the globe, become illegitimate. 1757 is the point in time when the verb to humiliate, for the first time in the English language, parted from the positive signification of to humble, and acquired the negative meaning of 'to violate the dignity or self-respect of someone.' [9]

The period of honour during human history was defined by the fear that is definitorial of the security dilemma, collective fear of attack from outgroups. Human rights introduce humiliation as defining negative emotion—feelings of humiliation as a reaction to failing respect for equal dignity. And these feelings of humiliation, in a context of human rights, are felt on the part of each individual qua being an individual, no longer qua being part of a collective. Human rights invite all human beings into one single human family where every individual member enjoys equal dignity. All are neighbours, no longer friends versus enemies. Former honour-humiliation (where only elites could invoke humiliation as a violation and underlings had to accept it humbly) transforms into dignity-humiliation that is illegitimate in all cases.

Human rights currently drive a process where 'normal predicaments' transmute into 'traumatic and humiliating violations,' and this permeates all levels, from global macro levels to inter-group, intragroup, and even intrapersonal micro levels. 'Domestic chastisement,' for example, transmutes to 'domestic violence'—a beaten wife, a subjugated underling in general, is no longer expected to quietly swallow lowliness and equate humiliation with due humbleness, but is encouraged to feel violated, abused, and humiliated in the sense of violation. Companies pay large amounts to consultants to train their employees to become team players who contribute with their creativity to the company's tasks in an empowered spirit of equal dignity, instead of distributing and accepting orders within an autocratic top-down system.

Clinical psychology, as well, is at the center of this transition, inspiring empowerment in clients who grew up in contexts where 'breaking the will of the child' still was regarded as 'prosocial pedagogy,' rather than 'antisocial abuse.' [10] While formerly only elites were allowed to define mistreatment as violation of their honour, now, this right is given to all underlings. The right to define humiliation as violation is removed from the masters and given to the downtrodden, marginalized, and underprivileged. Feelings of humiliation are indeed the very 'fuel' that drives the human rights revolution.

A host of recent research in the fields of psychology and neuroscience underpins that indeed, human rights are not only the appropriate normative adaptation to a globalising world, they are furthermore the adequate value system for a humane world. Old power-over cultures, including more recent outgrows such as 'rugged individualism' ideologies, are damaging to human beings. For example, much of the research on resilience points in a relational direction, suggesting that resilience grows through connection. [11] Jean Baker Miller and her colleagues at the Jean Baker Miller Training Institute (JBMTI) emphasise connection and mutuality as part of their Relational-Cultural Theory (RCT).

In sum, human rights are more humane than the old honour code; they are more in tune with a modern globalising world, more conducive to the need for creative solutions for global challenges, and at the same time more consistent with the long-term evolutionary background of the human species. The past ten thousand years could be regarded as a rather short period (in historical terms) of harsh adaptation to malign circumstances that ran counter to earlier evolutionary adaptations of Homo sapiens. [12] Ranking people, turning human beings into tools in the hands of masters, is not beneficial to anybody, not to masters, not to underlings, and not to society at large, not least because such strategies deprive society of what fully empowered human beings potentially can contribute to social and societal life.

Old Realpolitik is deeply emotional, contrary to their proponent's insistence that it is rational. It is deeply emotional because honour is a concept that has strong emotional anchorings. For the past ten thousand years, men were trained by society to be prepared for early honourable death in battle so as to protect their ingroup—only 'women' and 'cowards,' those who did not have the 'guts' to behave honourably, lamented the cost of armed conflict. Today, in a globalizing world, defending ingroups against outgroups is no longer a suitable concept. All humankind needs to cooperate, jointly, to solve new global problems. The suicidal aspect of honour is no longer concealable by the argument of ingroup self-interest. New Realpolitik has to consider this historically unprecedented situation. Only human rights offer a non-suicidal normative framework for world society in an increasingly interdependent world. This state-of-affairs is so novel that no history lesson can offer help, only clear analysis. History does not go in cycles, it does not repeat itself. None of our ancestors was able to see pictures of their Blue Planet from the perspective of an astronaut. None of our ancestors lived in a world with fabricated global challenges, and the relevant knowledge to tackle them.

Brave heroism and sacrifice in the old world of honourable old Realpolitik meant standing up against your enemies. It meant accepting to be part of a hierarchically organized ingroup, united in patriotic love for the ingroup, pitted against threatening outgroups. Brave heroism and sacrifice in the new Realpolitik of dignity means standing up united in humanizing love for a vision of one united family of humankind, where everybody deserves to be respected as equal in dignity, a world without enemies and outgoups, a world of neighbours, who together find a way to live together even if they do not love each other.

The Case of Genocide

The author focuses on the phenomenon of humiliation since 1996 starting from carrying out a four-year doctoral research project, entitled *The Feeling of Being Humiliated: A Central Theme in Armed Conflicts. A Study of the Role of Humiliation in Somalia, and Rwanda/Burundi, Between the Warring Parties, and in Relation to Third Intervening Parties*, from 1997 to 2001. [13] Hundreds of interviews in Somalia, Rwanda, and Burundi from 1998 to 1999 in Somaliland, Rwanda, Burundi, Nairobi, Kenya, Egypt, Norway, Germany, Switzerland, France, and Belgium made the base for developing a theory of humiliation that is transdisciplinary and entails elements from anthropology, history, social philosophy, social psychology, sociology, and political science. [14]

German history served as starting point for the research. It is often assumed that the humiliation of the Germans through the Versailles Treaties after World War I was partly responsible for the Holocaust and the Second World War. The results of the research confirm the original hypothesis that, indeed, humiliation plays a role for armed conflict and mass violence not only in Europe, but also outside of Europe, and not only in the past, but also today, with increasing relevance. In all three cases that were included in my doctoral research, Somalia, Rwanda and Germany, it was the fear of imagined future humiliating subjugation of one group at the hands of another that typically figured as justification for genocidal killings. In Germany it was the fear, projected into the future, of a future *Weltherrschaft des Judentums* (the world dominated by Jews).

In Rwanda it was the fear that future democratic power-sharing with Tutsis would mean Tutsi domination. And also

Somalia's future was regarded as threatened—by the 'arrogant' Isaaq tribe. [15] In all three cases, killing the alleged humiliators and their allies was chosen as 'solution'—by Hitler in Germany, by Siad Barre in Somalia, and by the extremist Hutu elite in Rwanda, all of whom portrayed themselves as 'saviours' and were initially widely welcomed and celebrated as such. However, as it turned out, the 'rational' self-interest of the perpetrators and their followers was ultimately undermined, not supported. Hitler took half of the world, including his own Germany and Austria, with him on a path of homicidal and suicidal destruction; Somalia's dictator Siad Barre had to flee in disgrace, leaving behind a country in chaos; and also the extremist Hutu elite in Rwanda lost precisely what they wanted to protect, despised by the world as the worst of genocidaires.

If we apply these lessons to contemporary world politics, we observe similar dynamics. In an ever more interdependent world it is no longer feasible to achieve security through exploding bombs, be it big-scale or small-scale. In former times, the mighty could hope to achieve calm and stability by keeping enemies at bay, and underlings humble, through applying a mixture of manipulation, routine subjugation, and, in case of attacks and uprisings, brutal retaliation and subjugation. In today's interdependent world, every single world citizen acquires the potential to turn into a 'Hitler' and pull the world into self- and other-annihilation. Anybody can download the construction plans for bombs from the internet, and anybody can maintain websites and global networks that instigate violence, locally and globally.

More even, the probability of people actually being attracted to this path of violence is heightened with ever more people expecting global solidarity, and equality in dignity, instead of division and subjugation. Feelings of humiliation emerge when equality in dignity is promised but not implemented, and when these feelings are instrumentalised by Hitler-like humiliation-entrepreneurs and translated into violence, world peace is in danger.

Statistics underpinning these claims abound. The *2007 State of the Future* report, for example, concludes that terrorism is a problem that the world is not yet tackling well. [16] And tellingly, much of what would have been dubbed 'aggression,' or 'uprising' earlier, has acquired the label of 'asymmetric conflict' today, at least in academic settings, [17] indicating how the call for equality in dignity has gained legitimacy. Yet, the new label alone does not render more constructive outcomes – the mighty reap 'terrorism' with their bombs, and all reap less security and quality of life rather than more, in a downhill cycle. The mighty and the weak in asymmetric conflicts have to understand that humiliating opponents by force no longer humbles and pacifies (as it may have done in former times). On the contrary, in the new context, ubiquitous cycles of humiliation risk leading to collective suicide.

Looking into the Future

At the current points in human history, what is lacking is not information about the cost of armed conflict. A simple Google Search provides ample insights. What is lacking is more clarity about the emerging new conceptual framework within which to gauge which cost is 'acceptable' and which not. Thus, not only the pure quantity of cost counts. It is the weighing of advantages versus disadvantages of paying a certain price. In the context of a strong security dilemma, almost any cost of armed conflict is considered acceptable. What is needed at the current historical juncture is a new framework for interpreting the advantages versus disadvantages of paying this price. This chapter aims at explaining this new framework.

The price of wars, globally, is being documented, for example, by The International Peace Bureau (IPB) in Geneva, Switzerland. It offers a wide variety of statistics on military spending. World military expenditures in 2006 reached a new high of US$ 1204 billion, reports the Stockholm International Peace Research Institute (SIPRI) at the launch of its annual Yearbook in 2007. This represents an increase of 3.5 per cent over the 2005 figure, and is 37 per cent more than a decade ago. The USA accounted for nearly half the total, with US$ 529 billion. These amounts constitute a huge treasury that should be re-directed to the fight against mass poverty and the threat of climate change, according to the IPB. The United Nations' Millennium Project (2005) has estimated that the annual costs of meeting the Millennium Development Goals by the target date of 2015 are of the order of US$ 135 billion per year, little more than 10 per cent of the money currently allocated to the military sector.' [18]

How can we explain that a world military expenditure of US$ 1204 billion is possible, at a time when the advantages to invest these funds more constructively are so obvious? Old Realpolitik conceptualises the world as a fragmented world, where security, or counterterrorism, means keeping 'enemies' out of ones ingroup or in 'secure submission.' And it is in the framework of this old Realpolitik that a world military expenditure of US$ 1204 billion is anchored. Today, ranked honour, with all its oratory of patriotic love, resolve, bravery and heroism, is still strong in three realms: in certain world regions (for example, where so-called honour killings are accepted as legitimate), in certain segments of societies (for example, city street gangs), and at macro levels, where international elites interact. Even though no longer as openly espoused as in former times, a state's 'honorable preeminence' [19] is still upheld by many diplomats, foreign policy makers, and military personnel. The average citizen, the common man and woman, are often much more attached to human rights.

In times of growing global interdependence, the old approach rapidly loses feasibility; indeed, it becomes increasingly counterproductive and self-destructive. In an interdependent world, unilateral action no longer stays unilateral, every action becomes a boomerang. Dishing out violence and humiliation to deter 'enemies' or keep them 'down' no longer pacifies the world, but comes back in kind. Humiliation no longer renders humble underlings but may produce enraged terrorists. New Realpolitik is global human security. A formerly fragmented world needs to unite in a new global ingroup, a global community, to tackle common challenges and give the survival of all humankind a chance. Global human security is safeguarded not by fighting against, but by standing up for, for a vision of one united family of humankind, where everybody deserves to be respected as equal in dignity, a world without enemies and outgoups, a world of neighbours, who together find a way to live together even if they do not love each other.

Notes

1. The term Realpolitik was coined by August Ludwig von Rochau (1810-1873), a German writer in the nineteenth century, following Klemens Fürst von Metternich (1773-1859) in his quest to find a balance of power for the European empires. See, for example, Natascha Doll, *Recht, Politik Und "Realpolitik" Bei August Ludwig Von Rochau (1810-1873): Ein Wissenschaftsgeschichtlicher Beitrag Zum Verhältnis Von Politik Und Recht Im 19. Jahrhundert* (Frankfurt am Main: Vittorio Klostermann, 2005).
2. William Ury provides a comprehensive description of this complex process. See, William Ury, *Getting to Peace: Transforming Conflict at Home, at Work, and in the World* (New York: Viking, 1999).
3. Ibid.
4. See, for an explanation of this approach Lewis A. Coser, *Masters of Sociological Thought: Ideas in Historical and Social Context.* (Fort Worth, TX: Harcourt Brace Jovanovich, 1977), p. 224.
5. Bruce G. Trigger, *Early Civilizations - Ancient Egypt in Context* (Cairo: AUC, 1993), pp. 53-54.
6. For details see, Norbert Elias, *The Germans: Power Struggles and the Development of Habitus in the Nineteenth and Twentieth Centuries* (Cambridge: Polity Press, 1996).
7. For details see, Norbert Elias, *The Civilizing Process (Volume 1:*

The History of Manners, Volume 2: State Formation and Civilization) (Oxford: Blackwell, 1994).

8. Robert W. Fuller, *Somebodies and Nobodies: Overcoming the Abuse of Rank* (Gabriola Island, Canada: New Societies Publishers, 2003).
9. William Ian Miller, *Humiliation and Other Essays on Honor, Social Discomfort, and Violence* (Ithaca: Cornell University Press, 1993), p. 175.
10. Alice Miller, *For Your Own Good: Hidden Cruelty in Child-Rearing and the Roots of Violence* (London: Virago Press, 1983).
11. Judith V. Jordan, Maureen Walker, and Linda M. Hartling, eds., *The Complexity of Connection: Writings From the Stone Center's Jean Baker Miller Training Institute* (New York: The Guilford Press. 2004).
12. Piero Giorgi, *The Origins of Violence by Cultural Evolution* (Brisbane: Minerva, 2001).
13. See Evelin Gerda Lindner, *The Psychology of Humiliation: Somalia, Rwanda/Burundi, and Hitler's Germany* (Oslo: University of Oslo, 2000).
14. I am the Founding Manager of Human Dignity and Humiliation Studies (see, http://www.humiliationstudies.org) and develop this network of academics and practitioners globally since 2001.
15. See a deeper discussion in Evelin Gerda Lindner, "Were Ordinary Germans Hitler's "Willing Executioners"? Or Were They Victims of Humiliating Seduction and Abandonment?: The Case of Germany and Somalia," in *IDEA: A Journal of Social Issues,* vol. 5, no. 1, 2000 and Evelin Gerda Lindner, "Humiliation and Reactions to Hitler's Seductiveness in Post-War Germany: Personal Reflections," in *Social Alternatives, 25, Special Issue: Humiliation and History in Global Perspectives*, First Quarter, 2006, pp. 6-11.
16. Jerome C. Glenn and Theodore J. Gordon, *2007 State of the Future* (New York: Millennium Project Publications, 2007), p. 6.
17. See the new journal *Dynamics of Asymmetric Conflict*, founded in 2008, published by Taylor and Francis, edited by Clark McCauley and Marc Ross, Asch Center, Bryn Mawr College, University of Pennsylvania, Philadelphia.
18. http://www.ipb.org/milspending.html. (A. O. 30 November

2007). See also *Joshua S. Goldstein, The Real Price of War: How You Pay for the War on Terror* (New York: NYU Press, 2004).

19. Donald Kagan, "Honor, Interest, and Nation-State," in Elliot Abrams, ed., *Honor among Nations* (Washington, DC: Ethics and Public Policy Center, 1998).

3

Long War and Long Peace in Northern Ireland

Neil Jarman

Northern Ireland has been the site of an extended armed conflict, locally known as 'the Troubles,' which lasted from 1969 until the main paramilitary organizations declared ceasefires in 1994. This led to a long drawn out multi-party 'peace process,' which resulted in a peace agreement that was signed on Good Friday 1998, the creation of a range of new political and human rights institutions and eventually in 2007 the formation of a devolved government. Despite the apparent success of the Northern Ireland peace process, which has led it to be considered as one of the major successes of recent peace building activity and a model for other conflict transformation work, the transition from militarized violence to peace has been a problematic and difficult period. The armed conflict ended without a clear victor, with no sense of conciliation between the wider British unionist and Irish nationalist communities and without any general agreement over the steps that were needed to consolidate the peace.

Since 1994 the peace process has progressed along a number of interlinked but distinctive paths. One path involved the participation of the political elite in an extended discussions and negotiations that focused on the content and implementation of the peace agreement. Another strand involved the business and commercial community in attempting to build on the 'peace dividend' to regenerate and redevelop the economy and infrastructure. Yet another path involved a grass roots process, which was often played out on the streets and in the different communities and organisations of civil society, as communities sought to influence the direction and content of the process and the new institutions. The various strands of the peace process were intimately linked, but they were rarely synchronized. Events on the ground have at times had a negative impact on the attitudes and actions of political leaders, and on the potential for economic regeneration, while the words and actions of the political leadership have at times encouraged, but at other times restrained or deterred, the actions of local activists and community leaders.

The difficulties were in large part because the violence that had dominated Northern Ireland for a generation left a legacy of suspicion, mistrust and antipathetic relationships between members of the nationalist and unionist communities. It generated strong feelings of mistrust and hostility towards the state and the security forces within working class communities. The early years of the transition witnessed not so much a peace process as a continuance of the conflict, albeit by other means. Violent attacks were scaled down, but hostilities were sustained at a lower level. Protests against parades and disorder at the territorial boundaries sustained tensions, while young people were often encouraged to participate in outbreaks of disorder. The period of transition also deepened the vacuum that existed in law and order, particularly in working class areas. The political transition was thus a period of uncertainty. It was a time of optimism but one that was frequently tinged with trepidation. In many ways the peace had to be built from the bottom up as much as from the top down and this process involved diverse groups, organizations and activities, including managing tensions and disorder on the ground, and building relationships with erstwhile enemies and opponents. [1] This chapter explores some of the elements of the different strands of the conflict and the peace process in Northern Ireland. [2]

Division and Conflict

Northern Ireland is, with England, Scotland and Wales,

part of the United Kingdom of Great Britain and Northern Ireland. But it is also geographically a part of the island of Ireland and has a land border with the larger Republic of Ireland. Northern Ireland is a small area of 13,500 square kilometres with a population of just over 1.7 million people; this includes a majority Protestant community of 895,000 people (53 per cent of the population) and a minority Catholic community of 737,000 people (44 per cent of the population). There is also a diverse mixture of minority ethnic, faith and national communities, which has been growing rapidly since the end of the conflict and now accounts for some 5 per cent of the population.

The conflict in Northern Ireland has essentially been over the political status of the region and the competing claims and aspirations of the two main communities. The Protestant community generally favour the political union with Great Britain. They regard themselves as British citizens and define themselves politically as unionists. Hardline unionists are known as loyalists since they proclaim loyalty to the British monarchy. The Catholic community generally favours the creation of a single united Irish state. They regard themselves as Irish people and define themselves politically as nationalists. Hardline nationalists are known as republicans since they strive for a United Irish Republic. These competing political identities derive from the close geographical proximity of Britain and Ireland, their entwined histories and the political influence and dominance that Britain has exercised over Ireland for much of the last millennium.

Until the seventeenth century, when England determined to extend its domination and rule over the island, the population of Ireland was predominately Roman Catholic and spoke Irish, a Gaelic language unrelated to English. In order to exercise their authority over Ulster, the particularly troublesome northern region of Ireland, the English encouraged Protestants from both England and Scotland to settle in the region from 1609 onwards. [3] This colonization led to the displacement of many Irish from their land. The Protestant succession in England and Protestant domination in Ireland were consolidated when King William III defeated his predecessor King James II at the battle of the Boyne in 1690.

Under the Protestant Ascendancy, Catholics were excluded from positions of authority, discriminated against, and socially, economically, politically and geographically marginalized. These processes were sustained both by law and with force. There were numerous attempts to limit British rule in Ireland and end discrimination against Catholics, which included unsuccessful armed rebellions in 1798, 1803, 1848 and 1870. The population and economy of Ireland were also decimated between 1845-1849 when the potato crop, the stable diet of the rural population, failed. Millions of Irish people died in the famines that followed or fled to start a new life in America. This was followed by a sustained and peaceful campaign for Home Rule from the 1870s onwards, which was largely supported by Catholics and opposed by Protestants. This campaign culminated in another armed uprising against British rule in 1916. The Easter Rising was unsuccessful in its immediate aim but provided the impetus for political developments that led to the division of Ireland into two political entities, the Irish Free State and Northern Ireland, in 1921.

The new Northern Ireland state had a majority of Protestants but with a Catholic population of around one third of the total of 1.5 million people. (In contrast the Irish Free State was overwhelmingly Catholic, but with a Protestant minority of some ten per cent of the population.) Partition led to a Protestant and Unionist government being established in Northern Ireland, in which the Ulster Unionist Party was to rule without interruption from 1921 to 1972. [4] Catholics remained politically marginalized and discriminated against under the new regime, while the overwhelmingly Protestant Royal Ulster Constabulary were able to draw upon extensive emergency powers to maintain law and order. There had been a long history of sectarian violence and inter-communal rioting in the north of Ireland dating from the industrialization and urban expansion of the early nineteenth century. This was, at least in part, linked to competition for economic resources and access to political power. But tensions and rivalries were also sustained and perpetuated by symbolic displays and cultural activities. The numerous annual parades, used by both communities to recall their history, demonstrate their strength and assert claims to territory, regularly triggered outbursts of rioting and disorder. [5]

This violence helped to sustain and emphasize the sense of difference between Catholics and Protestants, it also served to encourage and reinforce patterns of residential segregation and helped to sectarianize public space as controlled by one community to the exclusion of the other. Power and discrimination have always had geographical and territorial dimension in the north of Ireland, to complement the use of force and intimidation. Tensions over the discrimination of Catholics reached a peak in the 1960s when the Northern Ireland Civil Rights Movement, which drew heavily on the American model, began to challenge the Unionist government and demand equality for Catholics. [6] The focus of the civil rights campaign was particularly on issues of housing, employment and voting equality, while their public protests challenged the Protestant domination of public space. The civil rights protests led to increasingly violent reactions from sections of the Protestant community, were often constrained by the police, and were a factor in the emergence of the first loyalist paramilitary group, the Ulster Volunteer Force in 1966.

In 1969 increasing tensions and conflict between supporters of the civil rights campaign and sections of the Unionist establishment led to widespread rioting and disorder. One result was that the British Labour government decided to send troops to Northern Ireland to restore order. However, within a few months the violence had escalated further and was transformed into an armed conflict, while the focus shifted from the aims of the civil rights movement to a resurgence of republican demands for a united Ireland. The main combatants were initially the Irish Republican Army and the British Army, but the conflict soon involved a variety of armed groups, including the republican Irish National Liberation Army and the loyalist Ulster Volunteer Force and Ulster Defence Association. In 1972, the British government suspended the local devolved administration, and for the rest of the conflict Northern Ireland was subjected to direct rule from Westminster.

During the Troubles, the British government introduced several key pieces of legislation and made extensive reforms of local government, which were designed to reduce the scope for institutional discrimination of Catholics and to promote greater equality between the two main communities. However, the political polarization between Catholic nationalists and Protestant unionists ensured that enmity and violence were not limited to those involved in armed organizations. The conflict resulted in the death of over three thousand five hundred people, while many thousands of people were injured. Over the course of the conflict thousands of people were subjected to imprisonment. There was also widespread damage to property and the infrastructure of the region, and the local economy was seriously disrupted for a generation. The conflict also occasionally spread beyond Northern Ireland with attacks occurring in Great Britain, the Republic of Ireland and parts of Europe, particularly from the mid-1980sd onwards when the IRA increasingly focused on economic and military targets in Britain and Europe.

By the early 1990s the security situation had reached stalemate. The British security forces had been unable to defeat the IRA, while the IRA's military campaign showed no sign of achieving their political objective of a united Ireland. Loyalist paramilitaries also continued to attack republicans and often Catholics civilians as a way of, as they saw it, 'terrorising the terrorist.' Sinn Féin, the political wing of the Republican movement, had entered Northern Irish politics in the wake of the 1981 Hunger Strike campaign by republican prisoners and through the 1990s political activity increasingly took precedence over paramilitary activity. This eventually led to the declaration of an IRA ceasefire in August 1994. Before this position was reached, however, there was a long 'feeling out' period between the British government and Sinn Féin and the IRA from the early 1990s. Contacts between loyalist paramilitary groups and the British and Irish governments also began to grow at this time and their ceasefire followed in October of the same year. There followed an extended period of debate, dialogue and negotiation among local politicians, armed groups and the diverse communities of Northern Ireland, which was punctuated by periods of violence and crisis, and variously supported nurtured and encouraged by the British, Irish and American governments, with extensive financial support from the European Union. The period of transition from the ceasefires onwards is referred to as the peace process.

Humanitarian Impact of the Conflict

Although the Northern Ireland Troubles was a long-running conflict and was subjected to extensive international interest, the violence never reached the scale that has been witnessed in many other current or recent conflicts. In fact between 1969, when the British Army were first deployed on the streets and 1994 when the main paramilitary groups declared ceasefires, some three thousand five hundred and forty six people were killed. This figure includes civilians, members of the security forces and members of paramilitary organizations. [7] Although this figure is low compared with the violence in places such as Bosnia, DRC, Rwanda and others, it is important to bear in mind the small population of Northern Ireland, which is currently 1.7 million people, and the small scale of the geography, which ensured that the lethal violence impacted on a high proportion of the population, particularly in working-class communities.

Furthermore, the majority of the deaths occurred in the first few years of the violence. The most intense period of the conflict was the six years between 1971 and 1976 when one thousand eight hundred and forty three people were killed, fifty two per cent of the total figure. It is estimated that 54 per cent of those killed were civilians, while 21 per cent were members of the British Army and 9 per cent were members of the police, finally 13 per cent were members of republican armed groups and just 3 per cent were loyalist paramilitaries. It is also estimated that some thirty seven thousand five hundred people were injured of which 68 per cent were civilians, although this figure is likely to be an underestimate. [8]

There was also considerable displacement of people from their homes during the conflict due to direct violence or intimidation. However, no one was formally recognized as a refugee, since people were usually re-housed within a short period, although many people were forced to move from their home area and in some cases had to relocate to another town. One study estimates that between thirty thousand and sixty thousand people in Belfast alone (up to twelve per cent of the population of the city) were forced to move home between August 1969 and February 1973, [9] which represented the largest enforced movement of population in Europe since the Second World War. Belfast and other urban areas of Northern Ireland have long been extensively segregated, with Protestant and Catholic working class communities living in their own defined areas.

However, the violence of the Troubles served to intensify such levels of segregation and in 1999 the Northern Ireland Housing Executive, the public body responsible for social housing, estimated that ninety-eight per cent of public housing in Belfast was effectively segregated. The segregation was initially informally managed, but as the level of intimidation increased in the early years of the Troubles access across the boundary areas between Protestant and Catholic areas was controlled by the British Army by rolls of barbed wire. As the violence continued, more permanent barriers, referred to with some irony as 'peacelines,' constructed of sheet steel and later brick were built, while vehicle steel gates could control access along a number of roads.

Although it was always asserted that this was to be a short term measure, by 1994 more than twenty such barriers had been built across the city by the government, and while the paramilitary ceasefires brought an end to the armed violence it did not stop inter-communal violence and barriers have continued to be built to try to limit rioting and attacks on property. In 2008 more than forty official barriers have been documented and as many more defensive structures have been built in the course of process of rebuilding and regenerating communities. More significantly, none of the security barriers have yet been removed. [10] Thus, one of the major consequences of both the armed violence and the period of transition has been a deeper embedding of the ethnic segregation of the two main communities.

There has been a limited amount of research that has focused on trying to determine the economic and financial costs of the Northern Ireland conflict, in large part because it has been acknowledged that it is virtually impossible to disentangle the impact of the violence and the activities of the armed groups from other, wider factors. Fay, Morrissey and Smyth summarize the issues succinctly: "It is very difficult to separate out the impact of developments in the international economy, the effects of changes in the British economy, economic problems specific to Northern Ireland and the economic costs of the region's conflict. All were happening simultaneously and interacting with each other." [11]

Historically Northern Ireland has been a marginal and geographically remote region of the United Kingdom. It has had a less dynamic economy, a small consumer market, a lower standard of living and higher rates of unemployment than England, Scotland and Wales. Furthermore, the political domination of the Protestant unionist community between 1921 and 1972 was also reflected in their social and economic dominance, and in institutionalized discrimination against the Catholic nationalist minority, which resulted in greater levels of poverty and higher levels of unemployment among Catholics. These various forms of discrimination were important factors in increasing the alienation of the Catholic population and in the formation of the civil rights campaign in the 1960s, which preceded the descent into armed violence. [12]

Through the 20th century the Northern Irish economy had been based on heavy industry such as engineering, shipbuilding and textiles, all of which were struggling to survive in western countries. The conflict thus occurred in an economy that was already under pressure, and the political crisis ensured that Northern Ireland was not an attractive place for investors and exacerbated the economic problems rather than caused them. Over the course of the conflict the Northern Irish economy became more reliant on public expenditure and a higher proportion of people were employed in the public sector, while unemployment and poverty increased, both in real terms and in relation to the wider British economy. [13]

The pressure on the Northern Irish economy also increased from the mid 1980s with a more focused campaign by the IRA on attacking economic targets and in particular bombing the commercial centre of a number of urban centres. The economy continued to function, but the conflict undoubtedly had a negative impact in the region, although the high level of the financial subvention from the British Government mitigated the effects of the violence. [14] In particular it is worth noting the stagnation of the Northern Irish economy through the 1990s, which contrasted starkly with the dynamism of the Celtic Tiger economy south of the border, and it also contrasts with the relatively strong growth in the northern economy that has occurred as the peace process has steadily became more embedded.

The overall impact of the peace process on the local economy and of the local economy on the peace process has yet to be documented and must still be regarded as work in progress. However, particularly since the turn of the millennium the economy appears to be flourishing, with the Belfast skyline dominated by cranes and growing buildings, declining unemployment and a rapid growth in migrants from Eastern Europe, South Asia and the Philippines to supplement the indigenous workforce. A significant contribution to the process of consolidating the peace has been through the financial support provided by the European Union and other international bodies.

There has been a series of special EU support programmes since 1995, which to date had allocated a £640 million to Northern Ireland with a further £180 million of matched funding. Other major financial investments have come from the International Fund for Ireland, established by the British and Irish Governments in 1985, and the US based Atlantic Philanthropies, which together have been responsible for nearly £700 million investment between 1982 and 2004. [15] These finances have been used to fund a wide range of projects, including ones that focus on employment, education, regeneration, and structural development as well as activities associated with mitigating the impact of the conflict, and supporting the processes of peace-building and reconciliation, including work with victims and former prisoners. Collectively this diverse array of financial investment has been a major contribution towards consolidating the peace and encouraging people to think of the future, whilst not ignoring the unresolved problems of the past.

Negotiation and Agreement

The ceasefires paved the way for discussions which aimed to include all of the main local political parties: Ulster Unionist Party and Democratic Unionist Party, which draw their support from the Protestant community; Social Democratic and Unionist Party and Sinn Féin, which draw support from the Catholic community; plus the small cross community Alliance Party and a number of smaller parties. This process was supported by the participation of both the British and Irish governments, as well as the regular involvement of the American government. The transition to democratic politics and the practice of compromise was not easy or straightforward. Residual tensions, hostilities, and disagreements about the acceptability of the participation of political parties with relationships to the various armed groups by the unionist parties ensured that progress was slow. While some republicans believed too many compromises were being made in relation to their dream of a united Ireland. These tensions led to the IRA breaking its ceasefire in February 1996, although this was restored in July 1997. In contrast, the transition was aided by the growing electoral success of Sinn Féin, which was in part a result of the party's role in the developing peace process. By 2003 Sinn Féin had overtaken its rival the Social Democratic and Labour Party (SDLP) and had become the largest nationalist party and the second largest party in the North, while also becoming a political force in the Republic.

The extended period of negotiations involving the ten largest political parties led to the signing of the Agreement on Good Friday 1998. The Belfast, or Good Friday Agreement, was a wide-ranging document, but it included a number of vaguely worded sections (or elements of 'constructive ambiguity'), which were important at the time to ensure that all the parties would agree to the text, but only served to displace some problems to a later date. The Agreement was overwhelmingly endorsed in simultaneous referenda in both Northern Ireland and the Republic, but Protestants were more tentative in their support than Catholics - approximately 55 per cent of Protestants voted for the Agreement compared to 95 per cent of Catholics. This division within the Protestant community was made evident in the first elections to the new Northern Ireland Assembly when almost half of the unionists returned were opponents of the Agreement. This opposition among some unionists has continued to the present, it has been a factor in slowing progress towards the implementation of the Agreement, but it has also been a factor that has been used by unionist politicians to take a hard line in negotiations and improve the outcomes from their perspective.

The Belfast Agreement included provision for a devolved Northern Ireland Assembly of one hundred and eight members elected by Proportional Representation. The Assembly was to be headed by an Executive of ten ministers with legislative powers, although some powers such as defence and taxation would be retained by Westminster, while policing and justice were retained on a temporary basis. Positions on the Executive are allocated to members of the four main parties on proportional basis, which has effectively ensured that the government will be enforced coalition of the main parties, with little scope for an opposition or an alternative government. This system was designed to prevent a return to the previous system of majority rule, which would have allowed for the possible exclusion of nationalist parties from government. As a further safeguard all major political decisions must have the support of a majority of representatives of both communities, and to ensure that this could be monitored all Assembly members were required to designate themselves as 'Unionist,' 'Nationalist' or 'other.'

As part of the process of securing the Agreement the Irish government agreed to recommend changes to Articles 2 and 3 of the Irish constitution, which had asserted claims to the whole territory of the island of Ireland. The revised Articles would emphasize an aspiration towards unity: Article 2 stating, 'It is the entitlement of every person born in the island of Ireland … to be part of the Irish nation;' and Article 3 stating, 'It is the firm will of the Irish nation, in harmony and friendship, to unite all the people who share the territory of the island of Ireland, in all the diversity of their identities and traditions, recognising that a united Ireland shall be brought about only by peaceful means with the consent of a majority of the people, democratically expressed, in both jurisdictions of the island.' The British Government also agreed to replace the Government of Ireland Act claiming sovereignty to Northern Ireland. These elements effectively removed the assertions of both the British and Irish states to claim Northern Ireland as an essential part of their national territory, and instead left the constitutional status of the region in the hands of the people, with any change to be agreed by a majority vote in a referendum.

Furthermore, in order to provide for closer working relations between the various political units of the British Isles the Agreement created a North-South Ministerial Council to direct co-operation on a number of issues between Northern Ireland and the republic and established a British-Irish Council which would include Northern Irish Assembly Members and Members from the Irish Dail, the Scottish Parliament and the Welsh Assembly.

As well as creating a range of new political structures the Agreement also contained areas, which might be seen as a broader 'peace' settlement. The British and Irish Governments agreed to the early release of prisoners associated with the paramilitary groups, with the last prisoners to be released after a maximum of two years. The participating parties were also expected to use their influence to achieve the decommissioning of all paramilitary weapons within a period of two years if referendums on the Agreement were passed successfully in Northern Ireland and the Republic. The British government also agreed to reduce the numbers and role of the armed forces in Northern Ireland and remove emergency powers, which had been in force since the formation of Northern Ireland in 1921.

Policing had long been a contentious issue in the north, as over ninety per cent of officers in the Royal Ulster Constabulary were from the Protestant community and the current policing arrangements were unacceptable to nationalists. The Agreement therefore provided for the creation of an Independent Commission to make recommendations for future policing arrangements. Their report (the Patten Report) led to radical overhaul of all aspects of policing and the establishment a new Police Service of Northern Ireland, which was to be based on the principles of human rights, transparency and accountability. [16] The Agreement also provided for the creation of a complete review of the wider criminal justice system, the appointment of a commissioner with responsibility for dealing with issues affecting victims of the conflict, the creation of a Human Rights Commission, and an Equality Commission with responsibility for issues related to employment, gender, disability and race issues. These elements provided for the creation of a range of institutions with responsibility to facilitate the transition from conflict and to have a role in scrutinising government and holding it publicly to account.

In the implementation of the Agreement it became increasingly apparent that there was a distinct difference in how Protestants and Catholics viewed this process. Most Catholics considered that nationalists and unionists had benefited equally from the Agreement, but in contrast most Protestants believed that nationalists had gained most. Security related issues were a significant factor in the decline of unionist support for the Agreement: the paramilitary organizations retained their weapons and structures and continued to be involved in a range of activities, but the extensive reform of the police and the reduction in the military presence, were considered unacceptable concessions.

The issue of the decommissioning of paramilitary weapons, and in particular IRA weapons since Sinn Féin was entitled to two seats in the Northern Ireland Executive (loyalist paramilitary-related parties won only two Assembly seats and were not entitled to any Executive representation), became the key issue during the Assembly's first term. The failure to resolve this issue led to the suspension of the Assembly in

October 2002. Further Assembly elections in November 2003 saw the Democratic Unionist Party and Sinn Féin returned as the two largest parties, although the Assembly did not sit because of ongoing disagreements between the main parties. A major concern of the unionist parties has been the continued existence of the structures of the IRA, although the issue of decommissioning of weapons was eventually resolved when the organisation declared in July 2005 that it was ending its 'armed campaign' and in September it was announced that almost all of its weapons had been put beyond use.

These actions ultimately paved the way for fresh discussions involving the main local parties and the two governments, which led to Sinn Féin finally endorsing the police reform process in January 2007, the final significant hurdle to restoring the local government. New elections to the Assembly took place in March 2007. The results further consolidated the dominant position of the Democratic Unionist Party and Sinn Féin as the largest Unionist and Nationalist parties. In May 2007 the Assembly was reconvened with Ian Paisley, leader of the Democratic Unionist Party as First Minister and Martin McGuinness, deputy leader of Sinn Féin as Deputy First Minister. For many people this marked the end of the period of political transition and the beginning of a period of political consolidation for the new institutions.

Problems of Embedding the Peace

There was widespread support among the general population for the ending of the conflict and the creation of a framework for future peace-building and reconciliation. But there was deep hostility and suspicion between members of the two communities, and towards many of the political parties. There was, as has been noted, a significant minority who were opposed to the Agreement, this include sections of the paramilitary movements of both loyalist and republicanism. One of the underlying difficulties of ensuring the successful transition from armed conflict to a peaceful society based on democratic institutions was that there was no broadly accepted understanding of the nature, cause or outcome of the 'Troubles.' For Protestants the Troubles were primarily considered as a 'terrorist campaign' with the aim of forcing them out of the United Kingdom and into a United Ireland. For Catholics the struggle was primarily about obtaining equality and human rights for all people in Northern Ireland, but which also meant dismantling the unfairly enforced division of Ireland and re-uniting the geographical island of Ireland as a single state.

Similarly there was no agreement about the outcome of the conflict, which effectively ended in a political and security stalemate, in which the issue of the constitutional status of Northern Ireland remained uncertain in the long term. In theory, if or when a majority of the Northern Irish electorate decides to unite with the Republic of Ireland, this will happen. This has meant that there remains a fundamental insecurity at the heart of Northern Ireland relating to issues of political and cultural identity of the two main communities, and in which there is no common agreement about building for a shared future or uniting around common symbols.

This unresolved element of the dispute between Catholic Irish and the Protestant British meant that for many people the peace process did not signal an end to the conflict, but rather that the antagonism shifted to other dimensions of activity. On one side this involved a focus on politics, debate and negotiation, which resulted in the Agreement being signed in 1998, while on the other hand it resulted in outbreaks of community and street level tensions that were related to the contested domain of territoriality, culture and identity, and which served to sustain, and indeed extend, hostility and suspicion between members of the two communities. In particular the disputes over parades, which began in 1995, were immediately established as part of the rituals of the summer marching season, and at the same time punctuated the process of political negotiation towards devolved government on an annual basis.

Over the course of the transition the political and community levels of activity have moved in erratic and occasionally parallel paths, at times each has provided a positive influence of the other, at time it has been the opposite. One of the positive elements of the situation in Northern Ireland was the strong network of community-based organizations and NGOs that had been established over the past generation to work on a range of activities related to democracy building, community development, human rights and equality. These networks were generally positive in supporting the Agreement and became very active in helping to develop and support a variety of peace-building programmes. The community networks also provide a variety of links between members of the two main communities, between the communities and the political parties and between the communities and government, these could be used to communicate concerns and ideas, but also mobilise people to challenge actions that threatened to disrupt and reverse the moves away from armed conflict. In the terms of contemporary political theory, these groups had extensive social capital that could be mobilised through cross-community associational networks to contribute to building the peace. [17]

For many people the hostilities and antipathies between British and Irish, unionists and nationalists were still very raw, and suspicion, fear and mistrust of the 'other' ensured that progress in negotiating a political agreement was slow, while the slow progress in the political process in turn helped sustain the suspicion and mistrust. The tensions were increasingly played out on the streets, particularly in the summer months, which were marked by the numerous annual public displays of loyalty to the British monarchy in the form of parades of the Orange Order and other fraternal bodies. [18] The insistence of the Orangemen of their right to march through or past Catholic residential areas during 1995 and again in 1996 provoked opposition from nationalists, which increasingly led to serious rioting that proved difficult to contain or prevent.

In July 1996, the Northern Ireland was declared to be 'on the brink of the abyss' after a week of rioting that engulfed the entire province and threatened the viability of the peace process. Although order was eventually restored the pattern was set for the next several years as the 'marching season' served to raise tensions each summer. These resulted in rioting, inter-communal disorder, and attacks on people and property. In the eight years from 1996 to 2003 the police recorded 376 riots, 1,014 disturbances and 1,327 assaults in the northern part of Belfast alone, while between 1994 and 2002 they recorded 936 attacks across Northern Ireland on symbolic properties that served as a marker of the other community, such as churches, schools, Orange halls and Gaelic Athletic Association (GAA) clubs. [19]

The problems of street disorder were exacerbated by the high levels of residential segregation, and this was reinforced by the numerous walls and barriers that had been built to provide security at the interface areas, the sensitive boundaries between rival communities, but which also served to clearly demark the presence of the other community. Territorial boundaries were also marked by the flying of rival flags and by paintings and graffiti associated with the various armed groups. Often the problems of violence were initiated by young people who gravitated to the boundaries of community territories and start trouble out of boredom or simply for the *craic* [20]

Much of this violence was informally classified as 'recreational rioting' to distinguish it from forms of politically orientated violence, [21] but regardless of the inspiration of the violence, any disorder could still raise tensions between neighbouring communities and create wider problems. Managing the tensions at interfaces thus became a serious issue in trying to consolidate the peace. The issue however was complicated by the general lack of legitimacy of the police among the nationalist community and many within working class unionist communities. This relates in large part to the history of policing in Northern Ireland. [22] Over the course of the Troubles the police became increasingly militarised, as they were used as the front line in the conflict, initially against republicanism and the IRA, and later also against loyalist paramilitaries. Thus as the conflict drew to a close the police were regarded less as the neutral arbiters of law and order, and rather as a politicised security force.

The lack of acceptance of the police meant that there was a deficit in the effective management of the tensions on the ground. Although the police had responsibility for public order, the communities often viewed their intervention as provocative acts, and which often led to an escalation of the violence. One response was to draw upon the networks of community-based groups and to mobilise activists to manage the flashpoints and contentious parades. In the decade from 1997 onwards community-based policing became widely established activities in many interface areas, as people took responsibility for trying to prevent outbreaks of rioting by patrolling the street through the night and by stewarding crowds at parades. [23] The work of community activists thus contributed to reducing the levels of violence associated with the annual parades and with residential segregation. But also the reduction in inter-communal tension and in outbreaks of violence helped to provide space and opportunity for the politicians to negotiate the implementation of the Agreement, while working together in such peace-building activities helped to provide the basis for stronger working relationships between nationalists and unionists, republicans and loyalists, which in turn increased their capacity to engage effectively in managing disorder.

Although tensions remain in many areas, they no longer have the potential to disrupt the wider peace-building programme or the new institutions. One unexpected and unplanned outcome of the community-based policing was in the development of better relations between community activists and the police. Although the relationships were initially mutually wary and cautious, over time they improved, and the Police Service of Northern Ireland (PSNI) and the communities gradually established an effective means of working together. This in turn has helped to build mutual trust and understanding, which are important early steps in building acceptance of the reformed policing service.

Model for Peace-building

The Northern Ireland peace process and political transition has been regarded as a major achievement as far as one of the world's longest-running armed conflicts has been brought to an end and a democratic and broadly accountable political system has been established. The transition has been a slow process and not without its difficulties, but more than a decade after the signing of the peace agreement, a range of new political and human rights institutions have been successfully established and the economy is growing. There are a number of key factors that have helped to establish the peace in Northern Ireland and which might provide some guidance on the value of the Northern Ireland example as a model for other areas undergoing the same process of transition. These key aspects are the inclusivity of political participation, the involvement of the relevant national governments, a wider international involvement, an active role for local civil society, extensive financial and economic support, and a willingness to support and sustain the process over a number of years.

The negotiation process leading to the Agreement in 1998 was fully inclusive with all the main local political parties fully involved, including those with a close association with one of the armed groups. Initial multi-party talks in the early 1990s excluded Sinn Féin, the party with close links with the armed conflict, but once the IRA declared ceasefire in 1994, Sinn Féin were included in discussions, even though the main unionist parties initially refused to meet with their representatives face to face. Furthermore, as discussions progressed a much wider range of parties were involved and elections to a Northern Ireland forum in 1996 were structured to ensure that the ten largest parties were all involved, including parties associated with loyalist paramilitaries and the Women's Coalition, which was specifically established to promote the presence of women in politics.

Second, the British and Irish governments fully supported and participated in the process throughout its long duration and they provided support, guidance and influence, as well as making concessions to ensure the success of the project. The two governments had been working together since the mid-1980s to promote a resolution to the conflict, but for a long time Northern Ireland issues were regarded as solely British responsibilities, but once it was recognized that both interested states should have a role in the process – with the British providing support and encouragement to unionists and the Irish government offering the same to nationalist - discussions were able to move forward on a number of levels and be sustained more readily.

Third, there was an extensive international involvement in the process. The American government played an important role, particularly in the earlier years when Bill Clinton was in power and he designated Senator George Mitchell as a special envoy to the peace process. American interest highlighted the wider significance of the conflict and brought further sustained pressure to bear on local politicians to engage in constructive talks. The broader significance was also highlighted by the involvement of other international partners and actors including individuals from Canada, Finland and South Africa, among others, in key activities such as police reform and demilitarization. The international actors also provided a level of independent verification of progress on key issues that was used to reassure both to the two national governments and Northern Irish political parties.

Fourth, local civil society was a key actor in helping to support and build peace from the bottom up, to mirror the work of the political elite. Northern Ireland has an active civil society and it took an important role in promoting dialogue between the various groups and communities, of including ex-combatants in the process, in lobbying and working with politicians, and in responding to local crises and outbreaks of violence. Civil society groups also looked further afield and drew upon the experiences and ideas of groups in other conflict areas to develop work in Northern Ireland. Recent theoretical approaches to conflict transformation have highlighted the importance of grass roots peace-building activities to complement and support the elite level political discussions and this was certainly a factor in embedding the peace in Northern Ireland.

Fifth, the process received extensive financial support from the EU and the US, which helped embed both peace-building activities and projects and provide support for renewing and extending the infrastructure and promoting physical and economic regeneration. The economy had largely stagnated during the conflict and the opportunities for investment and business development had a positive impact on the local economy, promoting jobs and increasing the standard of living. The improvement in the local economy undoubtedly had a positive impact on peace-building as people had evidence of a wide range of benefits of the end of the conflict, beyond an end to violence and physical insecurity.

Sixth, the process was sustained, and key participants remained engaged, even though it stalled and appeared on the verge of collapse on a number of occasions. The broadly inclusive and multi-dimensional process generated after the ceasefires created a wider momentum for peace and change that was sustained even during times of violence and crisis. For example, the ceasefires broke down at times, armed groups killed people, there were extensive outbursts of inert-communal rioting, the demilitarization and demobilization of the armed groups did not happen according to schedule and the new devolved government collapsed on a number of occasions. Each of these had the potential to precipitate an end to negotiations and a return to conflict. But the various checks and balances through the participation of the British, the Irish, the Americans and local civil society all provided opportunities for ongoing discussion and created pressure to keep going until a more sustained peace could be established.

Some of these elements are obviously more transferable to other contexts and conflicts than others. The concept of inclusivity all parties in the discussions and negotiations, of a sustained process of engagement and of the potential positive role of civil society, are transferable to most contexts. But the sustained engagement of three governments and the financial support from the European Union, whilst important in Northern Ireland, are perhaps also unique to Northern Ireland, with the conflict's location in Western Europe being a factor that highlighted the importance of making the process work. In other conflicts, the interest and engagement of the major external powers all too readily dissipates once an agreement has been signed, and few if any other post-conflict societies have benefited from the scale of financial support that Northern Ireland has received. But these were clearly important elements in this process and should nevertheless become points of reference and citation for other contexts, even if a direct translation of practice is not possible.

The Northern Ireland experience suggests that a peace process is to be transformed into a of conflict transformation. That will benefit all parties and sections of society, and therefore will reduce the potential for a return to arms. However, this sustained and embedded process will take a considerable period or time, it will require sustained support from outside bodies, it will require investment, and local people must be able to have evidence of positive change for them. Furthermore, a process of conflict transformation must deal with the conflict on a number of levels, not merely ending the violence, but also offering the opportunities and potential for changing people's daily lives, both through addressing the structural causes of the violence and the inequalities and abuses that inevitably precede armed conflict. The process in Northern Ireland has been successful not only because it brought an end to armed violence but also because it offered people the possibility of a positive future beyond violence, and which would be based on a framework of rights and equality, rather than discrimination and inequalities.

Notes

1. John Paul Lederach, *Building Peace: Sustainable Reconciliation in Divided Societies* (Washington DC: United States Institute for Peace, 1997).
2. For broader ranging perspectives see Michael Cox, Adrian Guelke and Fiona Stephen, ed., *A Farewell to Arms? From 'Long War' to Long Peace in Northern Ireland* (Manchester: Manchester University Press, 2000); Roger McGinty and John Darby, *Guns and Government: The Management of the Northern Ireland Peace Process* (Basingstoke: Palgrave, 2002); Jörg Neuheiser and Stefan Wolff, ed., *Peace at Last? The Impact of the Good Friday Agreement on Northern Ireland* (New York: Berghan Books, 2003).
3. For a general history of the north of Ireland see Jonathan Bardon, *A History of Ulster* (Belfast: Blackstaff Press, 1992).
4. Michael Farrell, *Northern Ireland: The Orange State* (London: Pluto Press, 1980).
5. Neil Jarman, *Material Conflicts: Parades and Visual Displays in Northern Ireland* (Oxford: Berg, 1997).
6. Bob Purdie, *Politics in the Streets: The Origins of the Civil Rights Movement in Northern Ireland* (Belfast: The Blackstaff Press, 1990).
7. Marie-Therese Fay, Mike Morrissey and Marie Smyth, *Northern Ireland's Troubles: The Human Costs* (London: Pluto Press, 1999), pp. 136-139.
8. Ibid., pp. 158-161.
9. John Darby, *Intimidation and the Control of Conflict in Northern Ireland* (Syracuse: Syracuse University Press, 1986), pp. 58-59.
10. Neil Jarman, *Managing Disorder: Responding to Interface Violence in North Belfast* (Belfast: Office of the First Minister and Deputy First Minister, 2002), pp. 21-27. See also the

website of Belfast Interface Project: www.belfastinterfaceproject.org

11. Fay, et al, n. 7, p. 95.
12. Purdie, n. 6.
13. Fay, et al, n. 7, pp. 95-117.
14. Deloitte, *Research into the Financial Cost of the Northern Ireland Divide* (Belfast: Office of the First Minister and Deputy First Minister, 2007).
15. Ibid., pp. 25-27.
16. *A New Beginning for Policing in Northern Ireland* (Belfast: Independent Review of Policing, 1999).
17. Robert Putnam, *Bowling Alone: The Collapse and Revival of American Community* (New York: Simon and Schuster, 2000); Ashutosh Varshney, *Ethnic Conflict and Civic Life: Hindus and Muslims in India* (New Haven: Yale University Press, 2002).
18. Jarman, n. 5.
19. Neil Jarman, "From War to Peace? Changing patterns of Violence in Northern Ireland, 1990-2003," *Terrorism and Political Violence*, vol. 16, no. 3, Autumn 2004, pp. 420-438.
20. *Craic* is an Irish word with a meaning similar to 'fun.'
21. Neil Jarman and Chris O'Halloran, "Recreational Rioting: Young People, Interface Areas and Violence," *Child Care in Practice* (Belfast), vol. 7, no.1, January 2001, pp. 2-16.
22. Graham Ellison and Jim Smyth, *The Crowned Harp: Policing Northern Ireland* (London: Pluto Press, 2000).
23. Neil Jarman, "Vigilantism, Policing and Transition: Informal Justice in Northern Ireland" in David Pratten and Atreyee Sen, eds., *Global Vigilantes: Anthropological Perspectives on Justice and Violence* (London: Hurst, 2007), pp. 319-336.

Part II: The Asian Context

4

Challenges of Ethno-Nationalism in Balochistan

Aasim Sajjad Akhtar

In thinking about 'conflict areas,' there is always a tendency to assume symmetry on the various sides of the conflict in question. The term 'conflict' itself does not directly imply inequality in the possession of economic and political resources but rather posits two or more protagonists in competition over resources. In cases where 'conflicts' are a function of systemic subjugation, it is crucial to flag this point so as to ensure that any analysis of the 'conflict' in question begins by clarifying the asymmetries that define it. The subject of this chapter is the low-intensity war between the central government of Pakistan and ethno-nationalist forces in the south-western province of Balochistan that has raged since late 2004.

The present conflict marks a renewal of armed resistance by nationalists to the state after a period of almost 30 years. Through the 1970s a much more organized and widespread insurgency engaged tens of thousands of Pakistani military forces. More generally, the Baloch nationalist narrative claims that the Baloch nation has been subjugated by a predominantly Punjabi military establishment as soon as the state came into being. Nationalists have disputed the central government's refusal to accord the province autonomy since as early as 1948 when the then princely state of Kalat acceded to Pakistan. [1] It is therefore crucial to analyze the present phase of the conflict taking into account the underlying centralized and unitary nature of the Pakistani state alongside the counter-claims of ethno-national groups including the Baloch.

Sovereignty versus Federal Democracy

According to the 1940 Lahore Resolution which rhetorically underlies the Pakistan demand, the relationship between provinces and the centre was to be characterized by the principles of federal democracy thereby implying considerable decentralization of power. In particular the provinces were to have control over all but three basic state affairs- defence, foreign policy and finance- which would remain under the purview of the centre. When Pakistan was actually formed after the partition of the subcontinent in 1947, 'it was the Western colonial ideology of an indivisible sovereignty as underwritten by a centralized state structure' which prevailed. This can be attributed to various factors including the weaknesses of the Muslim League leadership that had spearheaded the nationalist movement, the incumbent power of the administrative apparatus of the state, the emergent imperative of defence against 'Hindu' India and the ethnic imbalance in the structures of power in favour of Punjabis and Urdu-speaking *Muhajirs* (refugees). [2]

Subsequently the political process was stunted and the power of the unelected 'military-bureaucratic oligarchy' consolidated. The state attempted to build national unity around the symbols of Islam and Urdu but this project had no takers from amongst the under-represented ethnic groups which included the Bengalis, Sindhis and Baloch. More generally the equation of religion to nation which underlay the Muslim League's 'two-nation theory' was challenged immediately after the inception of the state by ethno-national elites. The latter claimed that Pakistan was a multi-national state and that each of the separate nations that together constituted it had to be acknowledged as such and accordingly be given their due rights. These ethno-national movements repeatedly invoked the 1940 Lahore Resolution and emerged as the biggest challengers to the unitary state project. For its part the state continuously refuted the claims of the ethno-nationalists and accused them of undermining 'national security.' [3]

The oligarchy's fear of a democratic dispensation ensured that the first election in the country's history took place only in 1970, after which the state was dismembered due to the ruling military junta's refusal to hand over power to the Bengali-dominated Awami League which had secured an outright majority in the national assembly. Following the secession of the eastern wing a unique opportunity existed to undermine the unitary state once and for all and to establish a genuine federal parliamentary system of government. However, 'the dominant classes shunned a deeper introspection into the real reasons for the creation of Bangladesh in favour of rewriting national history.' [4] Only a few months after approving a new constitution with the consent of many ethno-nationalists, one that appeared to imbibe the spirit of the 1940 Lahore Resolution, the government of Zulfikar Ali Bhutto dismissed the nationalist-led provincial government of Balochistan. This action triggered the insurgency and confirmed that the post-colonial Pakistani state remained committed to a unitary nationalism that was anathema to the principle of federal democracy. [5]

The Contours of Conflict

The insurgency of the 1970s was put down by 1977 and ethno-national leaders eventually allowed to go into exile. Balochistan's historical grievances vis-à-vis the centre remained unresolved with low levels of development expenditure and a lack of representation at the higher echelons of the administrative apparatus of the state emerging as endemic problems. In thinking about the renewal of armed conflict since 2004, it is important to first acknowledge the longer-term structural situation as outlined here. The conflict was given fresh impetus by the government's attempts to assert its control over Balochistan's territory and natural resources, the latter emerging as the immediate causes of renewed violence.

More specifically the Musharraf regime's announcement that it was building three new military cantonments in the province, taking direct control over the Sui gas plant which meets over half of the country's domestic gas requirement, and unilaterally building a mega port in the southwestern town Gwadar have re-ignited the nationalist movement. Militants have targeted government installations across the province, focusing in particular on railway tracks and gas pipelines but more generally targeting any communication links between the province and the north. Since the beginning of the conflict in late 2004, there have been more than three thousand sabotage attacks, their intensity ebbing and flowing over time. The various (fragmented) sources through which information on the nature and successes of the guerilla attacks is disseminated have been unable provide any reliable estimates of the material costs of the conflict. Needless to say the damages have run into the billions of rupees but the government has been unwilling to disclose any figures in this regard. However, what is clear is that much of the damaged or destroyed infrastructure has yet to be rebuilt and there is very little that the government can do—in terms of military strategy—to stem such sabotage attacks.

The insurgents have also engaged government forces in various locations and the guerilla tactics that the former have employed have necessarily brought moderate results. An estimated 800 government troops have been killed over the past four years although this figure should be considered subject to 20 per cent error both upwards and downwards. In more recent times the intensity of the guerilla attacks has subsided somewhat which indicates that the government's claims of having significantly weakened the insurgency are at least partially correct. This raises an important point, namely that the conflict of the past four years is an even more asymmetrical one than during the 1970s.

While it is true that the insurgents have caused considerable damage to official property and taken the lives of government troops, it is also indubitable that the insurgency does not represent a challenge to the writ of the state in the way that a parallel insurgency in the Pakhtun areas of the country does. Indeed it is debatable whether in the Balochistan case it is accurate to use the word insurgency at all. Nonetheless, given the history of conflict in the province, and the widespread moral and political support that the insurgents enjoy amongst the majority of Baloch people, the government has wielded a considerable amount of force, deploying thousands of paramilitaries in the form of the Frontier Constabulary in the parts of the province that are most gripped by tension. In particular the areas around the Sui gas plant and yet untapped reserves of the Kahan hills are the heartland of the militants and it is here where the majority of pitch battles between the two sides have taken place. [6] There have also been a number of aerial bombardments of targets—mostly in the same areas—that the government has claimed are 'terrorist strongholds.' It is on account of these bombardments that the most loss of life has taken place.

The result has been the establishment of the government's writ in many parts of the province that were previously subject to a more autonomous structure of authority that dates back to the British period. Balochistan before its accession to Pakistan was administered as two separate entities, namely British Balochistan and the Kalat State. The former was considered an 'A' area subject to direct British control while the former was a princely state which was autonomous in matters of internal administration ('B' area). In effect the British ruled through intermediaries in these 'B' areas, namely tribal *sardars* (the Head) whose historical role was qualitatively altered by the colonial power. This system remained intact after Pakistan's inception. In 2004 in the period leading up to the eruption of conflict, General Musharraf asserted that the state wanted to extend its writ into the 95 per cent of the province that was still 'B' area. The police did not function in these 'B' areas as late as three years ago whereas it has now established a measure of control in most of the districts previously untouched by the state's administrative apparatus. Therefore, the insurgents have been incapable of preventing the state from achieving its immediate objectives. However, it can be argued that the state's growing presence has in fact enhanced the popularity of the insurgents due to the public disenchantment with what continues to be considered a colonial state. [7]

The Human and Intangible Costs

It is understood the costs of the conflict have weighed heavily on the civilian populations that are caught in the midst of violence. In particular, the bombing of villages has resulted not only in loss of life but also in large-scale displacement and dispossession of men, women and children with no meaningful resettlement option. The exact numbers are virtually impossible to garner given that the government has not released any official figures on the extent of the casualties and numbers displaced. In fact, the coverage of the government's actions in the area tends to be limited to sporadic and vague reporting of official initiatives to 'counter miscreants' in which the only information offered is the number of 'miscreants' that have been killed. [8]

Baloch nationalists estimate that more than 2000 innocents have lost their lives over the past four years whereas they are much more discreet about figures of insurgents killed. [9] Since August 2006, at least two of the major figureheads of the insurgency, Nawab Akbar Bugti and Nawabzada Balach Marri have been killed by the authorities. These are amongst the handful of well-publicized incidents in which civilian loss of life has been acknowledged even by official sources. Just as devastating as loss of life has been the destruction of livelihoods and permanent shelters. On this account even nationalist sources tend to have only a vague sense of the numbers involved but the estimate of displaced families runs into the thousands. [10] The most acutely hit area has been Dera Bugti in the months preceding and following Akbar Bugti's death. Virtually all of Dera Bugti town was deserted whereas most surrounding settlements were also cleared out due to the high-intensity attacks being conducted by the authorities. [11] Things having settled down somewhat, a fraction of the population of Dera Bugti has returned.

Balochistan's climate is mostly arid and rainfall is very sparse at the best of times. The primary livelihood source for most rural families remains livestock rearing. The destruction of homes has also meant the death of large numbers of livestock and therefore livelihoods. Even before the eruption of violence, many parts of the province were subject to an extended drought that had already created crisis-like conditions due to the death of livestock, destruction of a series of agricultural harvests and an acute shortage of water. Large numbers of men migrate into urban areas under ordinary circumstances and the elimination of the traditional source of livelihood has compelled many more to do so.

This development has put an additional burden on women to meet various burdens of running the household in the absence of a regular source of livelihood and—in some cases—lack of permanent shelter. In the summer of 2007, after years of drought, flash floods wreaked havoc in many parts of the province thereby exacerbating the problem of displacement. Following these flash floods as well as in the aftermath of major confrontations between insurgents and government troops, the authorities have refused to acknowledge the scale of devastation and have even denied the need for immediate relief. On repeated occasions aid from international agencies has been refused while attempts to gather information have been actively prevented presumably because any impartial investigation would yield conclusions not consistent with the government's depiction of events.

In some cases displaced communities have ended up living in destitute conditions on the outskirts of major cities. For example on the fringes of the provincial capital Quetta is the so-called Marri camp in which hundreds of families from the Marri tribe—which is at the heart of the conflict in the Kahan area—have been subsisting in makeshift tents in sub-human conditions. [12] There is a distinct shortage of working-age males in the area as many have been kidnapped by security agencies under the pretext that they are party to militancy in their home region. This means that women and children are forced into begging or quasi-criminal activities to make ends meet, if they can at all.

More generally the issue of 'missing persons' has become an extremely charged one in recent times. Hundreds of activists of nationalist organizations including the Baloch Students Organization (BSO) have been kidnapped since the beginning of the current phase of conflict. In some cases they have been released after many months incommunicado but in many more cases they are still missing. The government has repeatedly refused to acknowledge its detention of the missing persons although it is a widely-known fact that this is a cover-up. One of the major reasons for the falling out of the deposed Chief Justice of the Supreme Court and the military top brass was the issue of missing persons; the Chief Justice repeatedly summoned heads of the intelligence agencies demanding that they produce the missing persons before the court, thereby earning the wrath of an establishment that is very rarely shown up in this manner. [13]

The various humanitarian costs are necessarily the most acute fallout of the conflict. However arguably, if not more pressing, is the intensification of the long-held perception across much of Balochistan that the Pakistani state is little more than a colonizing entity that seeks to exploit the resources of the Baloch while undermining their cultural autonomy. The narrative of Baloch nationalism within Balochistan has been enduring because of a long history of marginalization and it appears that the recent phase of conflict has simply reinforced the belief amongst the Baloch people that they have no stake in Pakistan. This deep alienation fuels the militancy regardless of how organized or effective it is. It is common to hear ordinary Baloch remark that it matters little who the militants are, from where they receive support and what their objectives are, because as long as they are fighting Pakistani army they will enjoy the support of Baloch people.

Efforts at Peace (or Lack Thereof)

Ironically it was a military ruler, Zia-ul-Haq, that initially offered amnesty to leaders of the insurgency of the 1970s, releasing them from jail and allowing them to go into exile. This gesture might be construed as a peace offering on the part of the state, but it is more accurately thought of as an attempt by an illegitimate military regime to generate some measure of political support following its overthrow of Zulfikar Ali Bhutto's popular government. This is borne out by the fact that the structural injustices that have fuelled Baloch nationalism were not addressed meaningfully in the post-1977 period. When a semblance of electoral democracy was restored to Pakistan following Zia's death in 1988, various nationalist leaders that had been active in the 1970s insurgency shared power at the provincial level, Akbar Bugti and Akhtar Mengal amongst the more prominent who were chief minister in one or the other government between 1988 and 1999. However, throughout this period little, if any, attempt was made to dismantle the unitary state structure. Tensions between Balochistan (and other provinces) and the centre continued to simmer, and the nationalist idiom remained popular.

It was not until the Musharraf regime's decision to reconfigure the administrative arrangement and to acquire greater control over the province's natural resources that direct conflict was resumed. The military government's new posture has been built around the rhetoric of bringing 'development' to the province and accordingly in vilifying the 'sardari' system for keeping the Baloch people in a perennial state of deprivation. What is conveniently ignored in this official discourse of development is the fact that the 'sardari' system has been the preferred method of indirect rule by the state since colonial times. Perhaps more tellingly, the majority of

Baloch *sardars* have remained in the pro-government camp since the outbreak of hostilities in late 2004. In any case the development claims continue to be employed by the military regime even as the armed operation to do away with all forms of resistance carries on simultaneously.

The only meaningful attempt to engage nationalist forces in a dialogue took place in Dera Bugti in April 2005 when two major leaders of the ruling PML-Q party went to meet Nawab Akbar Bugti. The highly publicized visit produced a verbal agreement between the two sides to work towards an amenable solution to the conflict. The two PML-Q leaders were actually representing a parliamentary sub-committee that had been formed in September 2004 by the Senate to investigate the nature of the conflict in the province. Members of the ruling coalition were in the majority but opposition members including Baloch nationalists were also co-opted. [14] In the aftermath of the Dera Bugti visit, the parliamentary committee put together a relatively comprehensive report acknowledging that the central government has neglected Balochistan's 'development' needs in the past and that there is widespread resentment against the state across the province.

No sooner had the report been completed major military strikes were resumed by the government. It is a matter of conjecture that there may be major differences in the attitude of elements within the ruling regime on what the state's posture towards the Baloch nationalists should be. What matters is that the initial attempt at restoring some peace has clearly been foregone in favour of the use of force. Naturally nationalist forces have responded in kind while completely losing faith in the possibility of dialogue resolving the conflict. With the killing of Akbar Bugti in August 2006 with whom the initial peace was forged, it appears that the government has clearly indicated its unwillingness to compromise in any meaningful way with the insurgents. Despite the fact that insurgent attacks on government installations decreased in 2007, the government killed another major Baloch nationalist leader, Balach Marri, in November 2007, yet another indicator that there is almost no chance of the government initiating a fresh attempt at peace.

There has been very little in the way of international and or/regional peace efforts. This speaks of a variety of factors. First, the Baloch movement has been relatively small in comparison to other sub-nationalist conflicts in the region such as that in Sri Lanka or Kashmir as well as the most obvious conflict in adjacent Afghanistan. Second, there is virtual consensus amongst the big players in the region that pacifying Balochistan is necessary if the oil and gas of the Caspian region is to find a transport route to Arabian Sea and the Indian Ocean. [15] In particular, China has been at the forefront of the Gwadar Port construction while India has repeatedly indicated its interest in securing new sources of gas given its rising consumer and industrial demand. [16] Third, Iran has always supported the Pakistani state's attempts to crush Baloch nationalists given the fact that Iran is home to a sizeable Baloch population itself.

There are speculations about the various possible sources of support for the insurgents. The state has consistently propagated the idea (not necessarily at an official level) that either Afghanistan or India (or both) are covertly supplying the insurgents with weapons to undermine the sovereignty of Pakistan. In the 1970s the Soviet Union was widely believed to have supported the Baloch insurgency—at least to some extent —and thus there is also conjecture about Russia supporting the insurgents at the present juncture. In any case, what is clear is that there has been no attempt by regional powers to secure some kind of peace. Meanwhile multilateral agencies such as the United Nations have also remained dead quiet on the matter, in contrast to their stand on many other similar conflicts around the world. Even the rebuffing of aid offers by the Pakistani government has not induced any meaningful response. It would appear that the international community at large is generally uninterested in establishing peace in the region or at best considers this an internal matter that does not merit any intervention. This attitude smacks of complicity at best and downright hypocrisy at worst.

Current Scenario

The conflict in Balochistan appears farther from being resolved than ever before. As pointed out earlier, the intensity of the violence decreased somewhat through the year 2007 while the government established much greater control over large geographical swathes of territory. [17] However, the long-standing tensions that have characterized the relationship between the province and the centre seem only to have increased over the course of the past few years. Unfolding events in the Pakhtun areas have relegated the Balochistan conflict to one of secondary importance but this is not to say that the problem has become any less serious. The most telling indicator of this is the increasing alienation of educated youth from the centre and indeed from the Pakistani state more generally.

A visit to major educational institutions such as Balochistan University or Bolan Medical College provides an insight into the severe disaffection amongst young people. There is complete lack of faith in the 'development' claims of the state whereas there is also an unwillingness to entertain further dialogue with the government or even participation in what is considered a tainted political process dominated by a self-serving military. It is this feeling of total alienation that pulls young people towards the militant alternative as it not only corresponds to the historical narrative of the nationalist movement but also appears the only meaningful option in the face of a belligerent central government. Accordingly, the state views any and all nationalist activism in Balochistan as subversive, even in cases where youth are not actually affiliated with any militant organization. In other words, there is a complete gulf in the self-perception and attitudes of the protagonists that would seem to preclude any possibility of establishing peace.

While there is little chance of short-term reconciliation, the only option for peace in the long run necessarily involves an overhaul of the centre-province relationship and a reconfiguration of the ideological basis of the state more generally. In the first and last instance, this is contingent on the complete withdrawal of the military from the political sphere and the establishment of an unfettered and uninterrupted political process that allows the Baloch—and other ethno-national groups—an opportunity to actively participate in the decision-making process. This will reinvigorate faith in the 1973 constitution, or perhaps throw open the possibility of a new constitutional order that reflects the aspirations of all of Pakistan's nationalities. One can also hope that such an uninterrupted political process would permit a new generation of Baloch youth an opportunity to feel much more integrated into Pakistan rather than consider the state as an alien entity out to enforce its writ. It would appear that there is no other option if the Pakistani state is to reverse the trend towards fragmentation.

Notes

1. Many nationalists, including the brother of the Khan himself, insist that the Kalat state was forced to accede under the barrel of a gun.
2. Ayesha Jalal, *Pakistan: The Political Economy of Defence* (Cambridge: Cambridge University Press, 1990); Ayesha Jalal, *Democracy and Authoritarianism in South Asia* (Cambridge: Cambridge University Press 1995).
3. From its very inception, the Pakistani state has made 'national security' its raison d'etre. Hamza Alavi, "Pakistan and Islam: Ethnicity and Ideology" in H. Alavi and F. Halliday, eds., *State and Ideology in the Middle East and Pakistan* (New York: Monthly Review Press, 1987).
4. Mustapha Kamal Pasha, "Islamisation, Civil Society and the Politics of Transition in Pakistan," in D. Allen, ed., *Religion and Political Conflict in South Asia: India, Pakistan and Sri Lanka* (Westport: Greenwood Press, 2004), p. 116.

5. For a detailed analysis of the insurgency of the 1970s, see Selig Harrison, *In Afghanistan's Shadow: Baloch Nationalism and Soviet Temptation* (New York: Carnegie Endowment for International Peace, 1981). For a comparison of the movement of the 1970s and the present see Aasim Sajjad Akhtar, "Balochistan versus Pakistan" *Economic and Political Weekly*, vol. 42, no. 45 and 46, 2007.
6. Militancy has been spearheaded by a nebulous organization named the Baloch Liberation Army (BLA), the details of which remain very sparse. The typical pattern is such that sabotage attacks on government installations are followed by faxes to major newspaper offices in which the BLA claims responsibility. While insurgent strongholds appear to be in the Dera Bugti, Kahan and Kohlu areas, there have been skirmishes and sabotage attacks across the 30 districts of the province.
7. This normative assertion tends to be backed up by figures that suggest an increase in 'crime' after 2004, even in those districts that have been converted to 'A' areas. See *South Asia Intelligence Review* Weekly Assessments and Briefings, vol. 5, no. 47, 4 June 2007.
8. See for example http://www.dawn.com/2006/02/07/ top5.htm. (A. O. 23 January 2008).
9. This figure is generated on the basis of various interviews, newspaper reports, the *South Asian Intelligence Review* and information from websites maintained by nationalist groups like www.balochvoice.com and www.Asaappublications.com.
10. The district *nazim* (mayor) of Dera Bugti estimates that 100,000 people have been forced to leave their homes in his district alone.
11. The government repeatedly attributed the forced migration of thousands to the brutality of the 'sardari' system but it was clear that the intensive bombardment and shelling of the area is the primary reason for displacement.
12. Some of these families have actually been living in the camp since the early 1990s following their return from exile in Afghanistan that began after the end of the insurgency of the 1970s.
13. The predominant perception seems to have been that most of the 'missing persons' are professionals with an ideological leaning towards militant Islam. However, the majority of those who

have disappeared over the past few years are Baloch activists.

14. In actuality, the major nationalist parties eventually removed themselves from the committee as they felt that participation in the process was damaging their legitimacy in Balochistan given the fact that government attacks did not cease even after the committee issued its report.
15. This is what Ahmed Rashid has called the New Great Game. However, Balochistan's stability matters only insofar as Afghanistan becomes relatively conflict-free. See Ahmed Rashid, *Taliban: Militant Islam, Oil and Fundamentalism in Central Asia.* (New Haven: Yale University Press, 2001).
16. During a public seminar held in Islamabad during a visit of the secretaries of the Communist Party of India (CPI) and Communist Party of India-Marxist (CPI[M]) in 2005, CPI secretary A.B. Bardhan insisted that cooperation between India and Pakistan in the procurement of fresh sources of energy represented a great opportunity to enhance peace between the two countries. When asked about his feelings on the fact that Balochistan's gas resources were one of the major sources of the conflict in the province, Bardhan said 'this is your internal matter.'
17. Balochistan is a very large landmass with a very small population that means that large expanses of land are unpopulated at least in part due to inhospitable terrain and climate. Overall Balochistan comprises about 44 per cent of Pakistan's territory.

5

Maoist Insurgency in Nepal: Context, Cost and Consequences

Manish Thapa

Founded in 1769 AD, the Nepal is multiethnic, multilingual and multi-religious and one of the oldest states in the world. The 1814-1816 war with the British East India Company and the subsequent Sugauli Treaty with the East India Company defined the present day borders of Nepal that lies sandwiched between India and China. [1] It is renowned for spectacular natural beauty of mountains and culture of tolerance and peace symbolized by Lumbini, the birthplace of Lord Buddha, the apostle of peace. For this very reason, Nepal had once declared itself a Zone of Peace in the late 1980s. A rich culture notwithstanding, Nepal is a poor developing country with various social and economic ills. The prevailing political system was blamed for country's socio-economic ills. Democracy was seen as the panacea, and it became Nepal's great hope. Although political parties were banned, a pro-democracy movement was growing. From the outset, this was centred at educational institutions of higher learning.

Pro-democratic movement gathered strength in late 1989 and the late King Birendra finally acceded to their demands, giving the country a constitutional monarchy and multi-party democratic system. Despite introduction of Democracy, people's expectation that development would follow democracy did not materialize. Unemployment soared, and along with it, disillusionment and dissent. The country failed to achieve stability despite three parliamentary and two local elections. Twelve governments were formed between 1990 and 2002. Corruption became widespread and the fruits of democracy only served the purpose of dominant upper caste groups, in a country where there are more than 103 ethnic caste groups. A culture of impunity flourished as powerful leaders got away with the abuse of power. This period saw an explosion of identity movement as marginalized groups—including various ethnic, caste, religious and gender groups each of which faced political, economic, cultural and socio-economic discrimination—began to demand autonomy, reservations and proportional representations. In short, little of substance in improving the living conditions of the people occurred even after the dawn of democracy.

The Maoists seemed betrayed by the failed promise of democracy. In 1994, they abandoned legislative seats and their leaders went underground. Then in February 1996, they declared People's War, claiming that only a communist state could solve the country's ills, thus giving birth to Maoist Insurgency in the country. After a decade of the rising tide of Maoist insurgency, peace was destroyed, giving rise to widespread fear and sense of insecurity. The Maoists received considerable support in rural areas, especially from women and excluded caste and ethnic groups, and expanded rapidly. The Maoists also suppressed opposition with violent means and benefited from infighting in the formal political establishment. Likewise, the linchpin of the democratic system: election of the local bodies and the national parliament has been stalled. Educational institutions were in shambles and the economy was on the path to ruin, throttling badly needed development works in order to address widespread poverty, which further fuelled insurgency. The country's social and physical infrastructure, built over the years, was also gradually destroyed.

Nepal is now in the midst of the most successful Maoist insurgency the world has witnessed in recent decades. On 23 November 2001- after four months of cease-fire and peace talks- the Maoists walked out of the dialogue blaming the government for not responding to any of their conditions favourably. After the breakdown of the talks, the Maoists launched armed attacks on army barracks, police stations and other government offices in various districts of Nepal. Finally on 25 November 2001 the Maoists declared the formation of a 'People's Liberation Army' to carry forward the people's war. It was then that the government realized the police failure to control the insurgency, and the army was mobilized. The second round of peace talks between the Maoists and the government was announced in early January 2003 and was followed by a cease-fire by both sides on 29 January 2003. With talks continuing until August, the cease-fire lasted for about seven months. On the eve of the fourth round of talks on 17 August 2003 the Royal Nepal Army conducted a raid in Doramba village of Ramechap district where Maoist cadres were reportedly holding cultural programmes to spread the message of their politics. As many as 19 Maoist cadres were arrested and, reportedly, shot at point blank range in an execution style killing. The Maoists then walked out of the peace talks and hostilities resumed. [2]

King Gyandendra, who became the King after his Brother's entire family was killed in the palace massacre in 2001, dissolved the elected government in 2002 and took complete control of the country in February 2005 in a bloodless coup. This served as a breading ground for the Seven Political Party Alliance, struggling for the democracy in Nepal and the Maoists to work together. They agreed to launch a joint movement against the King and were successful in forcing him to relinquish power in April 2006 after a 19-day popular protest that mobilized people from all over Nepal. The Maoist and Government signed a Comprehensive Peace treaty in November 2006. Elections for the constituent assembly to draft a new constitution were held in April 2008, making Maoists the biggest party. Now the party has an upper hand in constitution making process.

Several scholarly debates and analysis were conducted in the past to understand the root causes of Maoist Insurgency in

Nepal. Given the magnitude of the crisis, the exploration of its causes and its success has become a subject of interest to commentators and scholars in Nepal and beyond. Popular wisdom holds that insurgency was a direct result of the increasing despondency felt by the poor and socially marginalized in the country. While there is an element of truth in these prevailing analyses, evidence suggests that the underlying causes of the origin of insurgency, its rapid growth, and continuing success are far more complex. [3] This chapter has attempted to look into the origin of this conflict from a different perspective including the socio-economic factors, trans-boundary factors, internal politics, etc. It will look into the Maoist Insurgency and explore its causes from a wider perspective to provide an intensive overview of origin of the Maoism in Nepal and its spread and multiple impacts.

Root Causes of Conflict

Lund and Mehler divide the root causes of conflict into four main areas- imbalance of political, social, economic and cultural Opportunities; illegitimate, undemocratic and inefficient governance; absence of opportunities for the peaceful reconciliation of group interests and for bridging dividing lines between groups and absence of an active and organized civil society. [4] Nearly all of the causes mentioned are present in Nepal.

Conflict between forces seeking change and those resisting it has been ongoing since the dawn of democratic awakening in the 1940s. After the declaration of the Peoples War by the Maoist, Nepal became a country under siege with violence. There is widespread consensus as to the root causes of the conflict in Nepal. The closely related grievances—inequitable socio-economic and political access, bad governance, corruption and widespread poverty—were used by the Maoists to justify their challenges to the legitimacy of the government. All these factors played a key role in motivating certain sectors of the population to join or at least support Maoists movement and their cause. [5] The new political order set up after 1990 failed to include all sections of Nepali society and nationalities and Dalits (untouchable caste). They remained—and they felt they were—outside both mainstream politics and the reach of development programmes. Traditional regional disparities continued and far flung areas like districts of Karnali Zone remained under-represented in politics, planning and the development processes. Meantime, the gap between the people in the rural and urban areas and between the rich and the poor continued to widen.

It did not take long for the insurgency launched simultaneously in three mid-western mountain districts of Rolpa, Rukum, Jajarkot and Gorkha, and Sindhuli in the east to spread. By the year 2000, Maoist violence had left no district unaffected and by mid January 2001, the Maoists had declared the formation of a provisional revolutionary district government in Rukum, Jajarkot, Sallyan and Rolpa districts. There are many theories on why the influence spread as fast as it did. Some attribute the spread of rebel influence to the involvement and support of the excluded groups—mainly women, minorities and the Dalits—but there is not enough evidence to isolate this as the main reason. As noted by Saubhagya Shah, the epicentre of the insurgency—the Rapti Zone in the mid-western Nepal—is not the most backward region in the country. He argues that "if social and economic marginalization alone were responsible for the emergence of the Maoist Movements, the hill districts of Karnali, Seti and Mahakali zones would be far more likely candidates, not only because of their grinding poverty and chronic food shortage, but also because of the nature of their terrain and their remoteness from the state centres." Even though difficult to generalize, what is almost clear is that the spread of Maoist influence has strong social and economic roots including the exclusion of the poor and the marginalized by the state, as opposed by government to it being only ideological or 'law and order problem,' or 'terrorism.' [7]

From one perspective, the Maoist insurgency in its mid-western stronghold areas can be seen as a renewal of an age-old confrontation between the Thakuri Raj and the radical left. The Thakuris (descendants of the rulers of the old principalities) and their clients had long dominated this area, and the nature of their rule at local level was repressive. This was in accord with the authoritarian regime at the centre during the party less Panchayat system (1962-1990). Even after the restoration of democracy in 1990, the former *Panch* system survived, reviving their power base under a new guise by responding to the Nepali Congress's policy of incorporating the traditional social and political elites in its schemes of party building during the early 1990s.

However, the sense of popular empowerment spread after the successful 1990 *jana andolan* (People's Movement) that introduced a new power base against the traditional forces. Both the CPN (UML) and the CPN (Maoist, formerly the UPF) emerged as the most influential left forces in the people's fight against various forms of the Thakuri Raj in this region. The equation among the left forces has changed in favour of the CPN (Maoist) because of the UML's movement from the left towards the centre, while the Congress Party was constantly heading towards the right from the centre of the political spectrum in the country. The local Thakuri-centrist alliances in the mainstream parties have never been strong under the democratic set-up. It deteriorated during the period of hung parliament (November 1994 to May 1999). As politics was concentrated at the centre in the game of government making and unmaking, the parliamentary parties grossly ignored the need for the party building at the grassroots level, thus providing occasion for a long drawn-out people's war. [8]

"In terms of caste and ethnic break-up, the country is essentially a conglomeration of minorities, with the two largest groups comprising 16 per cent (Chhetri) and nearly 13 per cent (Bahun) of the population. None of the other groups constitutes more than 10 per cent of the population. Regardless of the reality on the ground, Nepal was usually represented as a Hindu kingdom where different castes as well as ethnic, linguistic and religious groups have co-existed peacefully.

However, the subordinate groups began to question this picture of tolerance and pluralism, particularly since the restoration of multi-party democracy in 1990, when the open political atmosphere allowed the emergence of an energetic movement of ethnic assertion, whose leadership might regard Nepal as a pluralistic society, but one characterized by hierarchy, dominance and oppression." [9] "The future prospects of Maoism in Nepal will...depend largely on the extent to which the newly elected Nepali Congress government addresses the historic neglect and discrimination of the small rural communities which still make up the overwhelming majority of the population of the country...[which] means that a radical shake-up of the public administration system is in order to make both more representative of the ethnic diversity of the country and more responsive to the needs of peasant communities." [10] The above mentioned quotations clearly portray the complex scenario in Nepal.

A notable characteristic of Maoist movement is the degree of women's participation in guerrilla ranks. Women's political participation in the past had been limited to electoral areas, especially in voting and occasional candidacy in elections. It is a big surprise that Nepali women had joined guerrilla organization, taking up arms. It is a subject of analysis that why many rural women have been a part of Maoist Movement? What specific life experiences convinced or compelled the women to take part in Maoist activities? Although it is very difficult to verify the exact number but it is reported that women constituted anywhere between 30 to 40 per cent of Maoist military force, which according to conservative estimates total at least 10,000 people. Among female military personnel, it is reported that most came from ethnic and Dalit groups, but there were also women from the upper castes. [11]

Ideologically, the Maoist claimed to favour an end to the patriarchal organization of the society. In Nepali context, it appears that this position was exemplified by their demands for equal rights for women to inherit ancestral property. In the well-known forty-point demand submitted to the government just before the declaration of people's war, one point dealt exclusively with the patriarchal exploitation and discrimination against women. The Maoists asserted gender equality could be achieved only in a classless or communist society. This assertion accompanied by the sense of 'empowerment' that joining the cadres brought prompted the disadvantaged group of women to support the movement.

The geological structure of Nepal too has been suitable for guerrilla war operation. This is one of the important factors, which have led to the growth of Maoism in Nepal. Thousands of unemployed and ill-educated youths in the interior of Nepal have joined the Maoist forces. For many suffering from by caste and ethnic discrimination, facing lack of educational and employment opportunities, joining the Maoist armed movement provided a quick way to be counted and get an identity. There was also the added attraction of becoming involved in the pervasive networks of extortion and bank robbery operated by the Maoists to finance personal consumption and the guerrilla war that is said to have made the Nepali Maoist Movement the richest rebel group in Asia. [12]

After a decade of conflict, the rebel combatants became so used to the spoils of war and soldiering—power, prestige, resources—that it became an accepted way of life and living. There was also the fear that re-entry into civilian life may cost the cadres their lives, either at the hands of the Maoists or by the state forces scouring the countryside, for guerrillas. Hence, for them staying and fighting was ironically the safer alternative. This bred a whole class of professional young guerrillas who may or may not understand or even agree with the full political implications of what they were fighting for, yet fully understand and appreciate the sense of power, purpose and resources that being a guerrilla has placed at their disposal. This core group of young Maoist fighting cadre was the driving force behind the guerrilla war.

Similarly, given the precarious economic situation in the country, joining the Maoist Movement became an attractive option for young men and women in a growing number. The low level of societal development, especially economic development, which could provide a venue for the capable young people into the labour market, was not available. Whereas literacy rates have increased over the decades, more students failed the School Leaving Certificate (SLC) examinations (to be taken at the end of the tenth year of school). The movement for them appeared to be an alternative option. This is one of the reasons why the Maoists were able to recruit many youngsters in their Army.

The 1990 People's Movement meant many things to many people. However, for all people alike it ignited a level of expectations for progress and positive change unheard of in the aftermath of earlier political changes in Nepal. With political parties, media, activists and individual leaders joining the chorus, the belief was that political freedom and democracy would rapidly and easily translate into progress of the society. The idealism of the movement soon gave way to Nepali realities – parties poorly prepared to exercise democratic power, old patronage structures remained intact, limited scope left for sustained economic growth, the antiquated centralized state continued, and government lacked capacity, expertise or will to convert ideas into successful policy. Add to this the rampantly corrupt leadership of the two major political parties, i.e. Nepali Congress (NC) and Communist Party of Nepal-United Marxists Leninist (CPN-UML). These parties took turns to occupy the government to abuse power to an extent that citizens were disappointed and disillusioned with the 'fruits of democracy.'

The frustrations associated with the unfulfilled expectations of the people following the replacement of the absolute monarchy with multiparty democracy provided fertile ground for the Maoist movement. The lack of access to political and economic space has been compounded by bad governance and corruption. Despite enormous amount of funds being poured into Nepal for development, the proportion of Nepalese below the poverty line continued to increase. The decentralization process to improve governance and increase people's participation was implemented but largely remained ineffective. The United Nations Country Team of Nepal, in its Progress Report in 2002 has rightly observed that, "the legitimacy of these structures has rested more on legal requirements and the financial and organizational 'support' of the central government rather than on the stake holding of the local voters." [13]

Similarly, Saubhaghya Shah's observation portrays the reality vividly: "It remains Nepal's singular misfortune that the political forces are always engrossed with changing the regime, but never altering the substance of governance…For the political elites and counter-elites, establishing rule-based governance and institutional procedures has so far proved less attractive than simply overthrowing the political opposition and ruling through patronage and fiat." [14]

When the movement oriented political groups of the Panchayat era turned themselves into political parties, they failed to build their institutions in democratic manner. While almost all of them mouthed democratic slogans, none built mechanisms through which the illegalities of party leaders, ideologues and members could be disciplined through transparent, credible but decisive sets of intra-party rules and procedures. Some political misdemeanours were allowed to occur with impunity in each of the big parties—NC, CPM-UML and Rastriya Prajatantra Party (RPP). Personal aggrandizement, often in the name of helping the party, was overlooked. Although opposition parties often indulged in moral posturing, they too failed to come up with effective laws to tame excesses of the ruling party.

The CPN-UML, which led the opposition for most of the period, was unable to create a social environment in which the laws that would govern party finances—said to be the single most important source of political corruption in Nepal—could be passed. This kind of deceit on the part of the political parties contributed directly to a widespread disenchantment with the multi-party democratic set-up, and facilitated the political arrival and growth of the Maoist. [15] The fact is that Nepal has suffered for the past many years from corrupt, visionless leadership, rudderless and arbitrary state control, which has contributed in countless ways to the longevity of the Maoist Insurgency. Large ecological areas of the country have been sidelined in government measures to relieve poverty and encourage economic growth. These are, in particular, the mountain areas of the west and far west, where Maoist have begun their activities and taken the control.

The reasons described above, needless to emphasize, provide enough rationale as to why the Maoists have constantly gained the strength exploiting the weakness of its opponent, the state. The post-1990 politics was characterized by anarchy which was reflected in the major events that occurred in the past one decade or so- parliamentary elections being conducted four times, recommendation for the dissolution of House of Representatives (HOR)) made six times; special sessions of the HOR being summoned seven times, and fourteen times change in government. All these events occurred because the political sphere was excessively concentrated on power games. Besides, the political instability, frequent changes of government, politicization, division in the police force, erosion of ideology and decline in the credibility of political parties and their leaders- all these count for weakness of the state's crisis management capacity vis-à-vis the Maoist movement.

The situation in Nepal is perhaps more complicated than most other conflict situations since in addition to the multiparty system, the monarchy was also a major player.

This is especially true since the removal of the Prime Minister by the King in October 2002, forcing various political parties to not to participate in the governmental process. The institution of the monarchy was always ascribed a central position throughout Nepal's history. However, survival of such a central institution came in question and recently monarchy was abolished. King Gyanendra reached to the throne in the background of the Royal Massacre of June 2001, in which King Birendra along with his entire family was killed.

Unlike his predecessor, King Gyanendra has a problem of legitimacy. His popularity declined due to his ambition to become a 'Constructive Monarch.' The royal take-over of power that started in October 2002 invited confrontation with all the major political parties. This entry of monarchy in the power game had further worsened the stability of Nepal. Further, the state capacity to use the armed forces was limited by the fact that the Royal Nepalese Army (RNA) was not under the control of a civilian government. The party-military hostility was compounded by the factors of historical legacy, [16] constitutional ambiguity [17] and non-cooperation.

The exchange of heated words between civilian leaders and military officials accusing each other for the escalation of the Maoist crisis surfaced publicly several times. The Government's reaction to the movement was further complicated by the palace's separate dealing with the Maoist. Nevertheless, after the Royal Proclamation on 1 February 2005, RNA was active in forefront against the Maoist. The Maoists also cultivated internal contradictions and crisis among the same actors—particularly the palace/army and the political parties—to enhance its strengths and capacities. After Royal coup, the Maoists forged very good relations with the political parties and even signed a 12 point agreement in November 2005. This set a base for the April Revolution of 2006 that toppled the monarchy and led Nepal towards a new political development.

The Nepal Human Development Report 2001 observed,

"In Nepal, where society is comprised of many castes, creeds and ethnic groups, strong patrimonial and patriarchal systems have long existed to perpetuate the domination of the elite. Subsidiary governance will be realized only when people themselves become aware of their rights, and exercise them as citizens and members of civil society to promote individual and collective well-being." [18] Nepal's decade-long conflict between the government and the Maoist rebels disrupted the relationship between civil society, the state and the market. Successive governments during the time of the conflict took an authoritarian stance and tried to place restrictions on civil society groups, thereby reducing their room to manoeuvre. While civil society was thought to act as a check on the powers of the state, it was the state that set the parameters for civil society, considering it an 'evil society.'

Nepal's civil society failed to play a crucial role in mediating between the needs of special groups and those of the common good, between political and economic sectors for the welfare of the majority of citizens, who are poor, powerless, deprived, and, due to the decade-old conflict, alienated from the mainstream democratic and development process. After the February 1, 2005 Royal Proclamation civil society was seen as more active and influential than predicted. Though it was unable to intervene decisively in conflict, the role of civil society in the post conflict situation is expected to be crucial.

The regional dynamics also played a role in Nepal conflict, being a landlocked country, surrounded by India on three sides and China on the fourth. This geo-political situation has forced Nepal to be completely dependent on India for trade, commerce and access to sea. Without India's cooperation, Nepal's engagement with the rest of the world and its quest for stability and economic development cannot bear much fruit. This power arguably allows New Delhi to play a manipulative role in Nepal politics in a way, which serves its own interest. Thus, it is also important to understand the Maoist movement in a historical context and continuity, which has thrived due to the geopolitical situation of South Asia. It is also important to understand the crisis in Nepal from the historical context of India's role in Nepali politics, rather as a phenomenon nurtured at home by political, social and economic factors. According to some analysts, the Maoists are prime examples of India's 'strategic coercion' against the Nepali State. It is argued without a base outside Nepal, the Maoists would have found it very hard to continue their guerrilla war. [19]

There is also another dimension to the relations between India and Nepal. India has been supplying the Nepalese government with military hardware and training assistance. The Arms Assistance Agreement was signed in 1965 to assist in reorganization and modernization of the Royal Nepal Army with the objective of strengthening the security and independence of Nepal. The agreement was recognition of the military links between the two countries and it established India as the primary supplier of arms to Nepal. In 2004, India provided a grant of over US$ 14 million to Nepal in order to enable it to buy Indian defence equipment. India had a special interest in curtailing the activities of the Nepalese Maoists.

In India, the Naxalite movement that had begun in 1967 had metamorphosed in three decades into a major movement affecting almost 159 districts in over 12 states. The merging of the People's War Group and the Maoists Communist Centre of India in 2004 to form the CPI-Maoist has become a major cause for concern. What is even more disturbing to the Indian government is the evidence of linkages between the CPI-Maoists and the Maoists of Nepal. This strategic alliance had opened up avenues for movement of persons and materials. It also led to the creation of safe havens and the extension of training facilities for each other.

The Cost

All conflicts share certain features, though every particular situation is unique. They reflect change and clash of interests, which varies in each context and which, if not managed, leads to escalating strife. Nepal's conflict reflects political, cultural, social and economic clash of interests, which are related to and distribution of resources and power, value systems, social norms, ethnic, caste, class and gender inequality. The Himalayan kingdom of 27 million people has been wrecked by the Maoist insurgency for the last ten years. Fourteen governments have taken office since the restoration of democracy in 1990, and the great expectations of the *Jana Andolan* are yet to materialize. Furthermore, only a small segment of the society, i.e. elites, those who were already rich to begin with, seemed to benefit disproportionately during this period. The country still finds itself in near-complete disarray as a result of the ongoing political, social, and economic turmoil.

Socio-economic Impact: The insurgency has adversely affected every Nepali's life. Unfortunately, much of the discourse on the conflict in Nepal is concentrated on political aspects while very little attention has been given to the socio-economic cost of the conflict. When the first and second peace talks between the Maoists and the government took place in 2001 and 2003, the debate revolved exclusively around politics. Ten years of insurgency have weakened the Nepali state and society in numerous ways. It was the Maoist who brought the ceremonial army out of the barrack to become active countrywide for the first time in the modern era. The rebellion has retarded the economy and hit development activities. It has also made India increasingly powerful in national affairs as Kathmandu sought help from New Delhi to confront the rebels.

Over 14,000 Nepalese have lost their lives since violence began in 1996. Human rights violations have reached dangerous proportions with both, the rebels and security forces, reported to have engaged in various forms of atrocities such as torture, kidnapping and summary executions. [20] For a least developed country (LDC) like Nepal with a per capita income of around US$ 238 and more than 42 per cent of people living below the poverty line, [21] the cost of the conflict in terms of destruction of infrastructure, decline in economic growth as well as delivery of even the basic services to the most needy have been devastating. It is believed the insurgency has cost Nepal eight to ten percent of its GDP. 40 per cent of the Village Development Committee (VDC) buildings have been destroyed and following the dissolution of local bodies by the Deuba government, local commerce and development activities have come to a grinding halt. The infrastructure including power plants, electricity grid and telecommunication towers have been ruined. Nearly 2000 schools, mostly private, have also been periodically closed. Health centres and schools, which depend on government grants to VDCs, are without medicines and supplies. Widespread fears of Maoists and security forces, and lack of economic opportunities forced more than half a million people to leave their rural homes and migrate to district headquarters, Kathmandu and even India.

In areas most affected by the insurgency, there have been perceptible demographic changes. Women now head most households in the absence of men as many have left homes due to fears of forced conscription by the Maoists and routine harassment by the security forces. Evidence of increasing reliance on remittance notwithstanding, many overseas Nepalese are shying away from sending money to their families in villages due to fear of extortion. Initially, the Maoists were able to capture public imagination with strong opposition to perceived inequality and injustices-such as patriarchy, polygamy, child marriage, gambling and drinking. They also dealt harshly with individuals who they identified as corrupt, which often included village elites and the police. Much of this goodwill was squandered when they resorted to indiscriminate violence. During the insurgency, landmines were excessively used by both the sides to hurt each other. The use of the landmines was most common trick used by the Maoists to delimit the security force operations. Till now, there is no reliable information on the location of the landmines or casualties due to them. There is also proliferation of small arms and light weapons in Nepal during and after the insurgency.

Another area that has been affected drastically is the rural healthcare sector. While the Maoists have generally been supportive of immunization, these programmes have suffered largely in recent years due to poor levels of social mobilization. Many international donor agencies have completely withdrawn from Nepal due to the poor security situation. One study revealed that in the Maoist affected districts rates of malnutrition are exceptionally high, e.g. 62 per cent in Achham, 69 in Jajarkot, 78 in Jumla and 83 in Kalikot. According to the World Health Organization, any region with 40 per cent malnutrition rate is facing a serious public health concern. Even though the country is facing a humanitarian crisis of massive proportion, the rulers have paid scant attention to the pressing needs of the people. If the poor socio-economic conditions drag on, and nothing is done to alleviate poverty and suffering of the people, the good will towards the peace process would likely evaporate

Though civil war affects common people, its impacts are felt by men and women in different ways due to their gender roles and responsibilities. Any discussion of gender and conflict is immediately faced with the problem that it occurs within what is traditionally seen as a 'masculine discourse.' Most societies, such as Nepal are structured around patriarchal cultural traditions, and in the case of war, men tend to be the ones who take up arms and go to the battlefield while the women tend the home fires. [22] During the Maoists Insurgency, gender roles and social relationships in Nepalese villages have drastically changed. Due to displacement of male from village, the conventional roles of men and women have changed. For example, women have started to plough land in absence of their male members of the family, which was culturally forbidden. [23]

Significantly gender relations and gender roles are fundamentally altered, thus putting extra burden on women during conflict. At the same time, the conflict opens up opportunity for women to be empowered as several cultural restrictions such as unequal treatment and discrimination against women are changed. But at the same time, there was a drastic increase in the gendered violence such as increased cases of rape, both by the armed force and the insurgents. Both sides used rape as a tactic to intimidate the opposing side. There were also reported cases of increase in the HIV/AIDS as most of the female IDPs were directly or indirectly forced to enter commercial sex industry. Similarly, numbers of single woman also increased due to the armed conflict. They were left to fend themselves and children after the loss of husbands due to cultural practices of the society. [24]

Scenario after April Revolution of 2006

The Political parties started a non-violent democratic movement on the street in April 2006. This movement was neither fully planned nor fully spontaneous. It was founded on the loose political alliance forged by the parties and the Maoists in November 2005 with the hope that their joint peace plan would arouse people, who were disillusioned with the multiple failures of royal rule. Nepal's mainstream parties and the CPN (Maoist) have agreed to pursue a joint strategy against what they called 'the autocratic monarchy' and a plan for constitutional reforms. On 17 November 2005 a twelve-point agreement between the political parties and Maoists was signed.

This move fuelled the pro-democracy movement of April 2006. The movement was remarkable for the breadth of popular participation and the speed with which it gathered momentum – both beyond the expectations of the mainstream parties and the Maoists. King Gyanendra's capitulation on April 24, 2006 in the face of a mass movement marked a victory for democracy in Nepal and, with a ceasefire between the new government and the Maoists there started of a serious peace process. Forced to acknowledge the 'spirit of the people's movement,' Gyanendra accepted popular sovereignty, reinstated parliament and invited the mainstream seven-party alliance to implement its roadmap—including election of a constituent assembly to rewrite the constitution in line with the parties' five month-old agreement with the Maoists. This historical moment transformed Nepal's political landscape but ushered in a lengthy and challenging road to peace. [25]

Nepal's government, headed by the political party alliance and Maoist rebels signed the Comprehensive Peace Agreement (CPA) on 21 November declaring an end to the ten-year civil war, thus paving the way for inclusion of the rebels in mainstream politics and for elections to an assembly that would write a new constitution. The peace agreement charted the course towards elections for a Constituent Assembly (CA) following formation of an interim legislature and government including the Maoists. In a detailed agreement on arms management, the Maoists committed to cantonment of their fighters and locking up their weapons and the Nepalese Army (NA) was to be largely confined to barracks. The constituent assembly, to be elected through a mixed first-past-the-post and proportional system, was authorized to decide the future of the monarchy. Amid lots of doubts and suspicion, both processes fairly went well. The CA election established Maoists as the biggest political party. Later, monarchy was abolished.

The prolonged conflicts have a tendency to create dynamics of various actors' own stakes that thrive on violence and hence further fuel the conflict while ordinary people are overwhelmed by a sense of apathy, indifference and helplessness. We need to break this deadlock but the question is how? Can conflict be resolved by force or dialogue? Yet, how to convince those who are used to monopoly over power to share it without the use of violence? How to contain those who are bent on violence, without the use of the force? These are the complex questions. Only a leadership of wisdom and understanding will be able to address them.

The leadership dilemma and trauma of the people are complicated by force of globalization and accelerated by the dynamics of time and technology. In the meantime, Nepal falls deeper into quagmire of conflict and chaos in which Nepalese people suffer. Immanuel Kant, one of the world's greatest thinkers, in his treatise 'Perpetual Peace' asserted, "No treaty of peace shall be held valid in which there is tacitly reserved matter for a future war." Peace is not just the absence of war, but also epitomizes economic prosperity, social harmony, unity, and brotherhood among the multi-ethnic Nepali people. Studies have shown that sustainable peace in post-conflict nations is best achieved through purposeful development and democratization-which requires the recreation of democratic institutions to lead to a more open, participatory, and less tyrannical society. Thus, for the peace-settlement to succeed, Nepal must work on to institutionalize the pillars of democracy: free and fair elections; the rule of law and guarantee of basic human rights.

In 1996 the Maoists were a small, fringe party with no weapons, few active members and a support base limited to a few pockets of the remote countryside. Their ten-year armed insurgency transformed them into a powerful political force capable of standing alongside, and sometimes overshadowing Nepal's major established parties. This is one of the successful guerrilla movements that has sustained from jungle to the parliament. There is no denying the fact that the Maoist Insurgency, after all, is indicative of some underlying flaws in the historical structuring of institutions and allocation of political, economic and social resources in Nepal. It is possible and often necessary to find a silver lining in every problem, and the Maoist insurgency too brings its own share of opportunities for Nepal and Nepalese. It has advanced a historic challenge to Nepali society, state and its custodians to dare and repair some fundamental flaws in the nature and functioning of the nation and state. In the course of attending to the crisis induced by the insurgency the leaders are presented with a landmark opportunity to reevaluate and redesign all aspects of politics, governance, and democracy and to introduce structural reforms in the management of the state.

However, the cost of the conflict is huge and would continue to get reflected in Nepal in many years to come. Nepal still faces a lot of challenges ahead. The continued prevalence of widespread insecurity and violence indicate Nepal is far-from building a sustainable peace. Similarly, the integration of Maoists Combatants into the society is yet another challenge that has to be dealt very soon before it is too late. There are various other issues pending to be decided by the New Constitution including fulfilling the demands of various marginalized, underrepresented and underprivileged groups and demarking the federal structure, in the resource scarce country. Thus, unless the root causes of the conflict are addressed and the Maoists democratized, long-term sustainable peace in Nepal cannot be achieved and conflict may very well reignite.

Notes

1. Susan Hangen, *Creating a "New Nepal": The Ethnic Dimensions*, Policy Studies 34, Washington DC: East West Center, 2007, pp. 77-79.
2. Manish Thapa, *Back to Negotiation: Diagnosis and Prognosis for future Negotiation Process in Nepal* (Vienna: European University Centre for Peace Studies, 2007), pp. 10-16.
3. Rabindra Mishra, "India's Role in Nepal's Maoist Insurgency," *Asian Survey*, vol. 44, no. 5, 2004, pp. 627–646.
4. Michael Lund and Andreas Mehler, *Peace-Building and Conflict Prevention in Developing Countries: A Practical Guide (Draft Document)* (Brussels/Ebenhausen: 1999), p. 47.
5. Uwe Kievelitz and Tara Polzer, *Nepal Country Study on Conflict Transformation and Peace Building* (Eschborn: Deutsche Gesellschaft für Technische Zusammenarbeit, 2002), p. 10.
6. Saubhagya Shah, "A Himalayan Red Herring? Maoist Revolution in the Shadows of the Legacy Raj," in Michael Hutt, ed., *Himalayan "People's War": Maoist War in Nepal* (London:

Christopher and Hurst Publication, 2004), pp. 192-196.

7. Arjun Karki and Binod Bhattarai, *Whose War: Economic and Socio-Cultural Impacts of Nepal's Maoist-Government Conflict.* (Kathmandu: NGO Federation of Nepal, 2003), pp. 3-10.
8. Krishna Hachhethu, "The Nepali State and the Maoist Insurgency, 1996-2001," in Michael Hutt, ed., *Himalayan "People's War": Maoist War in Nepal* (London: Christopher and Hurst Publication 2004), pp.59-61.
9. Rajendra Pradhan, "Ethnicity, Caste and a Pluralist Society," in Kanak Dixit and Shastri Ramachandaran, eds., *State of Nepal* (Kathmandu: Himal Books, 2002), pp. 3-5.
10. Andrew Nichson as quoted in Deepak Thapa, "The Maobadi of Nepal," in Kanak Dixit and Shastri Ramachandaran, eds., *State of Nepal* (Kathmandu: Himal Books 2002), pp. 86.
11. Mandira Sharma and Dinesh Prasain, "Gender Dimensions of the People's War: Some Reflections on the Experiences of Rural Women," in Michael Hutt, ed., *Himalayan "People's War": Maoist War in Nepal* (London: Christopher and Hurst Publication, 2004), pp. 154.
12. Cited in Dhruba Kumar Shrestha, "Consequences of the Militarized Conflict and the Cost of Violence in Nepal," *Contributions to Nepalese Studies*, vol. 30, no. 2, July 2003, p. 184.
13. "Progress Report: Millennium Development Goals, Nepal," United Nations Country Team of Nepal, February 2002.
14. Saubhaghya Shah, "From Evil State to Civil Society," in Kanak Dixit and Shastri Ramachandaran, eds., *State of Nepal* (Kathmandu: Himal Books, 2002), p. 155.
15. Pratyoush Onta, "Democracy and Duplicity: The Maoists and their Interlocutors in Nepal," in Michael Hutt, ed., *Himalayan "People's War": Maoist War in Nepal* (London: Christopher and Hurst Publication, 2004), p. 138.
16. http://www.southasiaanalysis.org. (A. O. 12 December 2007).
17. Ibid.
18. *Nepal Human Development Report 2001* (New Delhi: Oxford University Press, 2002), p. 6.
19. Kalyan Chaudhari, "A Spurt in Maoist Attacks," *Frontline,* 28 April - 1 May 2001; Dipak Mishra, "Nepalese Extremists Being Trained in Bihar," *Times of India,* 16 April 2001. *Times of India,* 27 November 2001.

20. Amnesty International reported Nepal has the highest number of disappearance in the world. For details see, *Amnesty International Annual Report 2004*, www.amnesty.org. (A. O. 14 December 2007).
21. "Nepal at Glance", The World Bank Report, Kathmandu, 2005, p. 2.
22. Manish Thapa, *Institutional Approaches to Gender Mainstreaming in Post Conflict Reconstruction: A Case Study of World Bank* (Stadschalining: European Peace University 2006), pp. 11-12.
23. Bishnu Raj Upreti, *Armed Conflict and Peace Process in Nepal.* (New Delhi: Adroit Publishers, 2006), pp. 273.
24. Ibid. pp. 274.
25. For reporting on the early stages of the pro-democracy movement, see http://www.crisisgroup.org/home/index.cfm?id=4073&l=1. (A. O. 23 December 2007).

6

Justice or Reconciliation?: Prospects and Problems of Peace-building in Cambodia

Mneesha Gellman

Scholars and practitioners of peace-building repeatedly reinforce the notion that justice and reconciliation are integral to the reconstruction of post-conflict countries. [1] However, there is still no clear understanding about how these two concepts relate to each other. This chapter will discuss the prospects and challenges for peace-building in Cambodia within the framework of retributive justice versus reconciliation initiatives. The recently initiated tribunal for former Khmer Rouge leaders will be assessed, with particular attention given to the potential for such a justice mechanism to foment reconciliation among the general populace.

Cambodia is experiencing structural, social and political dysfunction that derives in part from the civil war time. The trial is one way that issues of justice are being addressed, but the trial itself faces many challenges and fails to adequately consider reconciliation. The international community and the Cambodian people will be better served if the trial is not an end product itself. Rather, culturally contextualized understandings of justice and reconciliation can embed these concepts into daily life in ways that local people can relate to.

These concerns lead to the central questions addressed in this chapter: can justice through a tribunal facilitate reconciliation for Cambodians and what additional mechanisms might be needed to further peace-building in the post-conflict reconstruction process? To focus these lines of inquiry, a brief overview of Cambodian social organization is provided, followed by a synopsis of the historical conflict that is still being dealt with today. This chapter initially explores why the Cambodian civil war still affects the psyche of the people, drawing on the quantifiable economic and human costs of war, and presents this as an argument for why both justice and reconciliation are necessary for the country today. The chapter also provides a detailed description of the Khmer Rouge Tribunal (KRT) that opened in late 2007, with an analysis of the obstacles it must overcome and ways in which its legal approach to justice may fall short of restorative justice values more useful for reconciliation.

Socio-Political Culture

Ethnic Khmer [2] people constitute nearly 90 per cent of Cambodia's population, with 5 per cent identifying as Vietnamese, 1 per cent as Chinese, and the 4 per cent 'other' [3] generally referring to indigenous tribal groups in the northeast provinces of Ratanakiri and Mondulkiri. Cambodian social structure today is a blend of traditional and bureaucratic power mechanisms. Described as 'patron-client communitarianism,' by Neher and Marlay, social relations entail duty to group over personal liberty, accepting suffering as *karma*, and the Buddhist life circle of *samsara* as a defining characteristic of life. [4] Patronage is a principal organizing system in Cambodian society, where people receive protection by following a person of higher status. [5] In this way, people who have acquired wealth in a village have an obligation to redistribute, in exchange for receiving status and having moral authority over their clients.

In traditional Cambodian culture, conflicts were confronted with a 'veiled threat', manipulation of the patrimonial hierarchy, or with one party (usually the weaker) withdrawing from the situation altogether. [6] Contemporary Cambodian researchers have also invoked the term 'neo-patrimonialism' to describe the mix of patrimonial and formal bureaucratic power structures that characterize Cambodian society in the post-2001 democratization process. [7]

Historical Background

Cambodia gained its independence from France in1953 after over a century as a colonial satellite. In the late 1960's, the United States, as part of its strategy to contain the 'communist threat' of northern Vietnam, orchestrated a power grab by puppet leader General Lon Nol to suppress a communist-sympathizer government gaining strength nearby. Lon Nol lasted in power from 1970 until 1975, when the Marxist-Leninist [8] Khmer Rouge army, known as *Angkar* (The Organization) overthrew the government and consolidated power.

In order to start anew on their independent path to 'modernity,' the Khmer Rouge reset the Cambodian clock to 'year zero' and embarked upon a highly idealistic program of reorganizing the entire country into self-sufficient agriculture communes. This program was a dismal failure. However, the wholesale execution of Buddhist monks, civil servants, and the urban educated class under the Khmer Rouge's rule from 1975 to 1979 was accepted by followers as necessary to cleanse society of bourgeoisie elements and the crutch of religion. [9] To visually make their point, Khmer Rouge soldiers systematically destroyed temples and other cultural sites that connected ancient Khmer culture to the present. Money, schools, religion, and private property were made illegal. Agricultural peasants, merchants, children, and many former Khmer Rouge comrades deemed suspicious of harbouring elitist tendencies were murdered under the leadership of Brother Number One, Pol Pot. Through *Angkar*, Pol Pot commanded the genocide of approximately two million Cambodians, either through direct execution or forced starvation and labour. [10] Disobedience or questioning of Khmer Rouge policies frequently resulted in being taken away to a 'study group' to be 're-educated,' generally understood as immediate execution.

While the systematic use of rape as a weapon of war has not been documented in Cambodia, forced gender and age segregation inflicted by the Khmer Rouge onto the populace resulted in unquantifiable suffering for families, particularly mothers separated from their children. There was no distinction between military and civilian populations as modern ethical codes of war attempt to create. Rather, the lines were drawn between the more than two million urban 'new people' relocated to the countryside and loathed as bourgeoisie by the Khmer Rouge, and the original rural peasants, the 'base people.' [11] In the end, both 'new' and 'base' people suffered together as the communist ideal of self-sufficient agrarianism descended into authoritarian mass murder.

In exploring the humanitarian dimensions of Cambodia's civil war, mention must be made of the Khmer Rouge's intense racism and persecution of ethnic minorities in the country. Although much of the violence was Khmer against Khmer, the Vietnamese, Chinese, Cham Muslim, Thai, Lao, and hill tribe minorities were particularly sought out for destruction. [12] Even in recent history, former Khmer Rouge leaders including Pol Pot have blamed any deaths that occurred under their leadership on the Vietnamese, and such remarks have perpetuated hostile Cambodia-Vietnamese relations. [13] This shows how ethnicity was manipulated as a fictitious boundary to perpetuate exclusion and pass responsibility for egregious crimes onto the demonized 'other.'

Conflict and its Actors

Although many overlapping conflicts exist within Cambodia consisting of multiple complex actors, for the purpose of this chapter, the central conflict assessed concerns the legacy of the civil war period. 'Civil war' refers to the time between 1970 and 1979 including both Lon Nol and the Khmer Rouge leadership. Although this is a narrower window than other scholars have defined for civil war, [14] the notions of justice for Khmer Rouge crimes were introduced in 1979 under Vietnamese leadership. The actors are limited here to those who previously sympathized with the Khmer Rouge forces or were cadres and leaders themselves, and those who were subjected to their rule and victimized under the Khmer Rouge regime.

Social reality for many Cambodians today is still coloured by the civil war, despite the termination of direct Khmer Rouge rule in December 1978. The liberation at that point by Vietnam was bittersweet, as it resulted in a decade-long Vietnamese occupation. Democratic Kampuchea, the name given by the Khmer Rouge, was renamed the People's Republic of Kampuchea, and a constitution mimicking Vietnam's was put in place in 1981, but the civil strife continued. [15] Vietnamese soldiers fought with Khmer Rouge guerrilla factions who were supported by China throughout the 1980s as part of China's anti-Vietnam agenda. [16] Vietnam withdrew its military in 1989, the Paris Peace Accords were signed in 1991 and the United Nations Transitional Authority in Cambodia (UNTAC) was in place from 1991-1993, but still there were few effective governance structures for Cambodian citizens to look towards in their hopes for restitution, reconciliation, and justice.

After the United Nations departure following the national election of 1993, many alleged perpetrators of past war crimes were incorporated into the new government under the guise of reconciliation through the government's compromise with opponents. Such actions have perpetuated the culture of impunity by eliminating accountability for grave crimes against humanity. [17] Even those Khmer Rouge factions who opted not to go into the government at this time were able to make a better living than most of their former subjects through exploitation of Cambodia's natural resources. Throughout the mid-1990s, nearly five thousand people continued to bear arms under the name of Democratic Kampuchea and Khmer Rouge guerrillas controlled approximately one fifth of Cambodia's territory, profiting from timber and gem extraction contracts with Thailand. [18]

As Thai support for the Khmer Rouge faded, the guerrillas continued to make themselves visible particularly in 1994, with several high profile kidnappings and executions of foreigners, and also in 1997, when they turned on their own leader, Pol Pot after he ordered the murder of a fellow cadre, Son Sen. Notably, Pol Pot was never charged by his troops for crimes committed during Democratic Kampuchea, only for the execution of Sen and his family. This exercise of power on behalf of his former followers led to Pol Pot's house arrest in 1997, under which he died, purportedly of natural causes in 1998. [19]

The culture of violence propagated by the Khmer Rouge continues today in many forms, particularly in the impunity that permeates society. Not only has there been no legal form of retribution against perpetrators in Cambodia, but other injustices are rampant, such as the vast socio-economic divide between rich and poor. Through to the present day, the majority of Cambodians experience poverty, with the average civil servant such as police and administrators living on US$ 28 per month. [20] The untended needs such insufficient government salaries generate are augmented by rent-seeking practices that prevent the regeneration of trust between the Cambodian government and its citizens. On the other hand, Cambodians employed by multilateral organizations such as the World Bank make up to US$ 500 a month, and the resentment such disparities bring plays out through robberies and acts of violence in the streets and neighbourhoods.

In this desperate situation, Cambodians are searching for their own style of socio-political organization that allows them to survive on a day-to-day basis, and many civil society groups are working in communities to generate a sense of stability. To highlight poverty as a legacy of Cambodia's civil war, this chapter next turns to a stark statistical portrayal of Cambodia's position in the global market to support the overarching theme of this book – that the cost of war has far outweighed the cost of peace.

The Cost

The following section comments on the enormous economic and human costs that have been caused by conflict in Cambodia. First articulated are relevant economic indicators that informally compare Cambodia to its two most intimate neighbours: Thailand and Vietnam. The section proceeds to a discussion of the human costs of conflict, including refugees and landmine victims.

In the realm of political economy, the cumulative effects of prolonged violence on Cambodia's current and future generations are illuminating. Thirty-six percent of Cambodia's population lives below the poverty line. [21] The World Bank estimates Cambodia's Gross Domestic Product (GDP) to be US$ 273, [22] one of the poorest Asian countries, ranking 122nd out of 177 in per capita GDP survey. [23] According to 2002 statistics, the country's economy is further pressured by an external debt constituting 65.5 per cent of GDP. [24] This high debt holds implications for Cambodia's ability to distribute funds for social projects such as education and health care as the government tries to increase exports in order to repay and service this debt.

Cambodia's overall Human Development Index (HDI) value is .583, placing it 129th out of 177 countries, just after the Solomon Islands and before Myanmar, both conflict-racked countries themselves. [25] The HDI Gender Empowerment Measure (GEM), which demonstrates the extent to which women take part in the economic and political happenings of a given country, is similarly low—out of 75 ranked countries, Cambodia is number 68. [26] In recent years, Cambodia's infrastructure of bridges, roads, and power supply plants have been estimated at 40-50 per cent of pre conflict capacity, suffering seriously from war targeting and neglect. [27]

Examining Cambodia's basic indicators in comparison with those of its closest neighbours dramatically highlights the impact that the civil war has had on Cambodia's population. In 2005, Gross National Income (GNI) in Cambodia was estimated at US$ 380, whereas Vietnam's GNI was US$ 620, and Thailand's was US$ 2750, more than seven times that of Cambodia. One difference accounting for a portion of this income difference is the way these three countries have been able to capitalize on the tourist industry. During calendar year 2005, Cambodia had 1,421,615 tourist visitors [28] compared to 11.52 million tourists in Thailand [29] and nearly 3.5 million in Vietnam [30] during the same time period. The continual perception of Cambodia as a volatile and dangerous place has stigmatized it in the international tourist market, and though this stigma is gradually decreasing, it will take considerable publicity and financing of tourist infrastructure before visitors flock to Cambodia the way they do to neighbouring countries.

Further statistical comparison is instructive in the burden Cambodia carries as a legacy of conflict. In 2005, the life expectancy at birth averaged for men and women in Cambodia was 57 years, [31] while in both Vietnam and Thailand [32] it is 71 years. [33] Also illuminating is the inflow of Official Development Assistance (ODA) to these three countries, a useful indicator of the gravity of need among populations. In 2004, Cambodia received US$ 478 million in ODA, comprising 10 per cent of its GNI. [34] Though Vietnam received considerably more aid the same year, US$ 1830 million, this comprised only 4 per cent of the country's GNI. [35] Thailand did not receive any ODA in 2004, in fact it contributed US$ 2 million as outflow of aid to other countries, and therefore ODA comprised none of the GNI. [36] The dramatic differences shown here illustrate the perilous financial position of Cambodia as the nation continues to labour in overcoming the setbacks of conflict.

The human cost of conflict is seen poignantly in the

landmine victims of Cambodia, which is one of the most heavily mined countries in the world. While exact casualty statistics vary, hundreds of people continue to be injured or killed each year from landmines; an average of 846 people died or were maimed annually from 2000 to 2005. [37] It is estimated that since 1979, there have been more than 40,000 amputations as a result of landmine explosions, and nearly six million landmines remain unexploded in the country. [38] Despite large expenditures on landmine clearance—US$ 27.3 million in Cambodia in 2002—the setbacks to Cambodia's development due to the destruction of the physical ability of the population are enormous. [39] The ongoing cost of caring for this disabled population is a constant reminder of the lingering effects of conflict on a country that is striving to move beyond its violent history.

The destruction wrought by war is seen not only in the bodies of Cambodians, but also in their rice fields. Before the war, Cambodia was regarded as a rice-bowl of Asia, that is to say it was a key player in the production of rice for export. [40] By 1975, five years into the civil war, rice production had decreased to 84 per cent of the 1970 level, and this former rice exporting country—which sold 500,000 tons of rice a year in 1964 and 1965—has fallen far behind neighbouring countries in rice harvests. [41] A related fact is that during the 1980's, when annual rice shortfalls reached between 50,000 and 200,000 tons, only 40 of the 400 agriculturalists qualified to manage rice production systems remained in the country—the others had either been killed under the Khmer Rouge, or had fled into exile. [42]

Finally, no measure of the cost of conflict in Cambodia would be complete without mentioning the status of refugees and IDPs. In 1996, near the end of Cambodia's three decades of conflict, there were an estimated 32,000 Cambodian IDPs and another 34,400 Cambodian refugees in Vietnam. [43] IDPs in Cambodia resulted from continued instability and violence from Khmer Rouge guerilla factions who prevented people, through force, threat or perpetuating a culture of fear, from either returning to their home areas or permanently settling in a new location. By the year 2000, these numbers had dropped, as the Khmer Rouge lost their power base with members defecting into the government in exchange for immunity from prosecution. Fifteen thousand Cambodians were still refugees at this point, but significantly, 36,000 refugees were repatriated from Thailand that year, and 22,000 Cambodian IDPs were resettled from the end of 1998 to 1999. At the end of 2003, 16,000 Cambodian refugees were living in Vietnam, many of whom are ethnic Vietnamese who fled Cambodia during anti-Vietnamese backlash from 1990-1995. [45]

The pervasive human insecurity for Cambodian residents, and among the diaspora and refugee population, confirms the argument put forth in this book that the cost of conflict is substantial. These costs should be taken into consideration when debating the worthiness of conflict prevention expenses in future, so that other countries may not suffer similar legacies of violence. The high cost of conflict is visible not only in the statistical indicators given here, but in the culture of impunity and violence that permeates Cambodia today. This chapter next investigates the potential for this less tangible cost of conflict to be mitigated legally, through a war crimes tribunal.

Impunity and the Khmer Rouge Tribunal

It appears that Cambodia's democratic mechanisms for governance are still very much in the process of being developed. The country is led by a constitutional monarchy with high levels of corruption and questionable commitments to building the rule of law. While constitutional structures generated by Cambodians are slowly replacing those of UNTAC, many laws and amendments governing land reform, human trafficking, and corruption remain sitting in various Ministerial offices, incomplete and un-ratified. The lack of rule of law allows conflict patterns to persist on many levels, but at the root of many conflicts is the fact that there has been insufficient closure on the violence of the civil war. To date, not a single person has been legally held responsible in a legitimate trial for the deaths of nearly a third of the Cambodian population. A trial of Pol Pot and Ieng Sary (Brother Number Three) did take place in 1979, under Vietnamese and international command, but this process has been derided as an illegitimate show-trial due to the fact that the defendants were convicted in absentia with no meaningful representation. [46] Therefore, the creation of another tribunal had to be carried out with the utmost precautions to ensure due process for all potential defendants to entrench its legitimacy in the public psyche and international eye.

The KRT that has been taking shape since 1997 is designed to address this culture of impunity. The KRT is an attempt to address a past conflict situation, by establishing justice where it has previously been forsaken. Bearing in mind the historical context and costs of the civil war, this section turns to the KRT to ascertain if justice can facilitate reconciliation for the Cambodian populace.

One of the most damaging characteristics of a civil war is that the agony of war does not stop when peace accords are signed, or when the international media present the conflict as over. The traumas of war linger psychologically throughout people's lifetimes, and can be passed on through generations by way of stories, absent family members, or post-war living conditions of poverty and displacement. In Cambodia, the lack of closure on the Khmer Rouge period has perpetuated the insecurity people feel in the post-war environment. The suffering of survivors has not been adequately acknowledged, nor any public apologies made by perpetrators. This scenario leaves survivors living as victims rather than as citizens moving forward in their lives. For this reason, some Cambodians and many members of the international community look to the KRT as a process to bring a sense of justice to the country, and with it, a sense of closure on the civil war period.

The operation of the KRT, if done in a transparent and ethical way, could mitigate the rampant culture of impunity currently in the country. Ideally, the KRT will provide a sense of justice to survivors of the Khmer Rouge period while honouring justice for those who died, and serve to educate Cambodian youth about this part of their national history. [47] However, war crimes tribunals are rarely quick undertakings, and Cambodia's case is no exception. It has been a ten year process just to create the court structure, and patience is required by all parties to see it through.

Outline of the Tribunal: In 1997, Cambodian Co-Prime Ministers Hun Sen and Norodom Ranariddh appealed to the United Nations for assistance in establishing the KRT, [48] but it took years for the preliminary details of the arrangement to be finalized. In 2003, an agreement between United Nations and Cambodian negotiators was reached, with detailed regulations about how training, financing, and operations of the Extraordinary Chambers in the Courts of Cambodia (ECCC) would take place. It was only in June 2007 that the KRT delegated court members finally agreed to rules for their conduct, including how international and Cambodian legal staff (excluding the judges) would work together. Continual discrepancies between Cambodian and international law make the investigations slow going, though resources such as the Documentation Center of Cambodia, which archives all documents pertaining to the civil war period, have proved invaluable to legal researchers. A further delay is the consistent need of funding for the KRT staff and overhead. It is estimated that the KRT will cost approximately US$ 60 million over three years, [49] significantly cheaper than other international tribunals, though already there are projections are that it will take significantly longer than three years to be completed, and therefore be more expensive. Currently there are five former Khmer Rouge leaders in custody, but none have been prosecuted.

In order to assess the potential of the KRT to bring a real sense of justice to Cambodia, it is helpful to understand the structure of the court. To address claims that Cambodia's legal system was not sufficiently independent from executive branch interests, and is generally subject to intolerable levels of corruption, the KRT has been set up as a hybrid court system. This means that there are two chambers of courts with a combination of Cambodian and international judges in each chamber. The Trial Court composed of three Cambodian and two international judges, will carry out the initial trials. After a verdict is passed, parties can appeal the decision to the Supreme Court, which has a seven-judge chamber with four Cambodian and three international judges. Defendants can be tried and sentenced in this final arena. To ensure that the verdict is not vulnerable to corruption within Cambodia, decisions in both chambers need to have a super-majority, with four out of five judges agreeing in the Trial Court, or five out of seven judges in the Supreme Court. [50] In other words, at least one international judge must side with the Cambodian majority for a verdict to be reached. The court draws first from Cambodian law and then international law if there is a specific provision missing from Cambodia's legislation, as is the case for the crime of genocide.

The hybrid court format has recently been used in Sierra Leone and East Timor, and is the most recent trend for tribunals attempting to balance local and international interests. Touted at one point by Deputy Prime Minister Sok An as being a way to ensure full participation by the Cambodian judiciary while maintaining international standards, this model also brings funding from outside donors to cover the estimated US$ 20 million per year of operation. [51] To some extent, both the international community and Cambodian elites consider the hybrid model a compromise. Internationals do not trust the ability of Cambodian judges to avoid corruption, and Cambodian elites want to maintain sovereignty as they shape their own retributive justice processes. [52] Yet the hybrid court structure has the potential for partially rendering justice by stepping out of the cycle of impunity that most Cambodians are accustomed to in their domestic legal mechanisms.

Challenges to a Successful Tribunal: To avoid idealizing the KRT as the solution to Cambodia's stalled justice and reconciliation process, the complexities of its implementation will be frankly addressed here. [53] Previously described forms of neo-patrimonial Cambodian social organization should be kept in mind when evaluating the KRT, as it is orchestrated by and for elites and its ability to be fair and independent is constantly questioned. The KRT is an inherently political sequence of actions that is engaged by actors based on their positions within the social hierarchy. Therefore, the first identified challenge to the success of the KRT is that it is an elite process understood more by internationals than Cambodian citizens, and will thus not be able to achieve a sense of justice for survivors.

A second challenge is that justice in a post-conflict environment can be seen as competing with other concerns such as stability or reconciliation, [54] and this has been utilized to deter Cambodia from seeking to implement the Tribunal. Prince Thomico, a member of the Monarchy who lost many of his family members under the Khmer Rouge, was recently quoted as saying 'I care more about peace and stability in Cambodia than finding out what happened 30 years ago…The future of Cambodia has nothing to do with this Tribunal.' [55] He added that he has no faith that the Tribunal will be a source of justice for himself to avenge his deceased family members. [56] However, the subversion of justice to stability does not always arise out of good faith.

While the structure of the hybrid court itself is tolerable for all parties, concern is mounting about the unfair treatment of the five former Khmer Rouge leaders currently in custody. Despite many NGOs calling for the Tribunal to bring justice to the Cambodian people, in some cases the same NGOs are decrying the lack of due process that the defendants are experiencing. Human rights groups and other political analyst think tanks in Cambodia have issued booklets discussing the unfair circumstances under which suspected war crimes perpetrators are being detained. Two of the defendants, Ung Choeun, known as Ta Mok 'the Butcher,' and Kaing Khek Iev, known as Duch, formerly the head of S-21, the infamous torture centre in Phnom Penh, had been incarcerated for years with no charges formally made against them.

Duch had been held for more than eight years in military prison before formally being charged and transferred to KRT custody in July 2007. [57] The rights of the defendants are weighed against the end product of justice. [58] This holds implications for reconciliation in that just processes can help all parties be more willing to rebuild, but further human rights offences will increase animosity. Thus, a third challenge to the success of the KRT is that even in Cambodia's pursuit of justice, the questionable treatment of those in custody leads to a continued sense of injustice. If the Tribunal is supposed to be a mechanism to dispel impunity, then the errors of the process leading up to it should be considered a hindrance of this purpose. The cycle of judicial incompetence and the lack of bureaucratic accountability that prevent Cambodians from rebuilding their social contract with the government continue in the process of attempting to achieve justice.

There has been widespread evidence of Cambodian public interest in a tribunal as a justice mechanism [59] perhaps in part related to cultural and religion based Buddhist notions of right action. In his survey conducted from 1993-2003, Cambodia specialist Craig Etcheson found that 80 per cent of Cambodians wanted to see Khmer Rouge leaders be held accountable for their past crimes. [60] In 2004, the Khmer Institute of Democracy found that 96.8 per cent of those surveyed favoured a trial, but 44.1 per cent also stated that no trial was better than an illegitimate trial. [61] Despite this widespread enthusiasm, fundamental questions of juridical operations remain unanswered and unexplained to the general population, which suggests the need for increased education and outreach around the KRT.

Specifically a fourth complicating factor in the KRT's success is the difficulty in deciding who should even be brought before the court in the first place. Many current political leaders are potential defendants, because a significant number of former Khmer Rouge leaders defected into the national government [62] and some were even offered immunity from prosecution under the banner of 'national reconciliation.' [63] The Cambodian newspapers had much to write about in September 2007, when the United Nations contingent of the Tribunal suggested that the King Father, the Patriarch of the Royal Kingdom of Cambodia, could also potentially be called upon to testify.

As in Thailand, the King is a holy and revered symbol of the nation who expects immunity from the undignified process of being called into court by international lawyers. However, the King may have previous behaviour under the Khmer Rouge to answer for in court. The fact that the public expressed outraged that the King should have to take part in the KRT and at the same time they want a legitimate justice process shows their fractured allegiance. The 'culture of exploitation, protection, obedience and dependency had deep roots in Cambodian social practice,' [64] and the reaction to the King illuminates the way that neo-patrimonial social relationships are intertwined with culturally foreign democratic practices.

There has also been discussion about whether current Prime Minister Hun Sen could be tried. Hun Sen, as a youthful commander of a Khmer Rouge faction, defected to Vietnam with his troops in 1977, and then resurfaced as a leader in Cambodian under Vietnam's rule in the 1980s. [65] In light of his past, Hun Sen's use of the word 'reconciliation' to describe a limited justice process can be seen as a tactic to avoid the real reconciling processes that could perhaps unearth his own role in Cambodia's violent history. By defining reconciliation as a political compromise to maintain stability, Hun Sen skirts his own responsibility in anything other than fostering legal justice through the ECCC. Certainly Hun Sen's relationship with Vietnam would not be viewed favourably by the staunchly anti-Vietnamese Khmer population, but he may yet be able to keep this fact out of the mainstream media while bringing a sense of accountability to Cambodia through the prosecution of other Khmer Rouge leaders. [66] Because of his strong control of all Cambodian ministries, including the Ministry of Justice, and the threat to stability his trial could bring, it is highly unlikely that Hun Sen will appear in the KRT.

A fifth problem with the Tribunal at this point in time, nearly thirty years since the end of the Khmer Rouge rule, is that many of the movement's top leaders have already died natural deaths before telling their stories. Therefore, the names that average Cambodians may most associate with their trauma will not be the ones going on trial. Sixth, the KRT is taking place in Phnom Penh, the capital city, where many people in the provinces have never been. Cambodia is still 80 percent rural and urban events remain isolated from the majority of the population. Despite promises to televise the Tribunal and making seats available in the Courts for the public, [67] it is hard to believe that the sense of closure for the urban dweller will be the same as for villagers in less accessible parts of the country.

Seventh, there is controversy around the viable charges against the defendants. Genocide is the preferred charge by many, but depending on the interpretation of the Geneva Convention on Genocide, this may not be applicable. The Convention describes genocide as 'acts committed with the intent to destroy, in whole or in part, a national, ethnical, racial or religious group.' This original definition does not consider the attempted extermination of any other groups such as political groups, economic or social class as being genocide. Because of this, the majority of Khmer Rouge crimes committed by Khmers against Khmers do not fit within the original legal genocide definitions, with the important exceptions of the targeting of Buddhist monks and the ethnic Cham Muslim minority. Although more recent definitions of genocide that could encompass Cambodia's situation have been attempted in other international tribunals, if the charge of genocide is brought against the former Khmer Rouge leaders, a probable defence may be that the accused actions do not fall within the definition. [69]

Crimes against humanity, a more readily applicable charge, is still serious, and if convicted would entail life imprisonment, as Cambodian law does not allow capital punishment. This charge includes 'knowledge of a widespread or systematic attack against any civilian population'. [70] However, the crimes against humanity definition is not without problems either, because the acts in question are required by the Genocide Convention to have taken place in a 'nexus of armed conflict.' While the Convention suggests that the prosecutors must prove that the period between 1975 and 1979 was 'war' or 'armed conflict,' recent decisions suggest that they may not have to. Because neither the International Criminal Tribunal in Rwanda (ICTR) nor the International Criminal Court (ICC) require a 'nexus to armed conflict' as a condition for crimes against humanity, it appears as though the international legal community has removed this requirement. In summary, this seventh challenge to the KRT is that the prosecutors will have to prove either a plausible framework for charges of crimes against humanity, or that Cambodian victims fit into categories that would still warrant the definition of genocide. The two prosecutors—one Cambodian and one international—will have to agree on a charge to move the proceedings forward.

Finally, there are several additional challenges facing the domestic Cambodian judicial system identified by the United

Nations Group of Experts Report, namely 'a lack of qualified legal professionals, a poor legal system infrastructure, and a lack of respect for an impartial criminal justice system.' [71] In fact, the Ministry of Justice records show that as of 2001, more than half of Cambodia's 120 judges had not finished high school, and only 15 judges actually have law degrees. [72] Two hundred and twenty-six judges and prosecutors are registered with the Supreme Council of the Magistracy as of September 2007, [73] and with higher education expanding in the country, this number should rise in coming years. The ability of Cambodian domestic courts to operate freely and without corruption is jeopardized not only by lack of education, but by low civil servant salaries, [74] and lack of resources and legal infrastructure. [75]

A conceptual challenge is that the KRT addresses social and political justice at the expense of economic justice in Cambodia, arguably a critical component to reconciliation. If people continue to live in poverty and amidst the conflict that poverty breeds, the national justice symbolically disbursed through the Tribunal may be inadequate to assist people in moving beyond their memories of the Khmer Rouge time.

Thus, the challenges to the KRT are immense, but there is popular support for it to take place legitimately. The rehabilitation of Cambodia's domestic judiciary requires multifarious ingredients, including political will, resource allocation, and partnership between international experts and Cambodian legal practitioners. In theory at least, this is exactly what the hybrid court model should be able to provide for Cambodia. Whether or not the resources brought in by the international community can avoid falling into corrupt hands remains to be seen. Connected to this, the political will of Cambodia's leaders to see the KRT through to providing legal justice for perpetrators and survivors of the civil war oscillates based on the temperament of the ruling party and Monarchy. Yet if these challenges are overcome and a clean KRT takes place, the benefit to the Cambodian psyche could be great.

The justice Cambodians seek as one of many steps on the path to reconciliation may be available to them in the coming years, but they may have to be willing to overlook the complicating factors that prevent the KRT from being a model trial. Justice achieved by perpetuating the unprofessional and corrupt legal system may not change the culture of impunity that has plagued Cambodia for so long.

No Justice, No Peace

When Cambodians say they do want a tribunal, it is hard to distinguish if they say this because they want *something* to address past violence and this is the only mechanism the national government has offered, or if it because they really think the KRT will be the most effective tool for justice and reconciliation. To an extent, the symbolism of a conviction is similar to the symbolism of reparations: the recognition of wrongdoing can be a relief to survivors, especially when they have spent so many years with the truth obscured. [76] But even the KRT accompanied by symbolic reparations such as memorials and apologies may not be sufficient for reconciliation.

Shifting the approach in Cambodia to restorative justice, a process focused on bringing harmony back to broken relationships, [77] could incorporate village level encounters between victims and perpetrators who need to find ways to coexist together. Restorative justice does have mechanisms to hold perpetrators accountable, but they are enacted with an emphasis on honouring the dignity of the victim rather than ensuring punitive measures for the perpetrator. This kind of justice may elicit more community buy-in than the national and international level KRT. Yet a tribunal on its own is not poised to bring reconciliation, 'a complex process involving perpetrators taking responsibility for the past, acknowledging wrongdoing, apologizing and eventually providing restitution to their victims, or some variation on this general theme.' Restorative attributes such as stimulating community dialogue about past violence within a social framework of legal and symbolic justice are steps towards reconciliation. Incomplete though it may be, the power of symbolism, and the strengthening of Cambodia's judiciary that may be achieved in the process of generating such symbols, should not be discounted.

As mentioned previously, the KRT is an elite event that is orchestrated by those in positions of power and will take place using an elite legal language that is not available to most of the Cambodian population. To find ways to address the need for justice, truth-telling, and reconciliation at the grassroots level, individuals and NGOs have advocated holding community-based dialogue panels to address ongoing trauma of the Khmer Rouge time. One suggestion was to hold a nation-wide town hall meeting in a central gathering point such as Phnom Penh's Olympic Stadium where former Khmer Rouge leaders could tell their stories and apologize in front of the King Father and the Queen, but this was dismissed as a security hazard. [78] More prominently, public forums to debate issues of justice have been recommended and in a limited way carried out by the Center for Social Development (CSD), one of Phnom Penh's most highly regarded national NGOs. [79] CSD's former director, Cheah Vannath has said that the path to reconciliation begins with dialogue, including those who identify with or as Khmer Rouge, to get to the real issues. [80] Victim-participation projects such as community truth-telling panels at the village level have also been proposed by the Khmer Institute of Democracy, an active participant in outreach around the KRT.

But the community-based panel concept faces challenges in its own right. Should NGOs be responsible for this activity when their budgets are already taxed by the job of providing basic services throughout the country where the national government is unable to meet this obligation to the people? There has been discussion about whether these panels should have any real role in justice processes, or if they are mode equipped to be space for therapeutic storytelling. In a comparison to the TRC of South Africa, there is no 'incentive' in the community panel model for perpetrators to tell their stories. Immunity from prosecution cannot be granted because the KRT will be prosecuting people simultaneously, and perpetrators at the community level already enjoy a certain level of safety from prosecution. But if the community panels exist as voluntary therapeutic space for survivors needing to talk about their past memories or trauma as the news from the KRT brings up old emotions, it is questionable whether this will be sufficient support for reconciliation to begin.

To be certain, a key step in the reconciliation process occurs when people feel that they can set down their past grievances and move forward. It is not clear whether real closure can be obtained through a combination of communal therapy in the village and some appearance of national justice through the KRT. Acknowledgement by perpetrators of past violence could make a difference in this process, and if the KRT makes space for this more restorative technique within its retributive measures, perhaps the necessary justice can be reached to then allow people to move into a deeper kind of reconciliation. By engaging at the village level, justice and reconciliation processes can take place through civil society programs that act as parallel grassroots initiatives to support the more elite and inaccessible KRT. Cambodia's conflict can be addressed in ways that allow citizens set down the past, but justice must be joined with reconciliation for real social transformation to take place. Cambodia's leaders may falter on this path, but the people continue walking.

Notes

1. Wendy Lambourne, *Justice and Reconciliation: Post conflict Peace-building in Cambodia and Rwanda* (Sydney: University of Sydney, PhD Dissertation, 2002); James Deshaw Rae, *Hello Malae, Goodbye Barang: Building Peace, Justice, and Reconciliation in Post-Conflict Cambodia and East Timor* (Hawaii: University of Hawaii, PhD Dissertation, 2005).

2. Khmer is both the Anglicized term for the dominant ethnic group and their language.
3. *The World Fact Book–Cambodia* (Washington DC: The US Central Intelligence Agency, 2007).
4. Cited in Judy Ledgerwood and John Vijghen, "Decision Making in Khmer Villages," in J. Ledgerwood, ed., *Cambodia Emerges from the Past: Eight Essays* (DeKalb, IL: Southeast Asia Publications, 2002), p. 128.
5. Siobhan Gorman, Pon Dorina and Sok Kheng, *Gender and Development in Cambodia: An Overview*, Working Paper No. 10 (Phnom Penh: Cambodia Development Resource Institute, 1999), p. 10
6. Grant Curtis, *Cambodia Reborn? The Transition to Democracy and Development* (Washington DC: Brookings Institution Press and The United Nations Research Institute for Social Development, 1998), p.129.
7. Kim Kimchoeun, Vuthy Horng, Netra Eng, Ann Sovatha, Sedera Kim, Jenny Knowles and David Craig, *Accountability and Neo-Patrimonialism in Cambodia: A Critical Literature Review* (Phnom Penh: Cambodia Development Resource Institute, 2007), p. 43.
8. The Khmer Rouge are occasionally described as extreme Maoists, see for example, MacAlister Brown and Joseph J. Zasloff, *Cambodia Confounds the Peacemakers: 1979-1998* (New York: Cornell University Press, 1998), p. 4.
9. Helen Horsington, "The Cambodian Khmer Rouge Tribunal: The Promise of a Hybrid Tribunal," *Melbourne Journal of International Law*, no. 5, 2004, pp. 462-482.
10. Varying statistics, from 1-3 million people have been presented by different authors. See for example, Brown et al, n. 8, p. 5; Craig Etcheson, *After the Killing Fields: Lessons from the Cambodian Genocide* (London: Praeger, 2005). To an extent, this is because some scholars include only executions while others count starvation and illness due to war conditions, but the disparity also reflects the lack of monitoring and accurate information reaching the international community at the time.
11. Ben Kiernan, "Introduction: Conflict in Cambodia, 1945-2002," *Critical Asian Studies*, vol. 34, no. 4, 2002, pp. 483-495.
12. Ibid.
13. David Chandler, *A History of Cambodia* (Boulder: Westview

Press, 2000), p. 233.

14. Craig Etcheson in his book *After the Killing Fields: Lessons from the Cambodian Genocide* (London: Praeger, 2005) defines the civil war as lasting from 1969 through 1999, when Khmer Rouge guerrillas disbanded after being granted the right to govern the Cambodian region of Pailin.
15. Chandler, n. 13, p. 233.
16. Ibid.
17. Wendy Lambourne, "Post-Conflict Peace-building: Meeting Human Needs for Justice and Reconciliation," *Peace, Conflict and Development*, no. 4, April 2004, p. 5.
18. Chandler, n. 13, p. 241.
19. Ibid., p. 243.
20. Duncan McCargo, "Cambodia: Getting Away with Authoritarianism?" *Journal of Democracy*, vol. 16, no. 4, 2005, p.101.
21. "Cambodia," United States Agency for International Development, US Government, 2005. http://wwwusaid.gov/policy/budget/cbj2005/ane/kh.html. (A. O. 23 November 2007).
22. Ibid.
23. "Human Development Report: Cambodia," United Nations Development Programme, 2006/2007. http://hdrstats.undp.org/countries/country_fact_sheets/cty_fs_KHM.html. (A. O. 23 November 2007).
24. "Cambodia," n. 21.
25. "Human Development Report: Cambodia," n. 23.
26. Ibid.
27. "Cambodia Information, "Royal Embassy of Cambodia to Japan. http://sunsite.nus.sg/SEAlinks/cambodia-info.html. (A. O. 23 November 2007).
28. "Tourism Statistics," Tourism of Cambodia, 2005. http://www.tourismcambodia.com/Statistics/index.asp?Year=2005. (A. O. 23 November 2007).
29. "Target of Tourism in Thailand 1997-2005," Tourism Authority of Thailand, 2005. http://www2.tat.or.th/stat/web/static_index.php. (A. O. 23 November 2007).
30. "International Visitors to Vietnam in year 2005," Vietnam National Administration of Tourism, Ministry of

Culture, Sports and Tourism, 2005. http://vietnamtourism.gov.vn/english/index.php?option=com_content&task=vie. (A. O. 5 December 2007.)

31. "Cambodia Statistics," United Nations International Children's Fund, 2005. http://www.unicef.org/infobycountry/cambodia_statistics.html?q=printme. (A. O. 23 November 2007).
32. Ibid.
33. "At a Glance: Vietnam," United Nations International Children's Fund, 2005. http://www.unicef.org/infobycountry/vietnam_statistics.html?q=printme. (A. O. 23 November 2007).
34. "Cambodia Statistics," n. 31.
35. "At a Glance," n. 33.
36. "Cambodia Statistics," n. 31.
37. "Landmine Monitor Country Report 2007 – Cambodia," *Landmine Monitor*, 2007. http://www.icbl.org/lm/2007/cambodia.html. (A. O. 5 December 2007).
38. Ouarda Merrouche, "The Human Capital Cost of Landmine Contamination in Cambodia," *Households in Conflict Network*, (Sussex: The Institute of Development Studies, University of Sussex, 2006), p. 8.
39. Ibid., pp. 2-3.
40. Harry Nesbitt, "Developing Sustainable Rice Production Systems in Cambodia: An Australian Contribution," 2003. http://www.regional.org.au/au/asa/2003/i/3/nesbitt.htm?print=1. (A. O. 23 November 2007).
41. Ibid.
42. Ibid.
43. "U.S. Committee for Refugees World Survey 1997–Cambodia," United States Committee for Refugees and Immigrants, 1997. http://www.unhcr.org/cgi-bin/texis/vtx/refworld/rwmain? (A. O. 23 November 2007).
44. "U.S. Committee for Refugees World Survey 2000–Cambodia," United States Committee for Refugees and Immigrants, 2000. http://www.unhcr.org/cgi-bin/texis/vtx/refworld/rwmain? (A. O. 23 November 2007).
45. Ibid.
46. Rae, n. 1, pp. 174-175.

47. Sok An, "Frequently Asked Questions," Royal Government of Cambodia: Khmer Rouge Tribunal Task Force, 2007. www.cambodia.gov.kh/krt. (A. O. 18 October 2007).
48. Kiernan, n. 11, p. 491.
49. Rae, n. 1, p. 178.
50. Horsington, n. 9, p. 472.
51. Sok An, n. 47.
52. Horsington, n. 9, pp. 467-470.
53. The numerical order does not correspond to the importance of the challenge.
54. Vannarith Chheang, "The Establishment of the Khmer Rouge Tribunal and the Issue of Justice," Working Paper No. 06-2, Ritsumeikan Asia Pacific University, Japan, 2006, p. 4; Alfred P. Rubin, "Legal Response to Terror: An International Criminal Court?," *Harvard International Law Journal*, vol. 65, no. 43, 2002, p. 2.
55. Kinetz, "Thomico Asks PM To Shut Down ECCC," *The Cambodia Daily* (Phnom Penh), 2007, p. 2.
56. Ibid.
57. "First Khmer Rouge Leader Charged," BBC News, 2007. http://newsvote.bbc.co.uk/mpapps/pagetools/print/news.bbc.co.uk/2/hi/asia-pacific/692. (A. O. 1 September 2007).
58. Mohamed Ali Lejmi, "Prosecuting Cambodian Genocide: Problems Caused by the Passage of Time since the Alleged Commission of Crimes," *Journal of International Criminal Justice*, no. 4, 2006, p. 306.
59. Lambourne, n. 1.
60. Chheang, n. 54, p. 6.
61. McCargo, n. 20, p. 104.
62. Michael Lieberman, "Salvaging the Remains: The Khmer Rouge Tribunal on Trial," *Military Law Review*, no. 186, 2005, p. 168.
63. Wendy Lambourne, "Justice and Reconciliation: Post-conflict Peace-building in Cambodia and Rwanda," in M. Abu-Nimer, ed., *Reconciliation, Justice, and Coexistence* (Oxford: Lexington Books, 2001), p. 319.
64. David Chandler, *Voices from S-21: Terror and History in Pol Pot's Secret Prison* (Australia: Allen and Unwin, 2000b), p. 149.
65. Chandler, n. 13, p. 222.
66. Lieberman, n. 62, p. 168.
67. An, n. 47.

68. Horsington, n. 9, p. 475.
69. Scott Luftglass, "Crossroads in Cambodia: The United Nation's Responsibility to Withdraw Involvement from the Establishment of a Tribunal to Prosecute the Khmer Rouge," *Virginia Law Review*, vol. 90, no. 3, 2004, pp. 924-926.
70. Horsington, n. 9, p. 475.
71. Chheang, n. 54, p. 16.
72. Ibid.
73. Prak Chan Thul, "Judge Shortage Illustrates the Slow Road to Justice," *The Cambodia Daily,* 2007, p. 2.
74. This problem is not confined to the judiciary but in fact plagues all ministries who have not yet adopted merit-based pay schemes.
75. Lieberman. n. 62, p. 173.
76. Nancy AmouryCombs, *Guilty Pleas in International Criminal Law: Constructing a Restorative Justice Approach* (Stanford, CA: Stanford University Press, 2007), p. 19.
77. Ibid. p. 141.
78. Nayan Chanda, "Cambodia: Unable to Confront the Past," in Y. Funabashi, ed., *Reconciliation in the Asia-Pacific* (Washington, DC: United States Institute of Peace Press, 2003), p. 125.
79. Lambourne, n. 63, p. 320.
80. Lambourne, n. 1, p. 335.

7

Causes and Consequences of Ethno-Political Conflict in Sri Lanka

Nirmanusan Balasundaram

This chapter analyzes the economic and humanitarian cost of Sri Lankan conflict, which is mainly ethno-political in nature. While analyzing the cost, it principally focuses on the Northeastern part of Sri Lanka as it is directly and worse affected region in the country. The author's residence in the region since birth has provided a unique opportunity to witness the horrendous consequences of violence, and first hand information to present the reality.

The Democratic Socialist Republic of Sri Lanka is a tropical island nation off the southeastern coast of the Indian subcontinent. The island lies to the northeast of the Bay of Bengal within the Indian Ocean. It is separated from the Indian subcontinent by the Gulf of Mannar and the Palk Strait. The total area of Sri Lanka is 65,610 sq km, in which land takes up 64,740 sq km and water 870 sq km. The Sinhala speaking majority community (74 per cent), Tamil national minority (18 per cent) and the Muslim community (7 per cent) are the significant communities in Sri Lanka, apart from Burghers and Moors (1 per cent). Tamil speaking people are majority in the Northeast province and Sinhalese are Majority in the South. Buddhism and Hinduism made their way onto the island from India. The dominance of the Sinhala majority, Tamil nationalism and the Islamic religious identity are some of integrated factors of the on going conflict.

Sri Lanka gained independence without any bloodshed from the British in 1948. Unfortunately, this small beautiful island continues to face bloodshed time and again. Legally speaking, it is one country, one sovereign state and one nation, but with two languages (Sinhala and Tamil), three main ethnic groups (Sinhala, Tamil and Muslim) and four religions in practice (Buddhism, Christianity, Hinduism and Islam)—arguably not all of them treated equally. This differential treatment has led to the rise of ethno-political conflict. The Tamil national minority community considers itself at the receiving end of discrimination, marginalization and suppression. For instance, Muslims from Jaffna in 1990 and Tamils from Southern Sri Lanka, especially from Colombo were evicted in mid of 2007. "The anti-terrorism laws fed into the deteriorating human rights situation in Sri Lanka that has resulted in hundreds of killings, abductions and disappearances, mostly of ethnic Tamils and some Muslims," says Ishbel Matheson, Minority Rights Group's Head of Policy and Communications. [1]

Since 1957 to 2007 around six major agreements were signed and five peace negotiations (in 1985, 1987, 1989-90 and 1994-95 and 2002-2003) took place between the Government of Sri Lanka (GoSL) and the dissenting groups including that of Liberation Tigers of Tamil Eelam (LTTE). Despite momentous involvement of international community in the last six years a peaceful solution to this conflict has so far eluded. The violent conflict has derailed the economic development of the country. For example, October 2007 attack of LTTE on Anuradhapura air force base led to damage worth millions of dollars. Mangala Samaraweera the leader of Sri Lanka Freedom Party (M) reportedly said: "The estimated damage from the Anuradhapura airbase attack is around US dollars 150 million (Rs. 17.1 billion). This would mean 30 per cent of the bond obtained from international banks at a very high interest rate." [2] In 1983 allocation for defence expenditure was 1.7 billion; 25 years later allocation for defence in the budget is 166.4 billion Sri Lankan rupees.

In 2002, the GoSL and the LTTE signed the Memorandum of Understanding (MoU) under the mediation of Norwegian peace brokers. This peace process helped in the decline of the humanitarian and economic costs to some extent. Unfortunately it was not possible to sustain this process as both Sri Lanka and the LTTE continue to fail to make use of the opportunities for achieving lasting peace. This common negligence by the stakeholders to the conflict has led to the stalemate of 'no war, no peace.' While the GoSL insists to retain maximum power under unitary state, the LTTE demands Self autonomy. Some other 'powerless' actors discuss about federal arrangements to find out a lasting solution to the prolonged conflict. As per the ground realities, both parties are preparing for a full fledged 'final' war. The people of Sri Lanka have almost lost their confidence on parties to resolve conflict. These affected people are waiting for the 'Just Peace Miracle.'

Brief Background of the Conflict

Following independence of Sri Lanka a political party called Thamilarasu Katchy known as Federal Party, which represented the Tamil national minority, started to claim Tamil rights. The claim appeared more powerful than the 1921 declaration of Tamil Eelam by Sir Ponnambalam Arunachalam. The Sinhala Only Act of 1956 is one of the foremost root causes of ethno-political conflict. In 1961 Tamil people's 'satyagraha' (nearest meaning- the love of truth) non violent struggle stopped all functions of government structures in the Northeast for three months. This was the first massive resistance against the government that was suppressed by force. The purpose of standardization in 1971 was to control enrolment of Jaffna Tamil students in university, thus leading to further frustration among the Tamil youth, who thought the non-violent struggle of Tamil political parties could not achieve their political goal. Continued discrimination by the Sinhala ruling parties, resulted in the establishment of Tamil militant movements in the Northeastern area of Sri Lanka.

The Tamil New Tigers (TNT) was established in 1972. In

1976, it became LTTE. Efforts of the Tamil moderates did not reach any constructive point. In 1977 parliamentary general election, the majority of the Northeast Tamils people voted for a separate state. After 1958 riots, the next riot against the Tamil national minorities took place in 1977. This riot added to the aggravation of Tamils youths. In 1979, GoSL imposed the Prevention of Terrorism Act (PTA). But, the Act could not control resistance against government. The burning of Jaffna library on 31 May 1981 was another tragedy faced by the Tamils and is often considered a turning point in the ethno-political conflict. Tamils view education and knowledge as the biggest asset that one could possess in life. The incumbent President Mahinda Rajapakse and late President Ranasinghe Premadasa and former President Chandrika Kumarathunga acknowledged the mistake of burning the Jaffna library and expressed their regret. It was one of the violent examples of ethnic intolerance of the twentieth century. The library at the time of destruction was one of the biggest in Asia containing over 97,000 books and unique manuscripts. President Mahinda Rajapakse said in 2006 "Burning the Library sacred to the people of Jaffna was similar to shooting down Lord Buddha." [3]

Political unrest escalated in the early 1980s as groups representing the Tamil aspirations moved towards organized insurgency. The LTTE was the strongest of these groups. There were also other competing groups, which were sometimes hostile to each other. On 23 July 1983 the LTTE ambushed a Sri Lanka Army (SLA) convoy, killing more than 10 soldiers. In response, the Sinhala majority unleashed riots against the Tamils in the South, resulting in the first ever humanitarian and economic crisis of Sri Lanka. Since then, it has become a pattern of war and peace process. The J.R. Jayawardene government sent troops to Jaffna in 1979. The Jayawardene government hoped to destroy the LTTE within six months, but now almost 24 years later the LTTE is running a de-facto state within Sri Lanka. There are many ongoing debates with regard to the nature of the LTTE, whether they are freedom fighters or terrorist.

However, majority of the Tamils feel that the LTTE is fighting for Tamil people's freedom.

Peace Process and Human Rights Violations

Since 2002 the six rounds of peace talks between the GoSL and the LTTE under the mediation of Norwegian peace brokers helped to calm down the situation. During the first round of peace talks between the GoSL and LTTE held in September 2002, at Sattahip naval base in Thailand, the LTTE announced that it would settle for 'internal self-determination' and 'substantial regional autonomy' for the Tamil population rather than the full independence—a major shift in the rebels' position. [4] However, the peace process could not move further due to intransigence of both the parties. Lack of commitment by both parties, limited facilitation role of Norway, national interests of regional and international super powers, resistance from the extreme parties, irresponsible acts of the media and lack of awareness among the public are the factors behind unsuccessful peace negotiations. The GoSL announced on 3 January 2008 that it has decided to abrogate the CFA.

The common people, who continue to live in the situation of protracted conflict, less understand the fact that 'peace processes are another face of war.' In Sri Lankan history, peace processes are lessons for failures as well as different faces of war. Six rounds of peace talks between LTTE and United National Front (UNF) government went on smoothly, but agreements related to humanitarian issues were not implemented. In the CFA agreement removal of High Security Zone (HSZ) was the most crucial and controversial aspect of the talks. Before the CFA, the LTTE held that the lifting of the government ban on them would be a pre-requisite for any possibility of peace talks. This lifting of the ban supported their claim for equal status, but this status was questioned during the 2003 Washington donor conference. The LTTE was not invited by the US for the donor conference. The LTTE saw this as unequal treatment by the US.

Subsequently, the LTTE was not allowed to participate in the Tokyo donor conference. This 'biased approach' also impacted the peace negotiations. Despite the Sri Lanka Monitoring Mission (SLMM) report accusing the LTTE for CFA violations, the Scandinavian truce monitoring mission has recorded over 100 per cent increase in CFA violations by government security forces and police. [5] On 31 October 2003, LTTE put forward their Interim Self Governance authority (ISGA) proposal. That was the first ever written proposal by the LTTE for finding a peaceful solution to ethno-political conflict, but the Sri Lankan authoritarians did not respond to it properly. Then President Chandrika Kumaratungga and Prime Minster Ranil Wickramasinghe could not address the LTTE demand properly ostensibly due to political differences between the two leaders.

The December 26, 2004 Asian Tsunami was a horrible incident. But the disaster proved to be a missed opportunity to bring the conflicting parties on a single platform. Many Sri Lankans, especially Tsunami affected people thought that post-Tsunami scenario will bring at least minimum peaceful solution to the ethno-political conflict. Memorandum of Understanding (MoU) for the establishment of a Post-Tsunami Operational Management Structure (P-TOMS) was signed between the GoSL and the LTTE on 24 June 2005. This led to increasing hopes towards peaceful solution of the conflict among three major communities.

But the Sri Lanka Supreme Court issued a stay order to block sections of the Post-Tsunami Operational Management Structure (P-TOMS) agreement signed between the government and the LTTE. The ruling was made by Chief Justice Sarath Silva after a case was filed by the Peoples Liberation Front known as Janatha Vimukthi Pearamuna (JVP) and Jathika Hela Urumaya (JHU) asking the Court to make the

P-TOMS agreement null and void. The stay order would remain valid until the Supreme Court reviews its decision. The Chief Justice also said that "an aid coordination committee, composed mostly of Tiger representatives based in the LTTE stronghold of Kilinochchi, is illegal and must be moved to an alternate location." [6] People meanwhile continued to suffer physically, mentally as well as materially because of prolonged conflict on the one hand, and the effects of the Tsunami on the other.

During the CFA period Sri Lanka military intelligence officers and Deep Penetration Unit of Sri Lanka army were targeted by the LTTE. Similarly Tamil parliamentarians, intellectuals, journalists and civilians were killed by 'usual unidentified gunmen' in government controlled areas. Soon after the election of a new president in November 2005, the violence escalated. Extra judicial killings, abductions, disappearances, arbitrary arrests, detentions and claymore explosions became common. International Human Rights organizations like Human Rights Watch and Amnesty International blame both the government and LTTE. Both parties have not taken appropriate actions to protect civilians from violence. Amnesty International Secretary General Irene Khan has urged President Mahinda Rajapaksa "to use his executive power to invite the United Nations to set up a strong human rights field operation in Sri Lanka, to investigate and verify serious human rights abuses committed countrywide." [7] With regard to most of the human right violations blames were ignored by the government and some of them were indirectly acknowledged. Defence Secretary Gotabhaya Rajapaksa (President Rajapaksa's brother) said in an interview on 12 June 2007 that the international community, especially the UK and other European nations, are bullying his country over human rights. "What I am saying is, if there is a terrorist group, why can't you do anything? It's not against a community... I'm talking about terrorists. Anything is fair." [8]

Former president Chandrika Bandaranaike Kumaratunga

condemned the trend of abductions and disappearances and observed that 'the government cannot act like a terrorist organization.' Fundamental rights which are a part of the Sri Lankan constitution are also dishonoured by the government, due to the enforcement of Emergency Regulations (ER) and Prevention of Terrorism Act (PTA). To quote the National Peace Council report, "Under the Emergency Regulations and Prevention of Terrorism Act, police and army were permitted to arrest and detain suspects without charge for up to 18 months, restrict visitor access and withhold information on the place and conditions of those detained. These regulations exceed the limits permitted under international law – in the International Covenant on Civil and Political Rights (ICCPR). It is estimated that 18,000 people were detained in 2000, alone under the PTA and ER." [9]

Many illegal actions are legalized by the government in the name of sovereignty. According to former United Nations Secretary-General Boutros Boutros–Ghali, "The time of absolute sovereignty…has passed; its theory was never matched by reality." [10] National security and territorial integrity are the areas of major concern to governments. However, state sovereignty can not deny a citizen's sovereignty and cannot be an excuse for their non-performance. Unfortunately Sri Lankan governments failed to fulfill national minorities' rights. Former president Chandrika Kumarathunga conveyed a national apology for 'Black July riots against Tamils' in New York in 2004 and accepted that denial of Tamil rights created ethnic conflict. "The Tamils wants equal rights and that there has been a continuous neglect of the frustrations of the Tamil people by the all governments since independence." [11]

Even opposition leader Ranil Wickramasinghe also stated the same thing, but the problem is that all these leaders blame each other for such denial of rights. Responsibility to Protect (R2P) concept finds major space in discourse in Sri Lanka in recent years. Gareth Evans, President of the International

Crisis Group has mentioned in his speech in Colombo in July 2007 that 'sovereignty is not the license to kill the people.' "Pro- government media are currently involved in promoting propaganda against R2P, and even the operations of the government show that they too don't like R2P. The GoSL has repeatedly asserted its responsibility to ensure state sovereignty. The equality in legal status of sovereignty also offers protection for weaker states in the face of pressure from the more powerful. [12] After the comprehensive analysis, from the International community point of view, R2P is vital for Sri Lanka.

Denial of the rights and oppression provided background for rise of separatism. Significant number of Tamil diaspora feel 'stateless' and would like to return to their ancestral homes. This feeling ensures the support for LTTE. According to Sri Lanka foreign ministry Tamil diasporas are feeding the LTTE. 2006 Human Rights Report has indicated that funding for the 'final war' was collected by LTTE in Europe. [13] The LTTE has been banned as a terrorist organization in 32 countries. [14] Likewise, Sri Lankan military officials were black listed in Canada. [15] Diplomatic confrontations continue between the United Nations and Sri Lanka with regard to establishing a human rights commission. The Chief Government Whip and senior minister Jeyaraj Fernandopulle accused John Holmes, United Nations under Secretary of Humanitarian Affairs, who visited Sri Lanka in August 2007 'of being a terrorist and bribed by the LTTE to carry out a mudslinging campaign worldwide against the Government.' [16]

Military Operations and Related Developments

Negative peace encouraged the 'Undeclared war' between GoSL and LTTE. Economic embargo on LTTE controlled area and closure of Maviaru sluice gate played a significant role in the escalation of this undeclared war. Fierce battles started towards the end of July 2006 in Trincomalee district. Sri

Lanka Air Force (SLAF) aerial bombings began in LTTE controlled territory after the LTTE attempted to assassinate the Sri Lanka Army commander Lt. Gen. Sarath Fonseka in April 2006. Since then more than thousand times SLAF bombardments have taken place on LTTE stronghold, Vanni region. In the recent air raids on LTTE control territory averagely 12 bombs were dropped per day, each bomb weighing 500kg. A survey conducted by the Intellectuals on Human Rights (IHR) has revealed that there are "more than half a million Sri Lankans displaced throughout Sri Lanka. Due to military operations public places like churches, hospitals, and children orphanages turns as Internally Displaced Persons camps which also get affected directly." [17]

Soon after the recapture of the east by the Sri Lanka army, a western aid agency volunteer who had visited to the east later told, "When I traveled to East from Colombo, both side of the main road, from Welikanda to Batticaloa I saw human catastrophe. The people who have been displaced from their villages are living under the trees without any basic needs. Shelling on one side, heavy rain and thunder strikes on the other side have traumatized the people. It reminded me Sudan." [18] Since 2006, more than 10 thousand Sri Lankan citizens including civilians, soldiers and cadres have lost their lives.

In East, resettlements have started, but IDPs are not re-settled within their native villages. The national minorities who have been living in those areas have expressed fear that another state colonization would befall on them. When strategic Sampur was captured by Sri Lankan security forces, President Rajpaksa said, "Our armed forces have captured Sampur for the welfare and the benefit of the people living there." [19] On 30 May 2007, the President established High Security Zone in the areas of Sampur and Mutur east, encompassing about 90 square kms. [20] Government regulations forbid any person, including local residents, from entering in the newly designated area without written permission from the competent authority. The Sri Lankan army in many cases perceives the humanitarian organizations as in favor of the LTTE. Hence, military interventions such as putting restrictions on humanitarian programmes have almost become unavoidable. All local and international NGOs engaged in development projects within newly captured areas in the Eastern Province confront a variety of restriction on their work. [21]

Present government believes that they can weaken the LTTE through military operations and after realization of the objective it can push the organization for talks on solutions. An interview given by Defence Secretary Gotabhaya Rajapaksa to the media on in 2007 stipulates the GoSL strategy. In that interview he said, "Government's aim is to weaken the LTTE. Our objective is to weaken them, we have to defeat them militarily, and we have to control Vanni. It is possible. We just have to squeeze them. Then a political solution becomes possible." [22] The current scenario in the Northeast of the country, thus, can be characterized with brutal undeclared war, while the rest of the country is experiencing tragic impact of this war. People in different parts of the Island carry different fears in their daily life. For example: an individual from the northeast holding the fear of aerial bombing, shelling, killing and abduction, whereas an individual from Southwest fear of bomb blast, rising cost of living, harassment through the check points. The impact would continue to rise disastrously if the solution is not sought.

The Cost

Nearly three decades of violent conflict has resulted in the loss of life of more than 75 thousand Tamil speaking people. The last 2 year of the Cease Fire Agreement (CFA) period, nearly 5400 Tamil people were killed. War-widows estimates were 22,963 in the eastern region in 2001. Before the CFA, in Jaffna alone there were 26,745 widows and around 400,000 women live in shelters across the country. [23] From 2005 November to end of 2007 about 1,200 newly war-widows were identified by unofficial reports in the Jaffna district. There are an estimated 30,000 female headed families in the Northeast.

Before 2002, 3,687 soldiers were reported missing in action. A particular attack calls 'Unceasing Waves-1' by LTTE on Mullaitivu Sri Lanka Army base led around 1000 soldiers missing in action. In 1998, a woman from Kandy said, "my son is in the Sri Lanka army. In September 1998, in Kilinochchi, about 650 of our children's bodies were lying dead. They were packed in plastic bags. But I do not know whether one of my children was among them. We could not even see the bodies. My child was a part of me, but I have been deprived of finding out whether my son is dead or alive." [24] Until, 2001, according to the Ministry of Defence 10,343 government soldiers were disabled. There are large numbers of children who have lost one or both parents as a result of the conflict. In Batticaloa (eastern district), 53 per cent of children have become victim of violence in terms of loosing a family member either through death or disappearance. As of today, more than 10,000 children are living in orphanages. Out of the remaining IDPs in Sri Lanka, it is estimated that 34 per cent are children. [25]

Since April 2006 to the end of 2007 about five hundred thousand Tamils became IDPs. According to the National Peace Council (NPC) 2003 research, around 250,000 of displaced were less than 14 years. Hundreds of boys and girls were recruited as child soldiers. Because of LTTE intimidation Sinhalese people from several border villages were also displaced. For the last seventeen years the evicted Muslims are living in Puttalam district as IDPs. Because of HSZ, for the last twenty years about 50 thousand Tamil people are living at Internal Displaced Camps in Jaffna district. One million Sri Lankan Tamils are living in Europe, America, Australia and Asia. Almost one hundred thousand Sri Lankan Tamils are living in Tamil Nadu, India. Thousands of them are suffering from post-traumatic stress disorder and other mental illness related to or resulting from the conflict. Over 9,000 troops continue to receive post-recovery treatment from the army rehabilitation unit. An estimated 30,000-40, 000 soldiers deserted the army during the conflict. They now face high level of unemployment having limited skills outside the military. The war extensively damaged housing, roads, bridges, commercial and state property, irrigation system, machinery, communications system, plantation and fisheries. The total cost of property damage amounts billions of Sri Lankan rupees.

In Northeast it is estimated that 1.8 million land mines are still active. Prior to 2002 CFA, both government soldiers and LTTE cadres planted land mines in the Northeast, especially in the Northern Province. During the CFA period some steps were taken at demining, which is expensive. Later, both the parties again started planting landmines. Since January 2006, 44 humanitarian workers have been killed in Sri Lanka. [26] United Nations under Secretary General for Humanitarian Affairs Sir John Holmes has stated 'there is a concern about the safety of humanitarian workers themselves and the record here is one of the worst in the world from that point of view.' Sri Lanka is the third dangerous country in the world for the journalists, an international media watchdog has observed. [27] The Minister of Mass Media and Information, Anura Priyadharshana Yapa stated that one journalist died in 2007 due to violence. Independence sources like Free Media Movement (FMM) of Sri Lanka and the Press Emblem Campaign report that in 2007, seven journalists were killed in Sri Lanka. [28]

From environmental point of view also, Northeast remains worse affected region in Sri Lanka. Deforestation – around 5 million trees were used for military fences and between 2 and 3 million palmyrah palms were cut down in the Jaffna peninsula, thus halving their population. In 2006 heavy battle from 11 to 19 August, Sri Lanka Army used 6,500 Multi

Barrel Rocket Launchers (MBRL) for a week towards LTTE controlled territory. The LTTE's shelling figures were not available. Since 2006 August, fierce shelling is exchanged between both parties on a daily basis. During the period of 2006 April to 2007, more than thousand times SLAF aerial bombardments have taken place in the LTTE controlled areas. During the air raids, at-least five to twenty bombs are dropped in those areas. This means minimum of 150 thousand kilogram aerial bombs were dropped in Northeast. According to the government sources, around hundred LTTE boats were destroyed. Based on media sources, during that period Sri Lankan Navy's 8 fast attack crafts were destroyed by the naval wing of LTTE known as Sea Tigers.

Agriculture and fishing are the main income sources for war affected Northeast. The war not only affected people in terms of loss of lives, but also it polluted ecology of the region including sea thus impacting the overall environment. The war also destroyed about 2000 schools, and out of 400 health institutions 55 were totally destroyed and 49 became defunct. Needless to add, the contribution of the Northeast to national GDP is much less in comparison to other regions due to obvious regions. War has destroyed most of the growth prospects of the region by affecting resources such as agriculture and fisheries. Besides direct violence, HSZ has made it difficult to access these areas for economic purposes. The war has also affected industrial sectors in the Northeast badly. The loss of output for the region during the war is estimated at Rs. 686 billion (based on 2001 prices). Over this period income per person dropped by around 40 per cent. Meanwhile government's investments in Northeast remain less in comparison to other provinces.

The LTTE attack on the central Bank of Sri Lanka on 31 January 1996 had significant impact on Sri Lankan economy and finance policy as this is the place where the gold reserves are kept and the country's financial policies are made. The consequences were less foreign investments and decrease in tourism arrival in Sri Lanka, two vital components of country's income. In the early hours of 24 July 2001, the LTTE's Black Tigers launched an attack on Sri Lankan Air Force base in Katunayake and the Katunayake Bandaranaike International Airport which shocked the country. LTTE's first air raid too took place on Katunayake air force base. Such attacks on airports or Colombo harbour have instantaneous effect on country's economy. Soon after the attacks on Colombo harbour, international shipping companies refused to send their ships to Colombo port. Same pattern emerged after the attacks on Katunayake airport. Passenger flights did not come to Katunayake international airport for a short period of time and the Government was forced to ban all night flights in and out of the country.

45.4 per cent of the population in Sri Lanka lives on less than two dollars per day. But the tragic part of the story is that, it seems, the key concern of both the GoSL and LTTE is about purchasing weapons. The money allocated for defence is higher than the allocations for all other sectors. Violence has also affected foreign investments and tourism. To quote the National Peace Council, 2003 report, "the war caused economic insecurity and instability that contributed to a lack of foreign investment and tourism. The loss of investors' confidence greatly affected the long term development and the growth of the economy. The loss of direct foreign investment is estimated at US$ 1,610 million. It is estimated that the economy lost US$ 4.4 billion from the decline in tourism." [29] Economic growth slowed down to 7 per cent in the third quarter in 2007. Director General of the Census and Statistics Department of Sri Lanka, Suranjana Vidyaratne observed that "We expect full-year economic expansion to slow down to 6.7 per cent this year from 7.7 per cent in 2006." [30] Inflation rate was 24.1 per cent in October 2007. Unemployment rate was 7.6 per cent in 2006. Mainly due to the increase in defence expenditure, the government's expenditure level has seen a greater increase than its earnings.

Analysts have pointed out that the government had printed currency notes worth of Rs. 45 billion from May to September in 2007 and was borrowing vast amounts from the state banks to fund its survival, thus causing high inflation. Economist Harsha De Silva noted unless the government stops printing money, the country would continue to record a high rate of inflation. In South Asian region, Sri Lanka holds one of the highest levels of inflation. Fast developing and closest neighbouring India has recorded only 3.2 percentage inflation in December 2007. China, country with largest population in the world recorded inflation at 2.4 percent at the beginning of the 2007. Based on recent political developments, Pakistan is one of the most dangerous countries in Asia. Its inflation level for the year of 2007 was about 7.8 per cent. Sri Lanka is smaller in comparison to India and Pakistan, but its inflation level and defence expenditure both are higher than both the countries.

According to Strategic Foresight Group representative, Ministry, Sri Lanka was the most militarized country in the South Asian region. In terms of the number of military personnel per million people, Sri Lanka has 8,000. Between 1996 and 2000, Sri Lanka purchased as many as 6.4 million small arms and light weapons. The average military expenditure as a percentage of GDP placed Sri Lanka at the top, with 4 per cent of its GDP in recent years, higher than India with 2.5 per cent of its GDP, Pakistan with 3.5 per cent and Bangladesh with 1.5 per cent of its GDP. [31]

Thus, the conflict has shattered Sri Lanka's economy, distorted its democracy and legal system, and impacted its sovereignty. [32]

Current Scenario

The undeclared war started three years after signing of the CFA and later the GoSL abrogated the CFA on 2 January 2008. As a result the Nordic truce monitors (Sri Lanka Monitoring Mission) have folded up their activities and left the country on 16 January 2008. This decision by the Government led to reactions from the international community. The US State Department spokesman Sean McCormack said the United States was "'troubled by the decision' and that it would make it more difficult to achieve a lasting, peaceful solution to Sri Lanka's conflict." [33] The United Nations Secretary General Ban Ki-Moon regretted the government's decision. His spokeswoman Michele Montas said; "the UN was 'deeply worried' that the withdrawal came amid intensifying violence in Sri Lanka." [34] Since the announcement, the NGOs working for peace are also facing indirect pressure to scale down their activities.

Sri Lanka is spiralling towards disaster. Within the first ten days of end of ceasefire two parliamentarians were killed and three claymore blasts took place in capital of Sri Lanka. On the other hand, aerial bombardments, claymore attacks and offensive operations of Sri Lanka security forces continue on LTTE strong hold Vanni region. At the end of 2007, the Tri-Forces Commanders expressed confidence that the LTTE would be extinct in 2008. The LTTE, in turn, warned bringing 'clarity' to the ethnic conflict in 2008 through a demonstration of military strength. The European Union has urged Sri Lanka to offer 'substantive devolution' to LTTE. In reality, 'urges', 'regrets' and 'concerns' of international community towards Sri Lanka has not created any concrete platform for durable peace in the country. Escalations of hostilities have just begun with disasters waiting ahead to unfold. The end of CFA and the ensuing developments have raised uncertainty, reaffirmed by the recent negative trends that only go on to demonstrate that lasting peace at this point is only a mirage. Primordial history shows that to seek a solution of conflict through war is un-realist; however the principal stakeholders of this ethno-political conflict are pursuing a war that is dreaded by the people, across all divide.

Violent conflicts result in instability not only in the socio-economic and political fabric of the country but also set a cycle of devastation for years to come. Sri Lanka is no exception to this imperative of conflict situation. However, one of the major roadblocks in the Sri Lankan conflict is lack of consensus towards peaceful resolution of the issue. Besides, extremism on part of conflicting parties too has contributed to the stalemate. Instead of rhetoric, realism should guide actions of both the government as well as LTTE, as continuation of violent methods would draw the country further towards the path of bloodshed and destruction.

Notes

1. http://www.minorityrights.org/?lid=4585. (A. O. 13 December 2007).
2. http://sundaytimes.lk/071028/Columns/political.html. (A. O. 28 November 2007).
3. http://en.wikipedia.org/wiki/Burning_of_Jaffna_library. (A. O. 6 January 2008).
4. Bruce Vaughn and Severn Anderson, "Sri Lanka: Background and U.S. Relations," CRS Report for US Congress, 16 May 2005, p.5.
5. http://www.island.lk/2007/06/17/news19.html. (A. O. 17 November 2007).
6. http://servesrilanka.blogspot.com/2005/07/sri-lanka-supreme-court-blocks.html. (A. O. 15 July 2005).
7. http://www.island.lk/2007/06/16/news2.html. (A. O. 16 November 2007).
8. http://news.bbc.co.uk/2/hi/south_asia/6745553.stm. (A. O. 12 December 2007).
9. *Costs of War, Challenges and Priorities for the Future* (Colombo: National Peace Council of Sri Lanka, 2003).
10. http://www.un.org/docs/SG/agpeace.html. (A. O. 12 December 2007).
11. http://www.asiasociety.org/speeches/kumaratunga04.html. (A. O. 22 December 2007).
12. *The Responsibility to Protect – Supplementary Volume to the Report of the International Commission on Intervention and State Sovereignty* (Canada: International Development Research Centre, December 2001), p. 7.
13. *Human Rights Watch Report*, vol. 18, no. 1(C), March 2006, p.

11.

14. http://en.wikipedia.org/wiki/Tamil_Tigers (A. O. 5 November 2007).
15. http://www.nationalpost.com/story.html?id=5b8f66c6-00ab-48b3-98f3-65601681bb56 (A. O. 14 December 2007).
16. http://www.dailymirror.lk/2007/08/16/front/1.asp. (A. O. 5 November 2007).
17. *The Daily Mirror* (Colombo), 17 December 2007.
18. Personal Interaction, name withheld, 15 November 2007.
19. http://www.presidentsl.org/data/html/news/200609/20060904news-1.htm. (A. O. 16 December 2007).
20. The High Security Zone was established under Emergency Regulations (section 5 of the Public Security Ordinance) published in Gazette Extraordinary No. 1499/25.
21. http://www.sangam.org/2007/10/Obstacles.php?uid=2578. (A. O. 16 December 2007).
22. http://www.themorningleader.lk/20071128/news.html#Gota (A. O. 21 December 2007).
23. *Costs of War*, n. 9.
24. Ibid.
25. Semu Bhatt and Mistry Devika, *Cost of Conflict in Sri Lanka* (Mumbai: Strategic Foresight Group, 2006), pp. 58
26. http://www.sangam.org/2007/08/Humanitarian_Workers.php?uid=2511. (A. O. 27 December 2007).
27. http://www.bbc.co.uk/sinhala/news/story/2007/12/071218_dangerous_press.shtml. (A. O. 27 December 2007).
28. http://www.pressemblem.ch/7545.html. (A. O. 27 December 2007).
29. *Costs of War*, n. 9.
30. http://www.colombopage.com/archive_07/December19185359JV.html. (A. O. 28 December 2007).
31. http://www.peace-srilanka.org/docs/Cost%20of%20Conflict%20Seminar%20Report.do. (A. O. 14 November 2007).
32. Whitaker P. Mark, *Learning Politics from Sivaram: The Life and Death of a Revolutionary Tamil Journalist in Sri Lanka.* (London: Pluto Press, 2007), pp. 3
33. http://colombo.usembassy.gov/. (A. O. 26 December 2007).
34. http://www.bbc.co.uk/sinhala/news/story/2008/01/080104_india_cfa.shtml. (A. O. 3 January 2008).

8

Kashmir Conflict: Causes, Costs and Prospects of Peace

Debidatta Aurobinda Mahapatra and Shailender Shekhawat

Despite diverse interpretations of the Kashmir conflict, its genesis and later developments, it is true that the conflict is one of most violent ones causing innumerable losses to the parties involved. Probably, it is the only enduring conflict in which two sovereign nation-states wielding nuclear weapons are involved. The conflict has led to the division of the Kashmir region, with major chunk remaining with India, and rest with Pakistan. The bilateral animosities, which not only manifested in four wars and many war scares but also in militancy within the Indian state of Jammu and Kashmir (J&K), brought large scale death and destruction in their trail. Though there are no expected lines in Indo-Pakistan relations over Kashmir, the recent developments towards resolution of the conflict however have indicated the transformation of the conflict from violent assertion of respective positions to amicable resolution of the conflict through dialogue and deliberation, with people's participation.

The Conflict in Nutshell

The Kashmir conflict started from the very beginning of the partition of the Indian subcontinent in 1947. Besides other factors, the geo-strategic importance of the region made it a point of contention between the two neighbouring countries, India and Pakistan. Pakistan's attempts to make the state 'independent' and India's attempts to maintain its territorial integrity impacted the development scenario in the state. This section attempts to analyze the causes of the vast Kashmir conflict briefly, while admitting the controversial nature of interpretations of the conflict and its causes. J&K (generally called Kashmir) was one of the more than 500 princely states of British India on which the British paramountcy lapsed on August 15, 1947. As per terms of the British withdrawal and partition of India, the rulers of all the princely states were given the option of joining either of the two dominions- India or Pakistan, taking into account the wishes of the people. Despite apparent simplicity of these principles, they were not easily applicable to J&K. The state had a predominantly Muslim population and a Hindu ruler. The problem was complicated as the region claimed by both India and Pakistan and both were neighbouring states. The issue of J&K became further complicated due to the political situation within the region. The ruler of the state, Maharaja Hari Singh, was facing opposition from his own subjects, primarily from the majority Muslim population. [1]

Maharaja's evasiveness about the political future of J&K worsened the already complicated situation. Hari Singh requested standstill agreement with both newly independent states. According to it 'the existing arrangements should continue pending settlement of details.' [2] While India asked for further negotiation, Pakistan agreed to the agreement. Much is disputed about the events that succeeded. To put pressure on Hari Singh, Pakistan many times stopped regular supply of material to the state. The uprising in Poonch against the ruler and infiltration of armed groups from Pakistan complicated the problem. Pakistan intending to 'grab J&K by force' [3] sent its troops disguised as local tribesmen. The developments forced Hari Singh to appeal India for help.

On 26 October 1947, the king signed the Instrument of Accession to accede J&K with India. Pakistan took the stand that the accession of Kashmir to India was illegal. On 27 October 1947, Indian troops were sent to J&K and a full-scale war started between India and Pakistan. The Indian government made formal complaint to the United Nations against Pakistan's 'aggression' on 1 January 1948. On 1 January 1949, the United Nations negotiated a ceasefire that left a considerable portion of J&K state in the possession of Pakistan. Since then the conflict over J&K became the longest border dispute. The current emphasis while talking about the Kashmir conflict remains largely focused on the Indian side of the state with little mention of the part of Kashmir that is under the control of Pakistan. [4]

Acute differences brought the two neighbouring states to the brink of war in 1950 and again in 1951. Conflict over the question of J&K flared up in a full-scale war between India and Pakistan in 1965. The war ended on 23 September 1965. The Soviet-brokered Tashkent Agreement was signed by the two warring countries on 10 January 1966 agreeing to a ceasefire and maintaining the status quo. The end of 1971 again involved India and Pakistan in another war. Although this war was not directly fought over J&K the fight did spread to it. On 17 December, both India and Pakistan declared ceasefire. They signed the Shimla Agreement on 2 July 1972 agreeing to settle disputes through bilateral talks and negotiations.

As per the agreement, the unsettled border in Kashmir that was earlier known as Ceasefire Line was rechristened the Line of Control (LOC) with some alteration in the earlier line. Thus, India and Pakistan share more than one thousand km long border in J&K. While the 198 km International Border (IB), extending from Kathua to Akhnoor, is recognized one, the 778 km LOC, extending from Akhnoor to Siachen Glacier, is a de facto border. The Shimla Agreement provided a comprehensive framework for normalisation of relations. It, despite tension from time to time, prevented a major clash between India and Pakistan until 1999, when the Kargil conflagration took place.

The onset of militancy in late 1980s in Indian state of J&K ostensibly with the support of Pakistan (as it failed to confront

India directly militarily) began an era of unending violence with only variation in the intensity. By 1989, a number of significant armed groups had begun to operate throughout the valley. A series of violent demonstrations erupted on various issues in 1988 such as the hike in power tariff and the demand for a ban on Salman Rushdie's *Satanic Verses*. A strike was organized on India's Independence Day and 'civil' curfew (as opposed to government-order) was imposed with burning of Indian flag and raising black flags. During numerous curfews imposed by the state, people came out in streets in huge processions, chanting the slogans of *azadi* (freedom). The withdrawal Soviet forces from Afghanistan in 1989 and the consequent diversion of Mujahideens towards India for violent activities with the support of Pakistan further worsened the situation, as Kashmir witnessed violence on almost daily basis, with the killing of innocent tourists, kidnapping, loot, arson, etc.

By early 1990s, the democratic political processes had totally collapsed in the valley and the mainstream political parties had almost disappeared. India accused Pakistan of interference in India's internal affairs. Pakistan, in turn, persistently accused India of denying the Kashmiris their right to self-determination and of systematic human rights violations. The tensions nearly resulted in apprehension of another war in 1986-1987 when India conducted a military exercise close to the border. In 1990, the two countries again reached the brink of war. The nuclear tests by India and Pakistan in May 1998 added further complexity to the conflict. The attacks of the *fidayeen* (suicide attackers) groups in the state of J&K again led to two consecutive war scares in December 2001 and May 2002. There are various reports from all over the globe that the area of undivided J&K that is in control of Pakistan is used by it to train and infiltrate the militants to create havoc in J&K. Attack on Indian Parliament on 13 December 2001 and on J&K Legislative Assembly October 2001, indicated the wide reach and sophistication in terrorist activities in India.

Kashmir conflict in fact is one of the most violent and much talked about conflicts in the global discourse, thus motivating the former US President, Bill Clinton calling the region 'most dangerous place on earth.' Both internal and external dimensions are intermingled in the conflict. The four wars, several war-scares and cross border firings in the past have witnessed deaths of thousands of the common people as well security personnel and militants, thus putting heavy burden on the public exchequer, besides paralyzing the socio and economic life of the state. The next section would, however, focus only on the cost of the internal conflict i.e. militancy in the India state of J&K.

The Costs

The economic cost of the Kashmir conflict cannot be confined to a particular sector of industry or investment prospects. It has affected the important sources of livelihood of local people such as tourism, horticulture and handicrafts industries. Besides exacting extensive damage to the infrastructure of the region, the violent conflict has discouraged private investment, pushing the economy towards stagnation. The conflict has caused extensive damage to the infrastructure. The basic infrastructure in terms of regular power supply, roads, communication system, and drinking water remains poor in the state. The findings of the pre budget Economic Survey 2007-08 in the state presented a very grim picture on all major fronts. [5]

As per the survey findings, the road length per 100 square km area in J&K is 35.71 kms as against 104.64 kms in the country. The state has 2060 such habitations, which have no road connectivity at all. The communication facilities too are inadequate. There is one Post Office for 60 sq km area as against national average of 20 sq km. Number of telephones per 100 people in the state is 7.76, well short of all India level at 13.57. The state is endowed with huge water resources but tapping of these resources for the benefit of the economy has not been done adequately. Having a hydro-electric potential of more than 20,000 MW, the state has so far been able to exploit only 1,478 MW, which makes only 9 per cent of the total power potential of the state. Ironically, the state with huge potentials of power has the largest power deficit in comparison to other states of India. The state government has to bank more on power imports from the Northern Grid of India and the arrears of which have crossed Rs. 1600 crore. The state is under acute electricity crisis and many times, there are 11 to 14-hour power cuts. Worse, as many as 25 per cent households in rural areas and 2 per cent in urban areas are without electricity. As many as 58 per cent rural population and 13 per cent urban population have no toilet facility. Safe drinking water is not available to 45 per cent people in rural areas and 4 per cent people in urban areas. There is just one medical centre for 3127 persons.

The state lag far behind in annual economic growth as compared to Indian national level, its per capita income is also well short of national average. Survey indicated that per capita income in the state stands at INR 17,174 per annum, much below the national average of INR 25,907 per annum. The state has also felt the direct impact of conflict in terms of huge damage caused by violent incidents, taking its toll on both public as well as private properties. From 1989 to 2002, over 1,151 government buildings, 643 educational buildings, 11 hospitals, 337 bridges, 10729 private houses and 1,953 shops have been gutted in some 5,268 attacks on infrastructure. The enormity of economic damage due to militancy can be gauged by the fact that the estimates of damage until December 1996 were approximately INR 4 billion. [6]

The militants have razed about 650 schools to the ground and the security personnel have taken possession of several hundred in the rural areas. [7] One of the consequences of such activities is low literacy rate in the state that stands at 54.46 per cent as compared to all India literacy rate of 64.8 per cent.

According to Census 2001, the state figures among last four most illiterate and educationally backward states in India. Only Arunachal Pradesh, Jharkhand and Bihar were behind J&K. The quality of education has also been seriously affected by indefinite strikes, intermittent closures and other disturbances, including several educational institutions being set on fire. The human resource too has suffered enormously in J&K due to large-scale displacement of Kashmir Pandits, Sikhs and Muslims from the Kashmir valley, as also of those from the upper areas of the Jammu region. Most of these people, living on relief provided by the government, are too far from engagement in any productive activity. The related issue of loss of creativity too needs to be seen as an adverse impact of violence stunting development prospects in the state. The lack of opportunities and overall dismal scenario has also led to significant migration from the valley. Many educated youth from Kashmir have started migrating to other parts of India in search of greener pastures thereby depriving the state of the human resource.

Tourism, one of the main industries in the Kashmir valley, has declined substantially since the late 1980s. The number of tourists visiting the state per year had gone down from 6-7 hundred thousand in the pre-militancy days to a few thousands in the following years. It is estimated that the state lost 27 million tourists from 1989-2002 leading to tourism revenue loss of US$ 3.6 billion. As per the records while as many as 557974 tourists visited the state in 1989, in 1993 the number reduced to 8026. In the year 2002, 27358 tourists visited the state. Since then the number of tourists keeps on increasing or decreasing depending on the level of violence at that particular point of time. However, the number of tourists has never reached even somewhere near to the number of tourists visited the state in pre militancy period. Another issue that remains almost elusive in the context of tourism sector is that while in the pre-militancy era the favourite destination was the beautiful Kashmir valley; the present period has witnessed increase in number of the tourists to Jammu region and Leh in Ladakh region of the state.

Violence has also directly affected other important sources of livelihood like agriculture, horticulture and handicraft industries. These sectors have become the survival mechanisms for the local people but are not flourishing ones. The state is known for wide variety of agricultural and horticulture products. However, the conflict environment has prevented people from maximally utilizing this gift of the nature. The forests of the state, which covered about eight thousand square miles, have also been among the principal casualties of the violence. During the height of the unrest, no government official dared to venture into the forests, which had become a hideout for militants. The armed groups exploited the timber resources to earn money. Consequently, the state's forest area is below the standard prescribed by National Forest Policy that states the total forest area in hilly states like J&K should be 66 per cent of the total land area. Official figures reveal only 50.97 per cent of the area in the state was demarcated as forests in 2006. The forests included a diversity of flora that includes silver birch, chinar (a richly verdant variety of the maple), conifers and deciduous trees. The damage of forests has deprived the state of many plants with medicinal values thereby negatively affecting the prospects of herbal trade.

Along with loss of forest, Kashmir has also lost the vast wildlife reserves including some rare species like the snow leopard, Ibex, antelope, Hangul (a sub-specie of Red Deer), Kashmiri Otter, flying squirrel, long tailed marmot, musk deer, black bear and blue sheep. More than hundred varieties of birds including quills, partridges, kites, eagles, pheasants etc. have virtually disappeared due to loss of natural habitat. The violence has also affected the timber industry.

J&K is having a subsidized economy wherein almost all the expenses of the state are borne by the Indian government. The state government is unable to generate resources for meeting the expenses of salary payment of the employees. The inception of militancy in the state that narrowed resource base further, has led to large-scale dependence on the Indian government. J&K, under its special category status, receives varied assistance from the Indian government. The Indian government also bears entire security related expenditure of the state, including expenditures on financial assistance to the conflict displaced, welfare activities, additional expenditure on police and security works and related activities. It also reimburses election related additional security related expenditure to the state. Between 1989 and 2002, New Delhi reimbursed a total of INR 23.6 billion as security related expenditure.

The economy of J&K is largely dependent on federal largesse as the state lacks own resource generation mechanisms as well as the much-needed private investment. In absence of private industries, the government is the only employer. The limited opportunities especially in terms of vacancies have led to rise in unemployment, thus fostering frustration among the youth. The violence in the state has led to sharp increase in unemployment. Unemployment rate in the state is 4.21 per cent as against 3.09 per cent at all India level. The Census of India 2001 shows that the rate of employment has decreased in the state after the violence became a norm of the everyday life in the late 1980s. The analysis of data shows the total worker population has decreased sharply as compared to 1981 from 44.3 per cent to 36.6 per cent. Citing unemployment and lack of infrastructure as main reasons for militancy, J&K Chief Minister Ghulam Nabi Azad has many times stressed the need to pay attention to these areas. The Chief Minister is confident that 80 per cent of militancy will go 'if we are able to give employment to the youth.' [8] In this context the survey conducted by a British group, Market and Opinion Research International (MORI) in the state in March 2002 is noteworthy. According to the survey, 93 per cent of the respondent believed the correct way to bring peace to the region would be economic development, which can provide more job opportunities and reduce poverty. [9]

The prolonged period of conflict in J&K has affected the society and politics of the state in many ways. It has resulted in a situation in which violence has become an integral part of day-to-day life of the people. The on-going violence in the state has taken thousands of precious lives. As per the official estimates, some 40,000 lives have been lost since the onset of militancy in 1989 though other estimates put the toll much higher. There are also hundreds of people who are 'missing' since a long time. Large-scale displacement from different parts of the state is an integral part of the Kashmir conflict. As per the estimates by the authors, thousands of families have displaced in the state. Though both internal as well as external dimension have led to displacement, in this chapter only the displacement induced by the former would be dealt with. [10] The militancy has led to creation of many different categories of displaced people, most of which are living in camps in the Jammu region. The first in this regard is the enmasse forced migration of Kashmiri Pandit community from the valley in the late 1980s. The Pandits claim that more than three hundred thousand people left the valley after the eruption of the militancy.

At present there are seven main camps in Jammu region in which many of the displaced Kashmiri Pandits are living. In addition to this identifiable displacement of the Pandits, many Kashmiri Muslim families have left the valley because of threat to their lives. They were forced to leave due to fear of the extremist forces operating in the valley. As per official records, in May 2002, 1,856 displaced Muslims were registered in Jammu. However, it needs to be mentioned that many of the other Muslims who also left the valley have not got themselves registered fearing disclosure of their identity. Many Kashmiri Sikhs also moved to safer places. In May 2001, as many as 1,903 displaced Sikhs were registered with the Relief Commissioner in Jammu.

There is also large-scale 'silent' inter-district displacement from the militancy-affected districts of Udhampur, Doda, Rajouri and Poonch. This displacement from hilly areas of Jammu region is considered silent since these people have not been able to draw attention of any one, be it government, media or NGOs. A majority of the displaced comprising Hindus as well as Muslims shifted to Jammu district. As per an estimate, from the Doda district alone around 30, 000 people have moved to Jammu after increased militant activities in the area in 1994-95. Besides, there has also taken place intra-district forced migration. Large number of people from the militancy affected far-flung villages in the districts of Udhampur, Doda, Poonch and Rajouri has taken shelter in the main towns. Though no authentic statistics related to this category, many families are living temporarily in the towns of Doda, Poonch and Rajouri.

Other humanitarian costs of the Kashmir conflict include negative impact on women and other vulnerable groups. The most widely documented victimization that women suffer is sexual violence. The conflict-ridden Berlin during Second World War, Sierra Leone, Bangladesh, former Yugoslavia, Vietnam, Mozambique, Afghanistan and Somalia may be cited as few instances wherein sexual violence in its ghastly form has remained a harsh reality. In this context, Kashmir is no exception. A number of cases of molestation, rapes, and even gang rapes have been reported in the region. Various human rights organizations have blamed the law enforcement agencies for failing to launch serious investigations into most cases of abuse and failing to prosecute the perpetrators. This vulnerable scenario has also fostered a sense of impunity among security forces.

There is, however, another angle wherein most of the reported cases are related to security forces and those done by the armed separatists never see the light of the day for varied reasons. Rape as a 'weapon of war' needs to be scrutinized more closely in case of Kashmir to highlight the use and abuse of women. In order to 'contribute' to the movement women came out in public to accuse the Indian security forces of sexual harassment. They made public testimonies of being raped by the security forces at the cost of facing long-term consequences of being socially ostracized. The example may be cited of Kunnon Poshpura village in which women were allegedly raped by Indian troops of the 5th Rajputana Rifles in 1991. This village, thereafter called as village of raped women, witnessed abandoning of the married women by their husbands and girls remaining unmarried after the episode for a long time. While the security forces abused them, the men of their own group used and later abandoned them. [11]

The widespread rapes have led to many unwanted pregnancies. The situation was further compounded by the diktat of the fundamentalist organizations against abortion. As part of their Islamic drive, in the initial phase the terrorist groups imposed ban on the abortions as well as contraceptives. Besides, due to the Islamic factor these may also be seen as an attempt to force women to produce more children that may later 'contribute' to the movement. However, how much suffering this ban might have brought to the women in Kashmir could be easily imagined wherein their choice to give birth was totally taken away.

There are also reports of sexual violence in the form of forced marriages at the hands of the armed separatists. Armed separatists have also reportedly used *mutah* (contract marriage) wherein after a fixed term the woman is deserted without any kind of compensation. Prostitution, either physically forced or economically coerced, evidently shows sharp increase in conflict-ridden zones. In this context, the sex racket exposed in Kashmir in 2006 needs to be critically analyzed wherein all pervasive disturbed situation provided a greater opportunity for flourishing of this 'business.' Women also continue to face eve teasing, etc. which affect their freedom of mobility. Women also suffer the gender-specific health problems due to both the experience of conflict itself and its impact on access to health facilities. Childbirth complications, arguably more likely in the stressful situations of conflict, lead to increased child and maternal mortality. The lack of privacy, especially in situation of conflict-induced displacement, makes the female bodily processes such as menstruation, lactation, etc. burdensome and uncomfortable. All this has been particularly observed in the camps of the displaced Kashmir Pandits situated in the Jammu region.

Further, there have been thousands of widows and half widows (women whose husbands are assumed dead but there is no proof to show they actually are). Half widows experience many of the same problems as widows but the absence of official recognition of their status has created specific problems for them ranging from leading a life of uncertainty to inability to claim compensation. Women also suffer the economic costs of conflict in gender-specific ways. In patriarchal societies like Kashmir, loosing husbands means not only emotional loss but also loss of social legitimacy and economic support. The loss of bread earner in a place where the economy has totally collapsed, unemployment looms large, the industrial development is not even for namesake the vulnerability of those women who had to become bread earners by stepping out of their homes could be well imagined. A survey conducted by the Sociology Department of the University of Kashmir has brought out the fact that the domestic violence has increased considerably in Kashmir and is on rise. With the breakdown of law and order, severe lack of confidence in the authorities and community pressure, bearing domestic violence in silence has become the norm.

Cultural violence also gets magnified during violent conflict. In such situations, women become vulnerable to attack or threats from their 'own' community. In the name of Kashmiri identity, many attempts have been made to inflict cultural restrictions. The most significant is the attempt to impose veil that was never a part of Kashmiri culture. Those not adhering to the prescribed dress code were targeted.

Sometimes acid was thrown and other times even women were reportedly shot on the legs. Beauty parlours were closed. The girls above the age of 14 years were warned against studying in schools and colleges. Diktats were issued to women to quit jobs in the state police. There are reports from Rajouri district of innocent women being killed for defying the diktat on veiling. There is also a noticeable increase in the psychiatric problems such as depression, anxiety, post-traumatic stress disorders and psychosomatic illnesses. The number of patients visiting hospitals in Srinagar for psychiatric diseases in 2003-2006 amounted to a staggering 45,000. [12]

The Peace Process

The ongoing peace process between India and Pakistan and between India and Kashmir has taken an 'irreversible mode.' The opening of trans-LOC routes for humanitarian and trade purposes within Kashmir has earned the epithets like 'mother of confidence building measures' and 'historic decision.' India under its National Democratic Alliance government led by Atal Behari Vajpayee, and Pakistan under Pervez Musharraf played an important role to take the peace process forward, with active support from the local people. In October 2003, India proposed ten confidence-building measures for improving people-to-people contacts and communications by road, rail and sea between India and Pakistan. It was followed by another positive development wherein a cease-fire came into effect on November 26, 2003 in the Indian state of J&K along the India-Pakistan border. The peace process is historic for two reasons. Firstly, it is the first formal truce between the two countries since the outbreak of militancy in the state. Secondly, it is for first time that firing on the borders stopped almost completely. The culmination of these developments was the agreement to initiate a peace in January 2004. In a joint statement, they proclaimed willingness to start a composite dialogue for peaceful settlement of all bilateral issues including Kashmir.

At the internal level, a major peace mission was launched to create conducive environment for negotiations. India announced a unilateral non-initiation of combat operations in J&K during the holy month of Ramzan on 19 November 2000. This initiative was extended twice up to 26 February 2001. Another important step was broadening the democratic activity by holding the elections. J&K witnessed assembly elections in 2002 that have been widely recognized free and fair. This was followed by Panchayat elections after more than two decades. The attempt has been a major one despite the fact that the voter turnout remained low in both the elections. After creating conducive environment the government of India reiterated its readiness to initiate dialogue with every group in the state that abjures violence. It started talks with the All Party Hurriyat Conference (APHC) wherein Indian prime minister met them twice. Government also organized round table conferences to accommodate varied voices within J&K on a single platform. It also set up five working groups to look into various contentious issues confronting the state. [13] The above attempts together with the external dimension of the peace process have created a historic environment wherein the hopes regarding the possibility of a resolution of the complex problem remain high.

Another important dimension of the ongoing peace process, besides engagement of India and Pakistan and that of New Delhi and Srinagar, is related to two Kashmirs. Involvement of people of J&K in the peace process gained momentum in the years 2005 and 2006. Besides the bus service between Srinagar and Muzaffarabad, the year 2005 also witnessed visits of many delegations from both sides of Kashmir. The people-to-people interactions have given a tremendous boost to optimism regarding the outcome of the ongoing peace process. It provides opportunity to people from both sides to revive old sentiments of belongingness and fraternity. The interactions also provided opportunity to the members of civil society to think 'out of box,' independent of the stances of their respective governments. Interactions with the civil rights activists and leaders from both the sides gives the impression that the people of region are fed up with violence and want to live in peace.

Conclusion

As the above discussions show, the Kashmir conflict has exacted heavy damage not only on national actors but also on the people inhabiting the region. Rather, the people have suffered the most from the direct violence, its collateral impact as well as its long-term social, economic and psychological consequences. Amidst the diverse interpretations of the roots of the conflict, the innocent civilians have endured the most of violence. The involvement of two nuclear powers, the terrorism factor ostensibly with the Pak patronage, the multi-ethnic and religious character of the conflict have made the situation complicated. The ongoing peace process, for the first time with the involvement of the local people, has taken forward the prospects of peaceful resolution of the conflict despite hurdles. It is for the first time that the people and civil society leaders of the region who spearheaded the peace campaign through 'round table dialogues' and 'heart-to-heart talks' to bring upon the respective establishments the realization that it is in peace, not in violence, lies the future of Kashmir.

Notes

1. Alastair Lamb, *Kashmir A Disputed Legacy 1846-1990* (Hertingfordbury: Rexford Books, 1992), p. 8.
2. See "Standstill Agreement with India and Pakistan," Verinder Grover, ed., *The Story of Kashmir: Yesterday and Today*, vol. 3 (New Delhi: Deep and Deep Publications, 1995), p. 106.
3. Jagmohan, *My Frozen Turbulence in Kashmir* (New Delhi: Allied Publishers, 2000), p. 85.
4. For details on Kashmir under the control of Pakistan see Debidatta Aurobinda Mahapatra and Seema Shekhawat, *Kashmir Across LOC* (New Delhi: Gyan Books Publishers, 2008).

5. *Daily Excelsior*, 7 January 2008.
6. "Infrastructure Costs." http://www.strategicforesight.com/cost_conflict/images/pg70.jp. (A. O. 10 February 2007).
7. During the survey in the Poonch district from 23 to 30 April 2007 the authors' witnessed that many public institutions have housed army contingent. For details of the survey see, Debidatta Aurobinda Mahapatra, "Poonch for Peace: An Eye Witness Account," *Kashmir Times*, 6 May 2007.
8. Quoted in *The Hindu*, 6 February 2006.
9. For details of the survey see, "Kashmir: The View from Srinagar," *International Crisis Group*, Asia Report no. 41, 21 November 2002, pp. 19-20. The group conducted a poll of 850 people in J&K in 2002 in anticipation of 2002 elections.
10. For details on the conflict induced displacement due to the Indo-Pak hostility see, Seema Shekhawat, *Conflict and Displacement in Jammu and Kashmir: The Gender Dimension* (Jammu: Saksham Books International, 2006).
11. Seema Shekhawat, "Women in Kashmir Conflict: Victims, Survivors, Peace Builders and Perpetrators," *The ICFAI Journal of Governance and Public Policy*, vol. II, issue 4, 2007, pp. 43-55.
12. For details of the impact of psychological as well as physical impact of violence of conflict in J&K since 1989, see *Kashmir: Violence and Death* (Amsterdam: Medicins Sans Frontiers, 2006).
13. During the second round table conference in Srinagar in 24-25 May 2006, Indian Prime Minister announced setting up of five working groups (WGs) to further the dialogue process in the region. While the first WG focuses on CBMs, the second focuses on strengthening relations across LOC, the third one deals with economic development of the state, the fourth WG aims at providing good governance to people and the fifth one aims at strengthening center-state relations.

9

Transcending Conflicts: Challenges and Hopes for Peace in the Philippines

Virginia F. Cawagas, Toh Swee-Hin and Ofelia Durante

In July 2000, then President Joseph Estrada ordered the Armed Forces of the Philippines (AFP) to attack the camps and strongholds of the Moro Islamic Liberation Front (MILF) in Central Mindanao. Abandoning the ongoing peace talks, the Philippine Government's fierce assault resulted in the capture of the MILF bases but also created nearly one million refugees and internally displaced peoples, mostly Moros or Muslims caught in the middle of the fighting.

In another part of Mindanao, ongoing clashes between the AFP and the 'Marxist' New People's Army (NPA) deep in the mountains have impacted significantly on the lives of Mindanao's many indigenous tribal communities. Some members of these communities have 'joined' the fighting either on the side of the military or the NPA guerrillas, while many were forced to flee from their ancestral domains.

In early December 2007, a group of poor landless farmers completed their nearly three months' protest march from the southern Philippines to the capital city of Manila. Frustrated by some 10 years of unresolved settlement of their claim to land ownership under the post-Marcos Comprehensive Agrarian Reform Law, the Sumilao farmers undertook their gruelling march to gain solidarity for their right to land and justice against the power of the landlord family and agribusiness corporation now controlling the land. Across the nation, the expansion of mining encouraged by the Government has seen an increasing number of foreign TNCs (transnational corporations) exploring or extracting minerals destined for the lucrative competitive global market. Many of these mining operations, however, have met opposition from local communities due to their negative economic, social, cultural and environmental impact.

These four scenarios exemplify sadly the continuing saga of conflicts in the Philippines. The Philippines is a beautiful island nation of happy, intelligent, resourceful and resilient people. They were once free people who became colonial subjects, for more than three centuries by the Spanish colonizers, then taken over by American rulers for almost half a century. For a brief period, the Philippines was also subjected to Japanese rule during the Second World War. In 1946, some sixty years ago, the Philippines emerged from more than four centuries of colonialism, to become an independent nation state. Most Filipinos cherish their bitterly fought freedom from Spanish colonial rule, American occupation, Japanese military rule and more recently the stirring people-power revolution (EDSA) that toppled the Marcos dictatorship. Certainly, these conflicts entailed militarization and physical violence, resulting in deaths, injuries and destruction of property and habitat. However, it is equally important to acknowledge the impact of conflicts that may not necessarily result in physical dimensions of violence. Millions of ordinary Filipinos remain victims of structural violence and conflicts reflecting economic, political, social and cultural manifestations of violence.

As peace researchers, peace builders and peace educators have emphasized, effective and sustainable resolution of conflicts requires critical understanding and analysis of root causes. More often than not, these causes are complex, multi-dimensional and inter-related. Faced with such complexity, the challenges and journeys to resolve conflicts in deeply fractured societies like the Philippines are inevitably difficult and slow. This essay will endeavour to clarify the major ongoing conflicts in Philippine society and highlight forces and factors that perpetuate and fuel them as well as initiatives and efforts to bring about a non-violent resolution and transformation of the conflicts. Progress in such conflict resolution initiatives however, has been uneven. For example, the 1996 peace accord between the Government and the Moro National Liberation Front (MNLF), which yielded a measure of political autonomy, regrettably has not fulfilled its promises of bringing peace to 'Muslim' Mindanao. An attempt would also be made to draw inspiration from a range of peace-building struggles to illustrate some signposts whereby the Philippines and the Filipino people are patiently and courageously transforming a long-standing culture of violence toward a culture of peace.

Armed, Revolution, Coup d'états or Non-violent Transformation

After centuries of Spanish colonization and decades of American rule, the Philippines inherited an economic and social system marked by great disparities in wealth, income and access to land. Political power was concentrated in the hands of a few elites, backed by large landholding families and business tycoons who benefited from post-independent modernization policies. These policies were based on the rapid exploitation of rich natural resources, carried on the back of a large but very low-wage labour pool of the Philippines. The conversion of large tracts of land from subsistence agriculture to agribusiness plantations (e.g., sugar, pineapples, bananas, etc.), massive logging of the bountiful rainforests, mining, and foreign investments in factories producing consumer goods for the industrialized ('North') world all contributed to the deepening of social and economic injustices.

Thus seeds of 'class' conflict was sowed as the marginalized poor began to confront such unequal societal orders at local and national levels. In the 1950s, the Hukbalahap or HUK movement was revived as landless peasants in Luzon waged an armed struggle for their land rights and access to a living income. With the help of counter-insurgency advice, supplied by its major ally, the US, the

Philippine government under then President Magsaysay was able to contain and militarily defeat the HUK rebellion. As an incentive to abandon further rebellion, the Philippine government offered land and financial support to many former HUK members to re-settle in the southern island of Mindanao. [1]

As successive Presidents promoted national development programs that enriched local elites and foreign corporations, while deepening poverty and inequalities, especially in the rural areas, it was inevitable that the resultant social discontent would catalyze further conflict. Another aggravating factor was the widespread graft and corruption among politicians and government agencies and their failure to deliver adequate basic services to ordinary citizens especially health care, schooling, housing, and infrastructure. In response to this marginalization of the rural and urban poor, a Marxist-Maoist oriented insurgency movement arose, committed to overthrowing the Government by armed revolution.

The 1969 formation of the New People's Army under a reconstituted Communist Party of the Philippines and the National Democratic Front that included a number of NGOs led to constant battles between the NPAs and the AFP, notably in the rural hinterlands. [2] An urban guerrilla group known as the Alex Boncayo Brigades [3] also targeted police, military and politicians accused of 'crimes' and human rights violations against the poor. With the imposition of martial law in September 1972 by the repressive Marcos dictatorship, [4] the scale of the insurgency and counter-insurgency cycle of violence intensified, accompanied by human rights violations committed especially by the military and para-military groups and also by the NPAs, through their internal party purges. The development paradigm pursued by government, the widening rich-poor inequalities, flagrant misuse of governmental resources, an authoritarian rule backed by military and police repression and externally-assisted counter-insurgency tactics - all these helped to attract recruits to the insurgency movement.

Over 1984-1986, a non-violent struggle emerged after the assassination of the opposition leader, Senator Benigno Aquino, culminating in the inspiring people-power revolution known as EDSA that finally deposed Marcos and his family and cronies. However, after the initial euphoria, there was not substantive change in development goals and strategies.

When Marcos called for a snap election, the NPA-NDF opted to boycott the opposition coalition and electoral process, and vowed to continue the armed struggle. [5] Shortly after EDSA (February 1986) and the ascendancy of Cory Aquino to power, the Government demonstrated a shift to more democratic governance, by releasing key NDF leaders from detention. Peace talks commenced between the Government and the NDF-CPP-NPA. The peace process was suspended when farmers protesting peacefully for land rights were allegedly massacred near the Presidential palace. During her term in office, President Aquino intensified the counter-insurgency campaign, and her 'all-out war' policy resulted not only in deaths and injuries of military and NPA combatants but also of refugees caught in or fleeing the crossfires. Many villagers have abandoned their rural abodes, ending up in urban slums.

As of 2008 an estimated 40,000 have died during this longest running Marxist-led insurgency in the world. [6] But the cost of this protracted armed struggle is not only measured in terms of lives lost. As Coronel Ferrer and Raquiza report: "No doubt, the war has taken its toll on the populace. One newspaper reported that since 1986, the insurgency has cost P21 million per rebel. There are at least 1.3 million internal refugees, created mainly by military operations. In 1990, an average of ten people was killed daily in the war zones." [7]

Succeeding Administrations, from President Ramos to the current President Gloria Macapagal-Arroyo, have made efforts to continue peace talks with the NDF-CPP-NPA, whose leadership remain in exile in Utrecht, Netherlands. However, the process has been slow, stalling and stalemating with no significant progress while ongoing skirmishes and battles are fought in various regions. The emergence of a number of breakaway factions due to disunity and leadership struggles within the NDF-CPP provided opportunities for the Government to attain locally-based peace accords. But the major segment of the NDF-NPA movement remain loyal to the Utrecht leadership, and hence the need to resolve the NPA-NDF-led insurgency remains as urgent as ever.

Clearly despite increased economic growth rates, expanding investments by transnational corporations, and accelerated urbanization replete with increasing number of malls, the continuing or even worsening poverty, inequalities, persistent graft and corruption, patronage politics and increased national indebtedness provide a fertile ground for social and economic discontent that constitute root causes of the insurgency and resultant debilitating conflict. [8] As elaborated in the next section, the paradigm of development that a South society such as the Philippines promotes plays a vital role in shaping the nature of conflicts as well as the possibilities for building a culture of peace. In recent years, a major complicating roadblock to the peace process has been the rise of extra judicial killings or several hundred assassinations of grassroots leaders from the peasantry, workers' groups, trade unions, NGOs, CSOs, and even churches. Responsibility for such human rights violations have been cast on some members of the military or police forces who in turn have denied complicity. To date, even with the highly negative report of the Special Rapporteur of the United Nations Human Rights Council on extrajudicial summary or arbitrary executions in the Philippines, the Government response has been viewed as inadequate. [9]

The slow and difficult progress of the peace process in relation to the NPA-NDF-led insurgency, however, has not deterred the growth of civil society initiatives to at least indirectly broker or encourage negotiations between the Government and the NDF-NPA movement. NGO and CSO leaders and groups, both Filipino and foreign, have sought to encourage both Government and NDF-NPA leaders to negotiate with sincerity and constructiveness. Furthermore, from an active non-violent perspective to peace-building, this civil society movement also continually emphasizes that addressing the roots causes of conflicts such as economic injustices and other manifestations of structural violence is vital when the parties in conflict sign a peace accord. Only then will peace be lasting and sustainable.

Most importantly, the good news is that many CSOs and NGOs have, at the grassroots, contributed to the building of a culture of peace in communities caught in the midst of the armed conflict. One exemplar lies in the zones or spaces of peace that have been created through the efforts of ordinary peoples and supportive institutions (e.g., churches, NGOs, Coalition for Peace) to at least maintain a place where peoples can live as 'normal' a life as possible, concentrating on their basic livelihoods and social relationships even as armed conflict is happening outside the zone. [10] While limited in direct impact to their designated areas and in a few cases, affected by internal disputes and the influence of external funds, such zones of peace nevertheless are inspiring exemplars of the values and practice of active non-violent transformation.

During the Presidency of Cory Aquino, the Philippines was also seriously affected by eight attempted coup d'états by some rebel leaders and soldiers in the military, including one major rebellion in late 1989 which nearly succeeded. Citing as reasons official graft and corruption and 'weak' governance, the military rebels under the banner Reform the Armed Forces Movement (RAM) have been able to galvanize sufficient support from officers and soldiers to try to forcibly overthrow the post-EDSA Government elected democratically under a new Constitution. [11] Each coup attempt, while confined to the Manila capital region, brought needless suffering to citizens caught in crossfires, destruction of property, and subsequent economic instability.

Since the time of President Aquino, the conflicts between sections of the armed forces and the Government have been simmering with tensions and continuing rumours of the next coup d'état. More recently, smaller uprisings by dissident officers and soldiers have failed to gain the support of the majority of the generals and rank and file. [12] However, as pointed out by peace advocates, this state of continuing internal unrest within the military have also heightened the dependency of the civilian leaders, including Presidents and the ruling party or coalition of parties, on the military for political strength and survival, which in turn undermines the state of democracy in the nation.

In response, peace-building advocates in Philippine civil society have implemented two strategies. Where opportunities arise, they have endeavoured to promote education for a culture of peace as well as human rights education for military and police personnel. Such education is seen as helping to strengthen the knowledge, values and capacities of soldiers and police officers in fulfilling their role as 'defenders' of democracy rather than as arbiters , using force, of who should rule and govern. At the same time, peace-builders equally emphasize the need to awaken the consciousness of the Filipino peoples and citizenry to be vigilant and to actively work in non-violent ways to uphold and nurture democracy in the nation at all levels of governance (local, provincial, national) and life. As later elaborated in the concluding section of this essay, this work of education for a culture of peace is vital in building social and political foundations on which peoples and institutions can and need to demystify ideologies and efforts to undermine democracy, whether by armed insurgents, rebel soldiers, and political elites, and to build a culture of democracy, human rights and justice.

Development Aggression or Just and Sustainable Development

Over the past six decades of post-independence nation-building, successive Philippine Governments have opted for a paradigm of national development that has been premised on modernization or as more commonly described today, 'globalization.' Under this paradigm, local, regional and national economic resources have been harnessed to fuel rapid growth and to focus on shift from primarily subsistence agriculture to commercialize or cash-crop agribusiness, industrialization, export-oriented manufacturing, free trade zones, urbanization, heavy external borrowings, reliance on foreign aid and transnational corporations, and the centrality of free-market mechanisms. In recent years, the integration of the Philippine economy to the globalized economic order has also seen an increasing flow of millions of educated Filipinos going abroad as overseas contract workers in Asia, the Middle East, North American and Europe.

Records in the Philippine Overseas Employment Administration (POEA) showed that from 1 January to 21 November 2006 a total of 1,011,148 Overseas Filipino Workers (OFWs) were deployed to different parts of the world. [13] The regular remittances of these OFWs to support their families have undoubtedly boosted the foreign exchange status of the country, and indeed if such financial transfers were to cease, the economy would be in very serious stress. In 2006, the accumulated remittances sent by OFWs through banks and commercial channels were US$ 12.8 billions. Not included in this figure were those sent informally through relatives and friends, which analysts estimated could be about 10 per cent more. [14]

This dominant paradigm of 'globalization from above' or 'corporate-led globalization' has over time laid the seeds and roots of conflicts due to the unequal distribution of resources and rewards among various sectors and classes of Philippine society. As earlier discussed, this is a major factor in the rise and perpetuation of the armed insurgency. In this regard, even though a majority of Filipinos still survive in the rural areas, the priorities of Governments with the collaboration of local and external private sector elites have meant a continuing neglect and marginalization of the rural poor. In turn, many poor rural Filipinos are increasingly forced to migrate to urban areas to search for alternative sources of income, often ending up as highly exploited urban poor labour eking an existence within the plethora of mushrooming slums.

Clearly, a major problem has been the slowness or failure, due to loopholes and technical deficiencies, of the post-EDSA Comprehensive Agrarian Reform Law to fulfil its promise to dismantle large landholding and redistribute land to the landless. [15] In the meantime, continuing conversions of subsistence farming land to commercial agribusiness, tourist complexes, golf courses and other activities primarily benefiting elites and the middle-classes, has reduced the Philippines's capacity to grow its own food and to be increasingly dependent on costly food imports. Poor landless or small tenant farmers and indigenous peoples increasingly found themselves displaced by estates or plantations of agribusiness cash-crops grown for export. Another manifestation of structural violence is reflected in the fisheries sector. Although surrounded by some of the most bountiful seas and oceans, the Filipino people generally lack equitable access to what by right should be cheap fish and other marine sources of nutrition. Instead, trawler fleets from other nations (e.g., Korea, Taiwan, Japan, and US) unsustainably exploit the waters off the Philippine islands. Poor Filipino fisherfolk in contrast remains one of the poorest sections in society.

Compounding the marginalization, especially of indigenous peoples, has been the growth of the mining industry that has attracted many foreign TNCs exploring and then extracting the rich and vast mineral wealth of the Philippines. Conflicts have arisen when the mining operations have been resisted by indigenous communities who view them as unbeneficial to the peoples' well being and also environmentally damaging.

As marginalized Filipinos, indigenous or non-indigenous,

argue, such development approaches and outcomes are better described as 'development aggression.' In addition, in order to provide the cheap energy required for such modern economic activities and industrialization, Governments at all levels have significantly invested, often with foreign aid, in infrastructural development (e.g., dams, geothermals, etc.). One example in the late 1980s that sparked controversy and conflict was the opening of the geothermal wells on Mt. Apo, the Philippines' highest mountain and the sacred ancestral domains of some 18 indigenous tribes or 'lumads.' Despite an organized opposition campaign by the lumads with support from environmental NGOs and church –based social justice groups, the project went ahead, displacing the lumads and catalysing ecological destruction in the pristine rainforest that is also a vital water catchment area serving several surrounding provinces. [16]

Turning to the urbanized and industrialization sectors of 'globalization from above,' the consequences of structural violence and unequal development are also visible. The urban poor provide cheap and exploited labour for factories and other businesses, earning barely enough to survive, lacking basic needs from food to decent housing, sanitation and basic healthcare. Organized unionizing to protect worker's rights are often resisted by factory owners, managers and business elites, sometimes leading to violence and repression exercised by private security firms. Among urban poor peoples, the harsh experiences of being evicted violently from their slum housing is sad reflection on the responsibility and accountability of Governments to provide one of the most basic human rights. As the late Cardinal Sin , Archbishop of Manila who played a pivotal role in the EDSA revolution, noted, homelessness is not a sin, and the poor should not be further be subject to the indignities of forced evictions while ever larger and more malls, business complexes and expensive apartment high-rises continue to dominate the skyline.

One inevitable consequence of unequal development, as is the case worldwide, finds its expression in the growing number of 'street children' in the Philippines. As parents are unable to earn enough income to provide basic nutrition, health care, housing and other social needs (e.g. schooling), children are forced by circumstances to 'work' on the streets such as selling newspapers, candy, cigarettes and other sundry goods, scavenging on garbage mountains, sweatshop labour and recruited or even 'sold' into prostitution and the drug trade. [17] The human rights of many Filipino children are therefore violated under this dominant unequal development paradigm even though the Philippines was one of the most active nations in sponsoring the United Nations Convention on the Rights of the Child.

Women in the Philippines likewise, as another vulnerable group, have also been subject to gender-based inequalities reinforced by the dominant development paradigm in conjunction with the patriarchal hierarchy of Filipino cultural traditions. While suffering from the 'double day' phenomenon, performing income generating jobs and also responsible for domestic work and raising of children, Filipino women additionally are victims of human rights violations through domestic violence. A more recent and disturbing phenomenon is the feminization of overseas employment and poverty. [18] However, in critically analyzing these structures of economic and social violence in the Philippines, there is no implication that all Government programs and the projects funded by official aid agencies always help to boost unequal systems and relationships.

Depending on their specific strategies and who controls and guides these programs, it is possible for a number of such initiatives to help overcome facets of injustices and hence resolve potential root causes that could lead to conflicts or even violence. Nevertheless, because official governmental and bilateral aid agencies tend to rest on key assumptions of the dominant development paradigm, it is the wide community of NGOs, CSOs and POs that have contributed the most to challenging and transforming structural violence a paradigm of development rooted on principles of justice, human rights, compassion and sustainability.

In sum, the range of conflicts generated by dimensions of structural violence in Philippine society have deep roots that need to be replaced by seeds and 'nutrients' infused with values, principles and practices of justice, sustainability and compassion. Policies and 'solutions' that only partially address or even ignore those root causes will fail in fostering just and lasting peace in the country. It is indeed also hopeful to see the courageous efforts by a small but growing number of progressive politicians working determinedly to reform existing legislation or to introduce new laws and policies that will facilitate the transformation of Philippine society toward a culture of peace.

National Assimilation or Moro Autonomy

On the southern island of Mindanao, the long-standing conflict has its roots on the struggles of the 'Moro' or Muslim peoples for independence from the Philippine nation. Regrettably, the Mindanao Independence Movement (MIM), organized in 1968 as an armed movement for independence, was used by rival politicians to establish their influence and control over their geographical and political territories. There were heightened clashes among Christian and Muslim paramilitary groups, resulting in killings and displacement of communities (both Muslim and Christian). When the MIM failed to take off, the MNLF was formally launched by Nur Misuari in 1971, which finally gained recognition and support from the international Islamic community. After the infamous Jabidah massacre in 1968, and the formation of the MNLF, then President Marcos waged a bloody war against the MNLF fighters, causing hundreds of thousands of deaths and injured and many more refugees, both Muslim and Christian. [19] While the combatants tended to be Christians on one side (military and settlers, some of whom organized para-military groups) and Muslims on the other (MNLF and Muslim communities), it is crucial not to see the conflict in simplistic 'religious' or 'faith' based terms.

The Moro struggle for independence sought to assert an identity separate from the non-Muslim majority comprising originally largely Christianized ethnic tribes from the central and northern islands. However, this identity was not only on the grounds of being Muslim. It was also a substantive sense of being marginalized by colonial (Spanish and especially American) and then Manila-based elites in their traditional territories. Over some 400 years, the Moros, who adopted Islam before the coming of Christianity through the Spanish-sponsored Portuguese 'explorer' Ferdinand Magellan, have understandably resisted the intrusion of colonizers and outside settlers into Mindanao. [20]

With their progressive loss of land and traditional political status, the Moros also challenged the role of modern Filipino schooling and education which largely valued Christian identity and cultures and looked down on Muslim and other non-Christian cultures as practised by the indigenous peoples. Importantly, the dominant development paradigm viewed Mindanao as the land of rich resources to be exploited for national growth while leaving Mindanaon provinces among the poorest and left-behind regions, especially those with Muslim majorities.

Hence the 'Muslim/Moro' conflict with 'Christians' need to be holistically understood within the parameters of economic, political and social disenfranchisement deeply felt by the Muslims/Moro peoples. This is not to say that over centuries of conflict, religious or faith prejudices, discrimination and enmities did not surface and over time, breed hatred, ignorance of the other, and distrust. Therefore, an effective resolution of the Muslim/Moro-Christian conflict needs to consider both the political, economic and social root causes and to overcome the tendencies of some leaders, on either side, to exploit the fears and deeply felt divisions and intolerances in order to gain greater power and 'unity of purpose' against the 'other' as the 'enemy.'

In 1976, with the signing of the Tripoli Agreement, Mindanaon wars ended in a truce and a partial peace deal brokered by Libya, a situation leaving the MNLF as one of the two major political organizations representing Muslim demands for initially secession and then autonomy. [21] This agreement yielded a 'stalemate' for almost 20 years, since the Government of the Philippines was alleged to have reneged in its commitment. This also resulted to a new group, MILF, a breakaway Moro armed group, who proposed an Islamic platform, adding to the cultural and political complexities of the conflict. [22]

Under President Ramos, a revitalized peace process, with the help of the Organization of Islamic Conference (OIC) as a 'mediator' for the negotiations, led to the signing of the GRP-MNLF peace accord in September 1996. Even though the MILF chose not to be involved, the 1996 accord was a dramatic step forward in peace-building in Mindanao. It gave the MNLF leader, Nur Misuari several windows for sustaining the peace accord such as: a stake in the democratic political system as the Governor of the newly referendum-established ARMM (Autonomous Region for autonomous Mindanao); the re-integration of some former MNLF combatants into the AFP; access to externally and Government-funded programs for post-conflict reconstruction and rehabilitation under the International bilateral agreements; and promises of tapping further Mindanao's rich natural resources for the benefit of the Moro peoples (e.g., improved literacy, schooling and social services; economic infrastructure, etc).

Regrettably, apart from the opposition of many Christian leaders and elites to the vision of Muslim or Moro autonomy, the design and implementation of ARMM and post-conflict rehabilitation and reconstruction policies, as well as internal problems of effective Moro leadership, did not equitably benefit a significant proportion of Moros or Muslims at the grassroots. This laid the ground for dissatisfaction and resentment of some former MNLF combatants, which together with the pushing aside of Nur Misuari as the favoured Moro leader, led to renewed armed conflict with his supporters. [23]

In the interim, the peace process has also been ongoing over the past ten years between the Government and the MILF in a bid to bring the other major Moro 'representative' group into the fold of the Philippine national order. In this case, Malaysia offered to host the GRP-MILF talks with the support of the OIC. During this period of talks, a de facto truce was generally respected by the AFP and the MNLF command, thereby sparing both Muslim and Christian peoples in Muslim-majority areas from being caught in armed crossfires. On occasion, skirmishes did occur though CSOs helped to organize a civilian monitoring committee to facilitate adherence to the ceasefire and to try to protect innocent civilians.

However, in July 2000, the growth of tensions over the disposition of AFP and MILF forces near a major highway in Central Mindanao eventually led to the ordering by President Estrada of an all out assault on the base camps or headquarters of the MILF. [24] In the ensuing battles, close to a million refugees were displaced, especially Muslims fleeing the bombs, bullets and fierce combat. Even in the face of disapproval by some of his Christian parishioners, the courageous and compassionate efforts by the Catholic priest Fr. Bert Layson to care for the needs of the refugees, including a majority of Muslims, exemplify how an authentic faith commitment can help to bridge intercultural hostilities and enmities. [25]

While the MILF camps were captured and the MILF leadership forced to flee, this effort to 'solve' the Mindanao problem by militarized force alone clearly did not have the expected outcome. Although militarily outgunned and battered, the MILF retained its strong support among Moros or Muslims who viewed the attacks as the central Government's attempt to eradicate Moro identity and rights. As in guerrilla war situations, the AFP's capture of the MILF bases could not prevent ongoing resistance by dispersed MILF forces. According to the 2008 Project Ploughshares report, from 100,000 to 150,000 people are estimated to have died and over 50,000 have been displaced since the war erupted in 1972. [26]

When President Estrada was ousted from office, the rule of his successor, President Gloria Macapagal-Arroyo provided a fresh opportunity to resume GRP-MILF peace talks, again hosted by Malaysia. The progress of these talks has, however, not been smooth. While the Government often declares a deadline when a peace accord will be completed, it has invariably been a false alarm as new obstacles arise, chief of which rests on the thorny issue of 'ancestral domain.' [27] Moreover, as the MILF-GRP peace process evolves, voices from Mindanao's indigenous peoples or lumads have been raised about the lumad's own indigenous rights to their ancestral domains. [28] To date, the MILF-GRP (like the previous MNLF-GRP) peace talks have tended to exclude considering the rights of lumads, who have indeed been inhabitants of Mindanao long before the advent of Christianity and Islam to the Philippines.

In reflecting on the Moro struggle for autonomy and the long and winding road towards a peaceful settlement, mention must definitely be made of the continuing patient and committed efforts of especially civil society organizations and networks to help facilitate the peace process. Through interfaith dialogues, forums and other community-based activities (e.g. reciprocal visits to homes and places of worship), Christian and Muslim leaders and respected practitioners are demonstrating to their followers and community members the importance of understanding of each other's faiths and finding shared values of peace, justice, love and reconciliation. Silsilah has further extended this shared understanding to common projects of solidarity (e.g. joint rebuilding of a church or mosque or school damaged by the armed conflict, or a basketball court for Muslim and Christian youth to interact peacefully).

While much of this interfaith dialogue work is in Mindanao, in recent years, the migration of Muslim communities to the Manila area has also led to valuable interfaith projects that help to overcome prejudices and fears among Christians to presence of the Muslim newcomers, including their right to build mosques. More generally, initiatives by peace movements and networks have also contributed to enhancing public awareness and support for a peaceful and just resolution of the Mindanao conflict over Moro or Muslim autonomy.

According to Tanada, in 2003, seven peace networks - the Agung Network, Bishops-Ulama Forum, Consortium of Bangsamoro Civil Society, Mindanao Peace Advocates Conference, Mindanao Peoples' Caucus, Mindanao Peoples' Peace Movement, Mindanao Solidarity Network and Peace Advocates Zamboanga came together to form a coalition—now called Mindanao Peace weavers—to more effectively address the conflict situation in Mindanao. [29] Mindanao Peace weavers is a convergence of major coalitions and networks of peace advocates in Mindanao. It currently represents the broadest network of peace constituency in the island cutting across NGOs, academe, religious, human rights groups, peoples' organizations and grassroots communities advancing a peaceful resolution of the conflict in Mindanao. It is also a formation of a peace movement where Bangsamoro, Indigenous People and Christian Settler communities, civic organizations, academic institutions, women, youth and religious sectors converge towards dialogue, unity and peaceful resolution of the conflict in Mindanao.

If Mindanao and in general the Philippines is to be a nation free of needless intercultural or interfaith antagonisms, divisions and enmities, there should be an appreciation of the need and right of diverse groups of peoples to assert their identities and to receive just entitlements to economic, social and political resources and representation within a multicultural nation. This of course requires a reciprocal attitude of any group to the needs and rights of other communities. The alternative strategy, which has been the dominant modus operandi, is to use political, economic and military might to try to effect the 'national assimilation' of marginalized groups, a strategy which on the evidence to date, can only result to an unending cycle of conflicts and violence.

Global Terrorism and Local Extremism

In 1992, the Abu Sayyaf, a small 'Muslim' group based in the island of Basilan in Western Mindanao gained international notoriety worldwide on major media channels when it kidnapped some tourists in a Malaysian diving resort. Committed to an 'extremist' interpretation of Islam and use of violence to attain their goal of establishing an 'Islamic' state in Mindanao, the Abu Sayyaf was founded in 1991 by Abdurajak Janjalani, a Muslim preacher who had trained as a *mujahideen* to end the Soviet Union's occupation of Afghanistan. Clearly influenced by the same extremist school of Islamic thinking embraced by the Talibans and by Al Qaida representatives, the Abu Sayaff has engaged in acts of violence and terrorism in south-western areas of Mindanao. [30]

Several well-publicized kidnappings of Mindanao people, including a number of Catholic priests, to try to raise funds, and continual skirmishing with the military, have served to give the Abu Sayyaf significant publicity evoking fear among the citizenry in the country. Clearly, the continuing presence of the Abu Sayyaf groups constitutes a festering source of extremist violence that needs resolution. However, what has compounded the problem is the official identification and attribution of the Abu Sayyaf as a link in the chain of 'global terrorism' under the auspices of Al Qaida. According to an analysis by the ICG, the Abu Sayyaf group has established links with the extremist Indonesian organization Jemiyah Islamiyah and with elements in the 'Al Qaida' network of globally financed 'aid and development.' [31] The Abu Sayaff problem has therefore helped to bolster the 'war on terrorism' in the Philippines, in part assisted by a continuing US military assistance and presence in Mindanao, despite the historic ending of the US military bases at Clark and Subic in November 1992 after a long grassroots campaign for nuclear disarmament and against the presence of foreign bases.

This approach inevitably heightens the scale of militarization in a part of Mindanao already affected by decades of conflict over the Moro struggles for autonomy. As the AFP seeks to militarily squash the Abu Sayaff, the continual pursuit and fighting has impacted seriously on the security of innocent civilians and in turn generates further enmity and distrust of the Government, as well as potential recruits for the group. Alternatively, if the Abu Sayyaf is recognized proportionately as a group focused on an ideology of extremism and violence learned initially from the Western-funded anti-Soviet war, followed by synergetic links with regional and international terrorist movement, then responses to diminish its influence need to be less militaristic and much more social, economic and educational in order to effectively tackle the root causes of the group's continual existence. It will also mean less scarce national economic resources needed to sustain this intensified level of militarization, and more freed up for enhancing social and economic development meeting the basic needs of all Filipinos, especially marginalized communities in Mindanao.

Hopeful Signs and the Challenges

This essay has sought to clarify various dimensions and components of the overall state of conflicts and various modes of violence that continue to be serious barriers to the building of a society attentive to the human security, rights and well-being of all Filipinos. Hopefully, a broad range of exemplars have also helped to illustrate how many committed individuals, communities, NGOs and CSOs and on occasion progressive governmental or private sector initiatives, have with perseverance, patience and hope made small steps forward in non-violent resolution and transformation of the conflicts.

However, given the vital role of education in nurturing a peaceful consciousness and action for peace at local, national and global levels, it is relevant to conclude our reflections with the theme of educating for a culture of peace. Developed by educators worldwide and through institutional programs under the auspices of UNESCO, Peace Education Commission—International Peace Research Association (PEC-IPRA), International Institute on Peace Education (IIPE), World Council for Curriculum and Instruction (WCCI) and numerous other institutions and networks, this broad multi-disciplinary and transdisciplinary movement has emphasized the holistic, multi-dimensional nature of conflicts and peacelessness and hence the need for an interdependent framework of education to promote understanding of specific conflict issues and themes. As conceptualized in a framework that we have found helpful in our many years of work in both North and South contexts, including the Philippines and especially in the Mindanao context, these dimensions include education for dismantling the culture of war, living with justice and compassion promoting human rights and responsibilities, building cultural respect, reconciliation and solidarity, living in harmony with the earth, and cultivating inner peace.

It was in 1987 when we cooperated in establishing the first graduate program in peace and development education in the Philippines and a community-oriented Peace Education centre at Notre Dame University (NDU) in Cotabato City. [32]

Located in the region of long-standing conflicts over the Moro struggles, as well as in a part of Mindanao well-known for large agribusiness plantations, the controversial Mt Apo geothermal project, and fairly close to the ancestral domains of numerous *lumads* or indigenous tribes and zones of active armed conflict between the NDF-NPAs and the AFP, Cotabato City proved to be a most relevant site to initiate education for a culture of peace.

From the courses and programs in formal peace education, this NDU initiative also expanded to non-formal educational and conscientization workshops with marginalized communities, local political leaders, councillors, civil servants, faith leaders, NGOs, CSOs and AFP soldiers and officers. Based on a critical and participatory pedagogical strategy that draw on a range of cognitive, affective and creative methodologies (e.g. simulations, role plays, street theatre, art, music, poetry etc), these peace education experiences served to not only deepen understanding of the root causes of conflicts but also helped to catalyse learners' commitment to personal and societal transformation for peace.

As mentioned in earlier sections of this essay, development NGOs have facilitated the empowerment of rural and urban poor Filipinos to recognize and overcome the economic and social injustices rooted in structural violence. Likewise, environmental NGOs have, through education and action, mobilized communities to resist further ecological destruction and implement more sustainable livelihoods. Women's organizations have also helped to educate women to struggle for their equitable participation in social, economic, cultural and political life. In the case of interfaith dialogue movements, education is indispensable in fostering the deep listening and learning that underpins the building of respect, trust and reconciliation. Clearly the foci of such grassroots and people-centered education for peace understandably emphasize the most salient issues and problems confronting the sectors in which they are active. Nevertheless, from a holistic paradigm of building a culture of peace, it will be essential for such educational initiatives to recognize the interdependencies and relationships among multiple conflicts and manifestations of peacelessness. For example, promoting ecological sustainability needs also to affirm the rights of indigenous peoples. Similarly, attaining social and economic justice requires that gender equity be upheld.

Besides the Notre Dame University exemplar, over the past nearly two decades, the receptivity and positive response by numerous Philippine and Mindanaon educational and social institutions (including some governmental and international aid agencies), NGOs, CSOs and POs to the relevance and utility of a holistic framework of education for building a culture of peace has been encouraging and hopeful. To name a few: Gazton Z. Ortigas Peace Institute (GZOPI); the Ateneo Peace Institute of Ateneo de Zamboanga University; Mindanao Peace-building Institute (MPI); Balay Mindanaw Foundation and Center for Peace Education of Miriam College.

Loss of peace is one of the most pervasive but heaviest cost of the armed conflict and we are increasingly convinced that a holistic and critical educational paradigm is the most effective way to face and transform conflicts, whether in the Philippines or in other North, South and global contexts. For Mindanao and the Philippines, which have been the focus of our essay, we acknowledge that many challenges remain. One challenge is the need to mainstream education for a culture of peace throughout the formal educational system nationwide as well in diverse non-formal learning environments and sites. Another is the importance of bringing together advocates from the various dimensions of conflicts and peace-building (e.g., just development, disarmament, non-violence, human rights, intercultural and interfaith dialogue, inner peace) to share their knowledge, understanding, capacities, skills, wisdom and spirituality in a unity of vision , solidarity and a shared hope that a peaceful world is possible.

Notes

1. James B. Goodno, *The Philippines. Land of Broken Promises* (London: Zed Books, 1991), pp. 40-49.
2. Art Ryan L. Seachon, "Insurgencies in History: A Blueprint for Future Strategy." http://www.army.mil.ph/OG5_articles/Insurgencies.htm. (A. O. 20 December 2004).
3. Ben Reid, "Philippine Left: Political Crisis and Social Change,"

Journal of Contemporary Asia Publishers, 2000, pp. 190-192.

4. Ed Garcia, *The Filipino Quest. A Just and Lasting Peace* (Quezon City: Claretian Publication, 1988), pp. 68-70.
5. Reid, n. 3, pp. 29-30.
6. "Armed Conflicts Report Philippines-CPP/NPA (1969- 2008)." http://www.ploughshares.ca/libraries/ACRText/ACR-PhilippinesN.html#Deaths. (A. O. 4 April 2008).
7. Miriam Coronel Ferrer and Antoinette Raquiza, ed., *Motions for Peace* (Manila: Coalition for Peace, Education for Life Foundation, GZO Peace Institute, Institute for Popular Democracy, Mennonite Central Committee-Philippines, NCCP, Leandro L. Alejandro Foundation, National Secretariat for Social Action, Justice and Peace, Peace Studies Institute, PRRM, 1993), pp. 22.
8. Sheila S. Coronel, ed., *Betrayals of the Public Trust* (Quezon City: Philippine Center for Investigative Journalism, 2000), pp. vii-xii.
9. Philip Alston, "Press Statement on Extrajudicial, Summary or Arbitrary Executions in the Philippines," Manila, 21 February 2007.http://www.extrajudicialexecutions.org/news/Philippines_21_Feb_2007.pdf (A. O. 12 March 2008.)
10. Soliman M. Santos Jr, *Peace Zones in the Philippines: Concept, Policy and Instruments* (Quezon City: GZO Peace Institute and The Asia Foundation, 2005), pp. 6-11.
11. Goodno, n. 1, pp. 193-209.
12. Rigoberto D. Tiglao, "Rebellion from the Barracks." http://www.pcij.org/HotSeat/military-rebellion.html. (A. O. 13 March 2008).
13. M. Jaymalin, "1 M Pinoy Workers Went Abroad this Year." http://www.philstar/show_content. asp?article=289958. (A. O. 3 December 2006).
14. "Remittances Hit Record High in 2006 at US$ 12.8B." http://business.inquirer.net/money/ breakingnews/view_article. php?article_id=49648. (A. O. 18 February 2007)
15. Mamerto Canlas, Marciano Miranda Jr. and James Putzel, *Land, Poverty and Politics in the Philippines* (Quezon City: Clareton Publication, 1988), pp. 37-60.
16. Albert E. Alejo, *Generating Energies in Mount Apo* (Quezon City: Ateneo de Manila University Press, 2000), pp. 195-234.
17. Vincent Cabreza, "RP Children Confirm Abuses for UN

Report," *Inquirer News Service*, Manila, 11 November 2005, pp. 1-2.

18. Cecile C. A. Balgos, ed., *Her Stories* (Manila: Philippine Center for Investigative Journalism, 1999), pp. vii-ix.
19. Marites Danguilan Vitug and Glenda M. Gloria, *Under the Crescent Moon: Rebellion in Mindanao* (Quezon City: Ateneo Center for Social Policy and Public Affairs & Institute for Popular Democracy, 2000), pp.2-23.
20. Macapado Abaton, *The Moro Armed Struggle in the Philippines: The Nonviolent Autonomy Alternative* (Marawi City: Mindanao State University, 1994), pp. 47-65.
21. W. K. Che Man, *Muslim Separatism* (Quezon City: Ateneo de Manila University Press, 1990), pp. 183-186.
22. Vitug and Gloria, n. 19.
23. "Misuari Posts Bail, Set to be Freed: Report." http://www.gmanews.tv/story/91615/Nur-Misuari-posts-bail-set-to-be-freed---report. (A. O. 10 May 2006).
24. "The Philippines: Counter-Insurgency Vs. Counter-Terrorism in Mindanao," *International Crisis Group*, Asia Report No. 152, 14 May 2008, pp. 1-9.
25. Roberto C. Layson, "Am Appeal to Continue the GRP-MILF Peace Talks," Speech delivered in Malacanang Palace, Manila, 25 October 2006, pp. 1-3.
26. Project Ploughshares "Armed Conflicts Report Philippines-Mindanao (1972-2008)." http://www.ploughshares.ca/libraries/ACRText/ACR-PhilippinesM.html#Deaths. (A. O. 4 April 2008).
27. Astrid S. Tuminez, "Ancestral Domain: The Key to a More Permanent Peace in Muslim Mindanao," Presentation at the Current Issues Briefing: Crunch time for the Mindanao Peace Process?, 8 February 2001.
28. Hilario M. Gomez Jr., *The Moro Rebellion and the Search for Peace* (Zamboanga City: Silsilah Publications, 2000). pp. 257-258.
29. Karen Tañada, A briefing paper by the Gaston Z. Ortigas Peace Institute, Philippines, for the "International Consultation on Religious Building Peace", International Alert, London, 5-6 October 2004.
30. Graham H. Turbiville Jr., "Bearers of the Sword Radical Islam, Philippines Insurgency, and Regional Stability." http://leav-

www.army.mil/fmso/documents/sword/htm. (A. O. 23 May 2005).

31. "The Philippines: Counter-Insurgency Vs. Counter-Terrorism in Mindanao," n. 24.
32. Toh Swee-Hin, Virginia F. Cawagas and Ofelia Durante, "Building a Peace Education Program," *Peace Education Miniprints, no. 38* (Malmo: Preparedness for Peace, 1992). pp. 1-25.

Part III: The African Context

10

Rwandan Genocide: Sociological, Economic and Psychological Consequences

Jean-Damascène Gasanabo

Today anyone looking for information on the 1994 genocide of Rwanda can find a large variety of source material. [1] Newspapers, magazines, radio and television programs, scientific articles, books, novels, and films are all widely available. Interested observers can find analyses on the tragedy from many different perspectives, ranging from the origins of the genocide, [2] to its planning [3] to the victims [4] and the survivors, [5] to the killers' stories and motives. [6] Even the role of the media has been examined in details. [7] However, as with any tragedy, the Rwandan genocide continues to be a source of anxiety, emotion and uncertainty.

The humanitarian dimension of this tragedy is significant, with the death—according to a United Nations estimate—of one million Tutsis and 'moderate' Hutus within a period of one hundred days between April and July 1994. Also, during the genocide and, mostly, afterwards, hundreds of people left the country to Zaïre, now the DRC. Many refugees died from cholera in the region of North Kivu while survivors could return to Rwanda in 1998. Today the victims, who were 'lucky enough' not to succumb, live with the trauma of what they witnessed and suffered. Clearly, the consequences of the genocide were catastrophic for Rwandan society and no one—whether in Rwanda or around the world—should forget this tragedy or ignore the lessons that it can teach.

Without question, restoring confidence and total

reconciliation between the Hutu and Tutsi groups will take time. Even if everyone recognizes the need for peace and security throughout the country, the road to justice is still long and full of traps. As an example, the re-establishment of the grassroots Gacaca Courts has provided with the opportunity to bring killers and victims face to face as well as offering a space for them to talk in mutual respect. Indeed, to acknowledge the crimes and to ask for forgiveness are fundamental acts towards national reconciliation. Equally important are the acts of courage by those victims who accept such apologies. However, sadly, the evidence shows that most of the killers still prefer to deny their criminal acts - ashamed to tell the truth in front of their relatives, neighbours and victims. And the process simply cannot work if no one comes forward for forgiveness. [8]

Finally, the economic disaster brought about by the genocide is also evident in the country. Offices, schools, hospitals, houses, shops and streets were all destroyed. The country's hydroelectric plants as well as its water supplies and other vital infrastructure were not spared. For this reason, after the genocide, the country's political leaders addressed the colossal humanitarian and economic catastrophe through the development of the 'Vision 2020.' The programme - seeking to answer the question 'Where does Rwanda go from here?'- charts a way forward for investments in infrastructure, education and other areas, with the objective to reduce poverty in twenty years (between 2000 and 2020). It also calls on all Rwandan citizens to get involved in the re-building of their country and attempts to invite and convince foreign private investors to invest and create companies in Rwanda. A mammoth task for a country with a reputation for strife and brutality!

The Roots of Ethnic Strife

Before the colonial period, members of the Twa *ethnic* group (largely fishermen and hunters), Hutus (mainly farmers) and Tutsis (mostly pastoralists) lived together sharing the same language, animist religion and customs. Major life-cycle ceremonies (i.e. weddings, births, deaths, etc.) were all similar among the groups. In addition, intermarriages were very frequent. From a social perspective, cattle-raising was considered the highest status occupation and was a sign of wealth. In part because of this preference, the Tutsis started being seen, informally, as the leaders of the country. The King was selected from the richest family of the Nyiginya clan and was therefore a Tutsi. His ethnic background, though, mattered little as he was generally recognized as the King of all Rwandans.

In fact, in the pre-colonial period Rwandan society was based more on 'family lineage' than on 'ethnicity.' At the beginning, lineage groups were autonomous and were headed by chiefs (so-called *Abatware*). In a particular region, these chiefs could become kings when they were recognized by other families and when they succeeded in bequeathing their titles and privileges to their descendants. According to Ntezimana, lineages "constituted slowly and painfully gained places of privilege, nearly exclusive, of identification and integration of families and people or, of 'collective memory.' They formed the starting point of distinct cultural communities, based on the promotion of the *Kinyarwanda* language, which served as a catalytic element for historical and national consciousness. It was also possible for lineages to weave solidarities or to enter into conflicts according to their interests. However, those conflicts were never a result of the Hutu, Tutsi and Twa subdivisions." [9]

The beginning of a sense of belonging to a Hutu, Tutsi or Twa group dated back to the eighteenth century, with the instauration of permanent armies. In that period, the chiefs of armies who identified themselves as Tutsis decided also to play the role of chiefs of lineages. To have access to some privileges, certain lineages identified themselves with those Tutsi military leaders. In addition, this ethnic consciousness stemmed from further factors such as the vertical administration of lands (*abatware b'ubutaka*) and of pastures (*abatware b'umukenke*) which began in the eighteenth century as well. [10] Some lineages benefited from alliances and conflicts. The Nyiginya dynasty and its allies became dominant throughout the country and the clan's allies had representation in all social categories. Prior to this point, there had not been strong ethnic identification and certainly no ethnically-driven violence. While there was some cultural identification expressing solidarity among Hutus, Tutsis, and Twas, this solidarity was mainly based on lineage. Another interesting aspect of inter-ethnic relations was the multi-class character of the clans. D'Hertfelt identified eighteen clans in Rwanda and noticed that Hutus and Tutsis were found in all eighteen while Twas were concentrated in only eleven. Interestingly, clans did not have any chief, lack internal organization and did not follow any particular procedure to resolve conflicts. [11]

From a political point of view, access to power came not from a person's ethnic group but from the affiliation of a lineage. Relations between the Nyiginya court and other kingdoms or Hutu principalities in the North, North-West or South-West of the country were not necessarily marked by hostilities. [12] In fact, the Nyiginya court maintained good relationships with the Hutu kings of Bukunzi and Busozo, [13] and there were other examples of cooperation.

The German and the Belgian colonial authorities (1895-1916 and 1916-1962, respectively) guaranteed, generally, respect for the indigenous social and political structure of Rwanda. They applied a policy of 'indirect rule,' keeping the King in power but using him as a puppet for their own ends. The colonial powers supported the King of Nyiginya and his clan because this allowed the Europeans to impose and extend their authority over the colonial territory. However, as part of this arrangement, the Belgians in particular intensified their help to the Tutsi-dominated monarchy, helping them to increase their control over regions such as Gisenyi, Ruhengeri and Cyangugu that had been dominated by Hutu groups. Thus, by contributing to the consolidation of the power of local Tutsi leaders, Belgium was able to strengthen its position in Rwanda.

Belgian Colonization, Cattle Ownership and the Expansion of Inter-Ethnic Tensions

In 1920 Jules Renquin, Belgian Minister of Colonies, concretized the practice of ethnic-based rule, by officially instituting a policy requiring that all local colonial staff be Tutsis. According to the decree, "[the Rwandan administration] must be composed of Tutsis only, as agreed with the King." [14] In his letter dated September 21, 1927, the Catholic Bishop Leon Paul Classe supported the instructions given by the above Belgian Minister: "Born to be Chiefs, the Tutsis have a sense of command… It is the secret of their installation in the country and of their seizure of it." [15] Of course, Bishop Classe's statement was full of serious errors. No one in the world was born to be chief and the Tutsis did not have control of the north of the country, which had historically been led by Hutu kings. Moreover, as mentioned earlier, Hutu and Tutsi groups were both in the army within the zones controlled by the Belgians. Still, the instructions of the Minister of Colonies, reinforced by the letter of Bishop Classe, were put into force between 1927 and 1931 through the Mortehan administrative reform that had the objective of concentrating power only within the hands of Tutsi chiefs while dismissing Hutu leaders. [16]

From a social point of view, cattle, traditionally, was an important source of wealth and status for Rwandans. There were two complementary ways to acquire this sign of wealth: either as a gift from friends, especially during major ceremonies such as weddings or through recognition of hard work, as a kind of work 'bonus' received from the rich. This latter system was called *ubuhake* and a person working for a rich person was an *umugaragu*, or client. More particularly, when a wealthy landowner was satisfied with the work of an employee, he offered one or more cows as a reward. This was part of a larger system under which the rich believed that they had a moral obligation to protect their clients when they might get in trouble. Having a number of clients was considered an honour and made the rich respected by neighbours and other upper class social peers. The practice of supporting clients also led to preference among the workers, who might choose to work with a particular landowner based on his reputation for rewards.

Interestingly, language vocabulary came to entrench and reflect the ethnically-oriented separation of power over time. In fact, in everyday life, the word "Hutu" came to be used synonymously with 'servant' or 'employee'—somebody who accomplishes a task to receive compensation—while the word 'Tutsi' came to mean 'rich in cattle.' Hence, during the colonial period, it was actually possible to change one's status and, from being an employee (a Hutu), one could become a rich man (a Tutsi) through the accumulation of cows. The majority, though, within both groups would live in similar social conditions. Without question, members of the Tutsi elite made profit off the *ubuhake* and created a kind of perpetual clientelism - essentially a Rwandan serfdom - which affected poor Tutsi and Hutu alike, even though, in theory, the elite was supposed to assure the protection of its clients. As a practice, it was finally abolished in 1954 when King Mutara III Rudahigwa recognized the oppression of the *ubuhake* by some who had taken advantage of it.

The social tensions between the Tutsi leaders and the majority of the Hutu and Tutsi population living in standard conditions began with the introduction of legislation by the Belgian administration on the *ikoro* (head tax) in 1917 [17] and intensified when in 1934 two further policies were implemented on the *akazi* (forced labour) and on the *uburetwa* (a kind of slavery or indentured servitude). These three acts led to widespread resentment among the population at large and had a negative impact on the power of the Tutsi elites. People were convinced that the laws had been enacted by the Tutsis to mistreat the Hutus. In fact, local administrators were asked to execute orders at the instruction of Belgian colonial authorities. However, the Hutu masses, understandably, felt a profound sense of exploitation and came to resent Tutsi authority. During this period, some Hutus and Tutsis went so far as to leave the country for a better life in Uganda. Meanwhile, the King Rudahigwa came more and more to need Belgian authority to maintain his position. Still, his efforts only served in the end to weaken his power. As already emphasized, the Belgian strategy was aimed wholly at maintaining the colonial presence and authority in the country and any support for the King was only secondary. [18]

Social Conflict and the Massacres of 1959

As in other African countries, Rwandan leaders started their struggle for national independence in the early 1950s. The Belgian administration and Catholic missionaries were sceptical about having the Tutsis and the King lead the country after independent statehood. They were afraid in particular that a new Tutsi-dominated government would not allow Belgian interests to continue their influence over the new government. Therefore, to destabilize the King and his administrators, some Catholic priests accused the King and his supporters of being communists. Meanwhile, the Hutu majority, with the support of some Catholic missionaries and of Belgian colonial authorities, accused the Tutsis of being 'foreign invaders.' [19] For the Hutu population, it was unacceptable that a minority group 'made of foreigners' would continue leading the country after decolonization. Hence, they began to express concerns about a 'problem between Hutus and Tutsis.'

To calm the population, on 22 February 1957 the *Conseil Supérieur du Pays* (High Council of the Country) published a document entitled '*Mise au point*' (to the point). This document was intended to clarify the situation and it was aimed at influencing a United Nations mission then visiting

Rwanda. In the document, King Rudahigwa recognized the inequalities among the population but minimized the importance of inter-ethnic issues, saying that both groups were represented at different levels of the administration. Moreover, he used the opportunity to call for Rwandan independence from the Belgians. Not happy with the above document, the Hutu elite published another one, two months later, on 24 March, entitled '*Manifeste des Bahutu*' ('The Hutu Manifesto'). Subsequently, in June, Grégoire Kayibanda, leader of the Hutu community and one of the authors of the Manifesto [20] created the *Mouvement Social Muhutu* (Hutu Social Movement) and, two years later, in October 1959, founded the PARMEHUTU. [21]

In July 1957 the King died under mysterious conditions in Bujumbura, Burundi. Some Hutus believed that he had been killed by Tutsis because he had abolished the *ubuhake*. By contrast, many Tutsis thought that his death was the result of a Belgian plot to give the Hutu groups the opportunity to take power.

In September 1959, two political parties known for their Hutu ethnic ideology – the APROSOMA [22] and the already mentioned PARMEHUTU—co-organized a political meeting in Butare (Centre-South of Rwanda) to call for support from the Hutu masses. In that meeting, Kayibanda declared: "Our movement concerns the Hutu—humiliated and despised, outraged by the Tutsi invader. If we want to help him [the typical Hutu], let us avoid confusion…Many want to know what APROSOMA means. We answer them that it means 'enemy of the King' and it is a monster which is going to devour the Tutsis. We have to light the way for the majority people. We are here to give the country back to its owners; it [Rwanda] is the country of Hutus." [23]

The tensions between the two groups continued until 1 November 1959 when one of the key Hutu leaders, Dominique Mbonyumutwa, was reportedly mauled by a group of young Tutsis. This was the spark that led to a series of killings of

Tutsis across the country and this event was by most accounts a true turning point in Rwandan history. For the first time, Hutu leaders called for a mass killing of Tutsis. In addition, for the first time, some Tutsis began to leave the country, becoming refugees in neighbouring States. Then, in municipal elections organized between June 26 and July 31, 1960, people voted overwhelmingly for the Hutu-oriented PARMEHUTU. In the Referendum of September 25, 1961, some eighty percent of the population voted to disband the monarchy and to install a Republic. Kayibanda became thus the first president of independent Rwanda on 1 July 1962. In December 1963, Tutsi refugees living in Burundi attacked Rwanda. In reprisal for those attacks, President Kayibanda supported the massacres of Tutsis in all areas of the country despite the fact that Vatican Radio qualified those acts as the 'most terrible systematic genocide since the Jewish genocide.' [24]

The 1994 Genocide and its Consequences

In a 2004 documentary entitled "*Kill all of them! Rwanda: Story of a Genocide 'Without Any Importance,'*" filmmakers Raphaël Glucksmann, David Hazan and Pierre Mezerette explored the world's reactions to the crisis and concluded that world leaders were universally slow in taking action. Still, once the crisis was over and calm had returned, the time came for counting the victims. In July 2000, the Rwandan Ministry of Local Administration, Good Governance, Community Development and Social Affairs initiated a survey to make a final, gruesome, count. It was decided to include the victims of genocide during the period October 1990-December 1994 and eventually there was an estimate of 1,074,017 people killed throughout the country. Obviously, this statistical work and result had political overtones. In her study, Verpoorten noted that the large number of Tutsi victims of genocide raises the question of how many Tutsis were actually in Rwanda at the time of the violence. [25] Many scholars believe that national censuses prior to the genocide had intentionally undercounted the Tutsi population, keeping alive the belief that the Tutsis made up a small, alien group – as opposed to a significant minority. According to the census of 1991, the number of Tutsis was 8.4 per cent. Still, for political reasons some believe that President Habyarimana's regime chose to keep the publicly acknowledged number of Tutsis under ten percent of the population.

Even today, the exact number of the victims is not known and will likely stay unknown for many years. Still, the fact remains that a genocide was committed against the Tutsis and this has to be acknowledged. Indeed, the common, public recognition of the atrocities contradicts both the denial of hard-line Hutus and some revisionist theories that claim a double genocide and which have been used to understate the violence perpetrated against the Tutsi minority.

Rape, HIV/AIDS and Psychological Trauma: During the 1994 genocide, Interahamwe militias raped many women. This act of violence also had a cultural component. According to Rwandan tradition, it was forbidden for soldiers to have sexual relationships while on the battlefield to avoid 'bad luck.' However, soldiers also believed that before going back home they could only purify themselves by having sexual relationships with foreign women. Thus, many militia members raped Tutsi women as a kind of purification ritual. A woman told her story: "We were at home when a militia group came. They killed my husband and his parents. They asked three Twas who belonged to the *Interahamwe* militia to take me and my sister-in-law and rape us, humiliate us, as a way of showing their contempt for the Tutsis. Other *Interahamwe* also came to violate us. The abuse lasted three weeks. We were able to escape only when they were busy killing a cow. Now we suffer every day living like this. They should have killed us instead of letting us live to suffer such tortures." [26] Many of these rapes also led to problems of HIV/AIDS. Yvonne was born in 1995, after her mother had been raped by *Interahamwe* militias. In 1998, when Yvonne was three years old, her mother died of AIDS. Yvonne was cared for by her grandmother, but no one thought to get her tested for HIV until 2005. Today she receives medicine and financial support from aid agencies. However, there are many orphan children who either refuse to get tested or do not have the access to health facilities.

In fact, the illness is only part of the battle. There is tremendous social stigma associated with the disease, and many young women living with AIDS still want to hide their condition. In public friends and neighbours generally refrain from saying anything to the concerned person, but in private prejudice against people with AIDS—even rape victims and their children—is strong. The Rwandan Ministry of Health has also recognized a high presence of HIV/AIDS in the country—a situation that has worsened because of rapes and because of corporal lesions from wounds by machetes and other cutting objects that were used on many victims of the genocide.

The genocide created special pressures on women. Men were disproportionately targeted by the killers, leaving many women alone to care for themselves and their families. Many widows were left without assistance because their families had been decimated. According to the national census of 2002, the population of Rwanda was 8,162,715. Women represented some fifty-two percent of the population, with roughly thirty-four percent forced to serve as heads of household in what had been a traditionally patriarchal society. Moreover, fifty-two percent of the population was estimated to be under eighteen of age and disturbing figures related to the huge number of orphans. Today between three thousand and four thousand children live in special centres for orphans. Incredibly, the census even showed some fifteen thousand cases where children under eighteen had been forced into roles as heads of household, and these family groupings accounted for over one hundred thousand children living without any supervision. [27]

A survey conducted by UNICEF in 1995 showed that roughly three thousand Rwandan children living in eleven provinces were suffering from trauma: ninety-five percent had witnessed scenes of violence; ninety percent had been in mortal peril and eighty percent had at least one member of the family killed in the genocide. Another survey was also conducted in 1999 by UNICEF in six provinces on a sample constituted by children in difficult circumstances- in centres for orphans, for street and living-alone children, for physically handicapped or with one or both parents in prison. This (unpublished) survey showed that ninety-five percent of these young victims had experienced violence; eighty-eight percent expected to be killed by machetes; eighty-eight percent was hidden because afraid to be killed; seventy-nine percent had lost one or many relatives; sixty-nine percent had seen injured people or being killed; sixty-one percent was threatened to be killed; fifty-seven percent had seen death and fifty-one percent had witnessed massacres.

Not surprisingly, psycho-social problems have become one of Rwanda's most serious public health issues. More and more people are still going to the *Service de Consultations psychosociales*-SCPS (Service of psychosocial consultations) as well as the Neuropsychiatrical Hospital in Ndera for mental and neurological problems. While overall the service usage remains low compared to the size of the trauma witnessed, it must be remembered that psychotherapy is still a very new medical treatment for Rwandans and it is not yet well understood by the populace nor integrated into the health care system.

Another survey conducted by the Psychosocial Consultations Service from 1 April to September 30, 2003 on ninety women and thirty men between eighteen and forty years of age showed the main problems shared by the survivors of the 1994 genocide and the main psychological disorders which they experienced. In particular, one can see that the main problems concerned the following factors: living with psycho-emotional experiences; remembrance of all losses and mourning; physical health problems; difficulties in living with others; social isolation; or work related problems. All the participants mentioned the first two major issues while other problems concerned more than sixty percent of the patients. Also, break-downs, anxiety, troubles of personality and cognition problems were mentioned by less that thirty-five percent of the patients. The results from the survey show that the genocide has dramatically affected the lives of those who experienced the atrocities—and the strong psychosocial impact persists even fourteen years after the genocide.

A synthesis of a statistical report on counselling programme and clinical supervision for the period 2000-2006 shows that 85 per cent of the traumas come from the genocide and fifteen percent had their origins in different sources such as violence, illness, family problems and drug use. [28] Women were more affected than men: 83 per cent versus 17 per cent. Many observers believe that this is because men were often killed immediately while women were first raped and beaten before been killed and, many of them who survived, were severely traumatized. In the 2006 survey the most traumatized people (67 per cent) were between twenty-one and forty-six years of age; 29 per cent were between twelve and twenty years old; only 4 per cent were more than forty-six years.

All these people shared a kind of common psychic pain because of what they had seen, heard and, in some cases, done in 1994. Hutus who were living in the country had seen horrors but few were able to come to grips with what they had seen and even fewer were still able to take responsibility for their actions. Survivors were prone to re-playing the scenes that they had witnessed and many complained that they could still hear the cries of the victims. Refugees from earlier crises suffered for having lost many family members. Refugees of 1994 suffered much pain - both in exile and upon return. And the *Interahamwe* and other militias, in prison or in freedom, had to address the pain of having committed atrocities-destroying their country in the process and then, losing control of the government. They left their own society in ruins and remained international outlaws—without a country and without prospects for a better life.

The Destruction of Rwanda's Economy: Each country needs qualified human resources to plan and prioritize projects for development. It also needs workers to contribute to production and to put decisions into actions. Throughout the genocide, Rwanda lost thousands and thousands of qualified staff in all domains. In the educational sector, thousands of teachers at the primary and secondary school level as well as at the university level were killed or left the country. After the genocide, lack of teachers and school material turned out to be a major handicap. In hospitals as well, thousands of doctors and nurses were either killed or condemned to leave the country. Even when international organizations such as *Médecins Sans Frontières* arrived to help, resources were insufficient to face the illnesses, injuries, psychological trauma and diseases (like HIV/AIDS) caused by the genocide. In the judicial area, many if not most of the country's judges and lawyers were killed and nobody remained to pursue the genocide cases. As regards the public administration, one can say that the situation was not so positive either, since the number of civil servants that was left was actually insufficient to deal with the administration of the entire country.

All these deaths and exiles caused huge problems in the Rwandan economy. Without human resources, it took even more time for the country to recover. Throughout its history, the Rwandan economy has been based on agriculture. However, primitive agricultural methods, the infertility of land, mudslides and other issues have kept productivity very low. The 1994 genocide made the condition of an already fragile agricultural sector even worse. The loss of population to genocide and exile meant that there were fewer people to cultivate. Furthermore, anti-personnel landmines and other explosive devices that had been used by the belligerents became dangerous for many people, especially in the suburbs of Kigali and other major cities. It became a handicap for field work because it was now dangerous to cultivate agricultural areas without the risk of being seriously injured or mutilated.

Before the genocide and during the colonial period, Rwanda had developed a reputation for its high quality exports of coffee and tea. The two industrial cultivations were almost the only sources of foreign currency. With the death and the displacement of the population, those who stayed in the country were preoccupied more by their survival than by the cultivation of export crops. Besides there were no government agencies to buy and sell the products in the international market. These two industrial cultivations were largely abandoned for a while and, consequently, the country lost huge amount of foreign currency. During the genocide, infrastructure was also destroyed. In 1994, twenty-one micro power stations were destroyed. Lack of water and electricity, especially in the capital Kigali and in other major cities, became problematic. The offices of the national and regional administration, banks etc. were ransacked and looted. Industries became defunct. With its twenty-six thousand square kilometres, Rwanda had only one thousand bituminised kilometres in 2002. All these roads and bridges were damaged during the 1994 tragedy. In 2002, roughly four hundred kilometres were considered to be in need of reparation.

Destruction of Culture: Before the colonial period, as noted above, Rwandans generally shared the same cultural, social, customary, moral and religious norms. This was possible given the small size of the country, the relatively small population, and the use of a common—and unique—language, Kinyarwanda. The word *abanyarwanda* (people of Rwanda) referred to Hutus, Tutsis and Twas and each of them recognized the other as being Rwandan. By living closely and by being members of the same clans, they developed and shared values such as *ubusabane* (helpfulness), *ubufashanye* (solidarity) and *ubuvandimwe* (brotherhood). They also helped each other through exchanging various services: for example, the practices of *guhingirana* (helping each other in cultivation); *kubakirana* (helping each other in building houses); *guhekerana abarwayi* (helping each other in transporting a sick person to a hospital); or *gutabarana* (helping each other in pain). All Rwandans aspired to *ubupfura* (being upright), *ubworoherane* (being tolerant), and *ubuntu* (being generous). All parents, regardless of ethnic background educated their children to avoid *ishyari* (jealousy), *ubugwari* (cowardice), *ubugome* (wickedness), and *umwiryane* (division), etc.

During the 1959 mass killing of Tutsis and the 1994 genocide, the extremist Hutus emphasized their ethnicity. They classified Tutsis as foreigners or invaders like the Belgian colonisers. [29] To be called foreigner in their own country was difficult for many Rwandan Tutsis to accept. That form of violence was new and damaged the everyday life of many Tutsis. The genocide destroyed the unity that Rwandans had built and in which they had believed for centuries. The value of *ubuvandimwe* (brotherhood) was destroyed. In the past, all Rwandans well called *bene Kanyarwanda* (sons and daughters of Kanyarwanda, eponymic ancestor of all Rwandans). Denying the national identity and giving voice to ethnic violence and mass killing have completely eroded and disrupted the social values which Hutus, Tutsis and Twas had shared together.

During the genocide, the most sacred value—*ubuzima* (life)—was clearly denied. Killing a Tutsi became normal 'work' and the impunity encouraged perpetrators to commit these criminal acts. Indeed, impunity explains the major reason why extremist Hutus did not hesitate to kill neighbours, friends and even relatives. The hatred vis-à-vis the Tutsis—taught through schools, in newspapers, on the national radio and through different meetings - was also expressed by the rapidity of the genocide as well as by the instruments and the methods used to kill. Victims were humiliated in different manners--for example by forcing son to have sex with his mother before being killed or gang raping women of all ages. During the genocide, rape and sexual violence became a kind of sport. The values of dignity, tolerance and solidarity were tragically and systematically shaken.

Current Scenario: The Reconstruction Attempts

When the new government was created on 19 July 1994, the first priority of Rwanda's leaders was to establish security in order to allow the public and private sectors and non-governmental organizations to restart their work. Security was also the *sine qua non* condition for Rwandans who took refuge in neighbouring countries to come back. Bringing back peace and reconstructing the damaged Rwandan social capital became part of the government's priorities. In that regard, the Institute of Research and Dialogue for Peace (IRDP) was created in 2001. The Institute's first mission consisted of conducting large scale consultations within the country and outside, among the diaspora, to collect different points of view and set up a kind of social map of Rwanda in the peace building process. This mapping exercise looked at the views of all social, economic and political levels of the Rwandan people. Debates were organized in the country at the grassroots, academic and political levels. From these platforms, some relevant questions were raised and concerned in particular "the relationship between Rwandan history and different internal conflicts, the genocide, economic development, the challenges posed by poverty, the appropriate type of democracy, the rule of law and the justice in repeated conflicts." [30]

The reconstitution of damaged social capital was an essential aspect of Rwanda's recovery. It reflected the country's desire to re-integrate vulnerable groups such as widows, orphans and refugees from earlier conflicts. In that context and for the social cohesion, it became an urgent matter to build social links between urban and rural regions and to avoid a massive population shift from the rural areas to the cities. Given the tremendous social need across the country, caring for the poor became a central focus of government and donor attention. In 1999, the Rwandan government created the National Unity and Reconciliation Commission (NURC) to lead national efforts in promoting unity and reconciliation—so essential for sustainable human development and lasting peace. Since its creation, it has conducted a series of local and national consultations and civic education at provincial and district levels, as well as at the national level. The first round of consultations found that bad governance and leadership as well as poverty and lack of justice were the main causes of the political problems in Rwanda. The NURC also organized a series of training sessions called *ingando* to promote unity and reconciliation. Each session is targeted at specific groups including youth, students, civil servants, university professors, politicians, and, recently, former-*Interahamwe* and other rebels, who returned from the DRC.

Interestingly, the decentralisation process offered an opportunity for the NURC to help the reconciliation process at the grassroots level. The decentralization of political, economic and social institutions established in 2001 became a central point for the democratization of structures of governance in Rwanda. The government's decentralization policy offered people the opportunity to work together at the local level where *inter-ethnic* divisions have been so destructive for years. It has also allowed local authorities to respond to local needs and the process shows signs of being able to help increasing the connection and the sense of accountability between the national government and the communities. The monitoring of the Gacaca jurisdictions is another important method of the reconciliation process. Gacaca were designed to help neighbours to talk to each other in an environment of mutual respect and to provide the space for indicted genociders to explain the circumstances under which they participated in the genocide—and to provide an opportunity for the victims to forgive.

The main challenges to this process continue to be the prevalence of denial and revisionism of genocide within the country, in the Great Lakes region and in other states. [31] In Rwanda, the NURC intends to implement a multi-sector approach to achieve its aims. Efforts are put together with various concerned ministries, such as the Ministry of Justice, the Ministry of Education and the Gacaca jurisdictions with a view to combating the genocide ideology. Civic education programmes stressing the value of living in peace, in unity and in reconciliation are supported and expanded at all levels of society to foster social cohesion.

Rwanda's Vision 2020 placed a high priority on improving public health, including an emphasis on mental health. As part of this work, the Neuropsychiatric Hospital of Ndera was rehabilitated and it is now a national reference in hospitalization. Besides, a mental health department was created at the Kigali Institute of Health (KIH) and a department of psychology was initiated at the University of Rwanda. A capacity building programme was created for professionals who are in charge of mental health problems. As Rwanda commemorates the genocide each year in April, the national mental health programme supervises the national mourning. During 2008, the Ministry of Health plans to revise the national policy of mental health and to give more attention to the victims of AIDS.

After establishing security in the whole country following the genocide, poverty reduction became a national priority. The Government of Rwanda has set out a programme for wiping out poverty within twenty years. The program, introduced in 2000, has six key objectives on the road to 'fundamentally transforming Rwanda into a middle-income country by the year 2020.' [32] These key objectives include: Good political and economic governance: with an emphasis on security, human rights, decentralisation of administration, economic management and macroeconomic stability; Rural economic transformation: through decentralization and the introduction of new technologies to provide sustainable livelihoods and access to service outside cities; Development of services and manufacturing: re-establishing Rwanda as a regional trade and service centre, strengthening the use of information and communication technology (ICT) and encouraging the development of tourism; Human resource development: increasing human resources, improving education and establishing a better health care; Development and promotion of the private sector: through further liberalisation, privatisation and enhanced public-private partnership; Regional and international economic integration: by joining the Common Market for Eastern and Southern Africa (COMESA); by being a member of the East African Community; and by exploiting the opportunities offered by the World Trade Organization and the Africa Growth and Opportunities Act (AGOA).

The above six key objectives were grouped into three cross-cutting themes: gender equality; protection of environment and sustainable natural resource management; science and technology. Based on this ambitious plan, Rwanda has been granted a loan of sixty-five million US dollars by the OPEC Fund for International Development to finance agriculture, energy, transportation, water supply and sewerage, and multi-sectoral projects as of March 11, 2008. [33] The Arab Bank for Economic Development in Africa (BADEA) has also given out a loan of eighty-two million US dollars as of November 27, 2007, to finance various projects including energy and transportation. Other donors as well believe in Rwanda's capacity to recover and to make possible the living in mutual respect of all Rwandan citizens.

Conclusion

The 1994 genocide in Rwanda was planned and organized in the name of the Hutu community. Indeed, a substantial number of Hutus has already been acknowledged as having played a part in carrying out the atrocities. The genocide left an indelible stain on Rwanda's collective memory and those

Rwandans who have experienced the violent events will live with the wounds until the end. After the genocide, the work done by the NURC and by the government's efforts have enabled the country to look back on the crisis and to seek healing and treatment. It has taken time to absorb the enormity of the violence, time for the perpetrators to come forward through the Gacaca process, and time for the victims to realize that not all Hutus participated in the genocide. In fact, some Hutus even risked their lives protecting the Tutsis. Even many Hutus were killed for refusing to participate in the heinous crime of killing the innocent people.

Building confidence among the population has become more challenging than building the economy and reducing poverty. Changing the mentality of destroyed people needs centuries! But without sincere efforts to address the country's psychological trauma, the kind of large-scale economic transformation called for by Rwanda's leaders is unlikely to be successful. Healing Rwandans and enlisting the support of all —across ethnic and class lines—is a crucial component of achieving the country's Vision 2020. Many Rwandans, within and outside the country, as well as foreign observers recognize the efforts and progress that have been made since the genocide to bring Hutus and Tutsis together again. However, despite this progress, some Rwandans persist in proclaiming their wish to continue the 'work' of genocide that they did not finish in 1994.

Recently, a Rwandan was talking to a Belgian man in Brussels (believing that the latter was French): "You helped us, thank you. They are not all the same, only the Tutsis. One could kill all those cockroaches. What a shame, a few of them are still alive. The work is not finished." [34] The supporters of the genocidal ideology continue to deny the 1994 genocide of Tutsis. Books, [35] articles and comments on the internet deny or justify those atrocities as well as discuss the so-called 'double genocide' as a way of downplaying the genocide in Rwanda. The fear for most observers is that in denying an internationally-recognized genocide extremists could be planting the seeds for a return to a policy of discrimination and atrocities. All Rwandans as well as the international community should vigorously condemn this attitude, keeping in mind the words of Italian writer Primo Levi, who was 'lucky enough' to come back from Auschwitz: "Do not forget that it happened. No, do not forget it." Let us hope that the forces of hate and division will never again lead our future – in Rwanda or anywhere else for the costs are too much to bear.

Notes

1. In this article we shall use the term 'genocide' to refer to the period April-July 1994, bearing in mind that a controversy still exists on this issue.
2. Prunier Gérard, *Rwanda Crisis: History of Genocide* (Paris: Dagorno, 1997).
3. Merlvern Linda, *Conspiracy to Murder: The Rwandan Genocide* (New York: Verso, 2004).
4. Mukagasana Yolande, *Les blessures du silence* (Paris: Actes Sud & MSF, 2001).
5. Hatzfeld Jean, *Dans le nu de la vie : récits des marais rwandais* (Paris : Seuil, 2000).
6. Hatzfeld Jean, *Une saison de machettes* (Paris: Seuil, 2003).
7. Thompson Allan, *The Media and the Rwanda Genocide* (Ottawa: CRDI, 2007).
8. Hatzfeld Jean, *La stratégie des antilopes* (Paris: Seuil, 2007)
9. Ntezimana Emmanuel, "Histoire, Culture et Conscience Nationale : le cas du Rwanda des origines à 1900," *Etudes Rwandaises*, vol. 1, no. 4, 1987, pp. 462-497.
10. Ibid.
11. D'Hertfelt Marcel, *Les clans du Rwanda ancien* (Butare: INRS, 1971). By contrast, Nyagahene Antoine mentions twenty-seven clans in his book, *Histoire et peuplement. Ethnies, clans et lineages dans le Rwanda ancien et contemporain* (Villeneuve d'Ascq: Presses universitaires du Septentrion, 2001).
12. Vansina Jan, *Le Rwanda ancien. Le royaume nyiginya* (Paris: Karthala, 2001), pp. 156-157.
13. Ntezimana Emmanuel, "Coutumes et traditions des royaumes du Bukunzi et du Busozo," *Etudes Rwandaises*, 1980, pp. 15-39.

14. Rumiya Jean, *De la royauté au Sultan Belge du Rwanda* (Paris: Univesité Paris I, PhD dissertation, 1983), p. 79.
15. De Lacger Louis, *Le Rwanda* (Kabgayi: Editions diocésaines, 1933), p. 523.
16. Mortehan was Belgium Resident of Rwanda at the time.
17. Overdulve Cornelis Marinus, *Rwanda, un peuple avec une histoire* (Paris : L'Harmattan, 1997).
18. Harroy Jean-Paul, *Rwanda : De la féodalité à la démocratie, 1955-1962* (Bruxelles: ARSOM, Hayez, 1984), p. 246.
19. De Lacger Louis, *Le Rwanda* (Kabgayi : Editions diocésaines, 1933), p. 41; Paternostre de la Mairieu, *Le Rwanda: son effort de développement* (Bruxelles: De Boeck, 1972), pp. 42, 308. Later, once independence was achieved, the Rwandan History Textbooks (Histoire I, 1987, p.14) mentioned that the Tutsis were warlike invaders. For more details, see the author's doctoral dissertation, Mémoires et histoire scolaire: le cas du Rwanda de 1962 à 1994 (Genève: Université de Genève, 2004).
20. Grégoire Kayibanda was the Private Secretary of Bishop André Perraudin—a Swiss citizen, Apostolical Vicar of Kabgayi, Archbishop of Kigali and editor of the church newspaper *Kinyamateka*. He became Rwanda's first President following the country's national independence.
21. PARMEHUTU is the Party for the Emancipation of the Hutu People - an ethnic political party as its name indicates.
22. 'Association pour la promotion sociale de la masse' (Association for the social promotion of the majority people), meant for the Hutu. A political party created on 15 February 1959.
23. Musangamfura Sixbert, *Le Parti MDR Parmehutu. Information et propagande, 1959-1969* (Université Nationale du Rwanda à Ruhengeri: Mémoire de Licence, 1987), p. 70; Jean-Pierre Chrétien, *Le défi de l'ethnisme, Rwanda et Burundi: 1990-1996* (Paris : Karthala, 1997), p. 71.
24. Linden Jan, *Christianisme et pouvoirs au Rwanda (1900-1990)* (Paris: Karthala, 1999), p. 363.
25. Verpoorten Marijke, "Le coût en vies humaines du génocide rwandais: le cas de la province de Gikongoro", *Institut National Etudes Démographiques*, vol. 60, no. 4, 2005, pp. 401-439.
26. Mukarugambwa, *Les conséquences psychosociales du viol des mères de famille pendant le genocide de 1994. Cas du Secteur Mugina, District Kamonyi* (Université Libre de Kigali: Mémoire

de Licence, 2007), p. 44.

27. Speech by the Minister of Family and Gender Promotion, broadcasted on 14 June 2004.
28. "Synthèse de rapport statistique 2000-2006. Programme counselling et supervision Clinique," (Kigali: ARCT-Ruhuka, January 2007).
29. Paternostre de la Mairieu, n. 19.
30. http://www.veritasrwandaforum.org/dialeg/DIR06_fr.pdf. (A. O. 7 April 2008).
31. "Economic Development and Poverty Reduction Strategy, 2008-2012," *Ministry of Finance and Economic Planning*, Kigali, 31 August 2007, p. 86.
32. "Rwanda Vision 2020," *Ministry of Finance and Economic Planning*, Kigali, 2000, p. 11.
33. www.opecfund.org. (A.O. 10 April 2008).
34. See the Belgian newspaper *Le Soir*, 5-6 April 2008, p. 11.
35. See for example Péan Pierre, *Noirs fureurs, blancs menteurs* (Paris: Mille et une nuits, 2005) or Philpot Robin, *Ca ne s'est pas passé comme ça à Kigali* (Paris: Duboilis, 2004).

11

Congo in Crisis: Violent Conflict and its Consequences

Seema Shekhawat

Democratic Republic of Congo (DRC), situated at the heart of the west-central part of sub-Saharan Africa, is surrounded by Angola, the Republic of Congo, the Central African Republic, the Sudan, Uganda, Rwanda, Burundi, Tanzania across Lake Tanganyika and Zambia. The country is the site of one of the world's worst ongoing humanitarian crises. The conflicts of 1996 and 1998 have resulted in massive disruption of the social, political and economic fabric of the country. [1] For over a decade the country has been mired in conflict with devastating effects on its civilian population.

The country emerged from what has been called 'Africa's First World War' in 2003 with the establishment of a transitional government. With the signing of the formal peace accord in December 2002, the war has come to a halt but has given way to several local conflicts. Amidst the conflict scenario, the country held its first reportedly free and fair elections since independence in July 2006. However, the persisting humanitarian crisis in the DRC is among the most complex, deadly and prolonged ever documented. The situation at present continues to be dismal with cost of the violent conflict in terms of death and destruction, disease, malnutrition, mass displacement ever rising.

The Historical Background

DRC, formerly referred to as Congo Free State, Belgian Congo, Congo-Léopoldville, Congo-Kinshasa and Zaire, is the third largest country by area on the African continent. This former Belgian colony had a brutal colonial history. The Congo territory was acquired formally by King Leopold II of Belgium in 1885. He named it the Congo Free State and exploited the vast natural resources for personal gain. In 1908, the Belgian parliament took over the Free State from Leopold following the international pressure. From then on, it became the Belgian Congo, under the rule of the elected Belgian government. Conditions in the Congo though relatively improved following the Belgian government's takeover, the overall scenario remained dismal. As an analyst argued, 'Belgian colonialism was unparalleled in the continent in its control and penetration of African society, organised by the 'trinity' of bureaucracy, capital and the church.' The desire for independence came to the people of DRC with neighbouring countries getting liberated. As Lemarchand argued, "the political developments that occurred in other African territories stimulated the political awakening of the Congolese. It made them all the more aware of the miasma that seemed to govern Belgian colonial policy, and hence intensified their desire to change the status quo." [2] But the sense of independence could not bring the much needed sense of unity among the people due to the policies adopted by the colonial masters.

The country became independent on 30 June 1960 but the post-independence era was marred by mutiny and secessionist movements. Earlier in May 1960, Patrice Lumumba led Mouvement National Congolais (MNC) won the parliamentary elections. Lumumba became the Prime Minister and Joseph Kasavubu, of the ABAKO (Alliance des Bakongo) was elected President. To quote MacNulty: "Unlike Africa's other major colonial powers Britain and France, Belgium had done little to promote a local elite to govern on its behalf and assume the reins of state power. As a result, there was not the smooth transition to Western-favoured regimes which largely characterized independence elsewhere; instead, the Congo began rapidly to implode, the new administration faced with mutiny and multiple secessions which foreign interests did much to foment." [3]

The problem got aggravated with the fact that the cold war era brought the fight between east and west to the country. While then Soviet Union supported Lumumba as the legitimate leader of the country, the US challenged the notion. The resource rich country also could not get economic freedom with powerful outsiders continuing to keep control on the economy of the country. To quote MacGaffey, "the colonial African elite thus lacked education, administrative and managerial experience, and wealth. At independence, the Belgians handed over political but not economic control, so that the new dominant class based its power on control of the state, while ownership of the economy remained in the hands of the big and foreign mining and plantation companies." [4]

The mutiny and secessionist attempts led to a political crisis with Kasavubu and Lumumba getting engaged in a power struggle. Kasavubu dismissed Lumumba, who was later assassinated in 1961. Moise Tshombe became Congo's Prime Minister in 1964. Following five years of extreme instability, Lieutenant General Joseph-Désiré Mobutu, ousted both President Kasavubu and Prime Minister Tshombe in a 1965 coup and began his thirty-two years of rule. In the name of democracy a one-party system was established wherein periodically election were held with the incumbent head of the state the only candidate. Mobutu was guilty of severe human rights violations and political repression. He consolidated power by co-opting potential rivals and exploited country's vast natural resources to make wealth for himself as well as his allies. He declared the Third Republic in 1990, whose constitution was supposed to pave the way for democratic reform. The reforms turned out to be largely cosmetic, and Mobutu's rule continued. By the 1990s the country's economy was near collapse due to economic mismanagement, corruption and authoritarianism. This led many to conclude that conflicts in Africa, including the one in the DRC, are due to 'bad governance.' [5]

The history of the conflict in the DRC can be traced back to the genocide that took place in 1994 in Rwanda. Some of the militias responsible for killing thousands of Tutsis and moderate Hutus fled across the border to DRC. Rwanda wanted DRC to stop these militias launching attacks on Rwanda and twice sent its own troops in order to stop preparation of attacks on it and to protect the Banyamulenge, members of the Tutsi ethnic group in DRC. Rwanda helped create the Allied Democratic Forces for the Liberation of the Congo (Alliance des Forces Démocratiques pour la Libération du Congo-Zaire, AFDL) in DRC to gain some kind of legitimacy for its presence in another sovereign country. Uganda also sent its troops to DRC in due course of time. The Allied Democratic Forces for the Liberation of the Congo under the leadership of Laurent Kabila and backed by neighbouring Rwanda and Uganda ousted Mobutu in May 1997. The ascendancy of Kabila led to the end of first conflict in DRC. The forces of the neighbouring countries however continued their presence in the country ostensibly to preserve their national security.

After a brief calm, differences between Kabila and the neighbouring allies aggravated to a no compromise situation. [6] There was also disappointment at popular level with the government behaving in an authoritarian manner by deviating from its promise of providing a genuine democracy and combating corruption. [7] The second conflict broke out in the country in August 1998. The Congolese government was supported by Angola, Chad, Sudan, Namibia and Zimbabwe, and on the other side Congolese rebels were backed by Burundi, Rwanda and Uganda. What complicated matter further is that there are many different militia groups in the east, each claiming to be defender group for their community. From 1998 to 2003, the country suffered from the devastating Second Congo War, the world's deadliest conflict since World

War II.

One of the major reasons for the conflicts in DRC is the vast natural wealth. The unstable situation provided fertile ground to the vested interests to exploit the natural wealth of DRC with impunity. As Reyntjens wrote, "Entrepreneurs of insecurity are engaged in extractive activities that would be impossible in a stable state environment. The criminalization context in which these activities occur offers avenues for considerable factional and personal enrichment through the trafficking of arms, illegal drugs, toxic products, mineral resources and dirty money." [8] In July 1999, a cease-fire agreement was signed in Lusaka by the DRC Government, the major rebel groups, and the foreign countries involved. A UN peacekeeping force (MONUC- the French acronym for the UN Mission in Congo) was deployed in 2000. However the violent activities by various groups did not come to a halt.

In January 2001, President Laurent-Désiré Kabila was assassinated and his son, Joseph Kabila, took over. Later in 2001, the Inter-Congolese dialogue was initiated to set the stage for a transition to democracy. Peace negotiations continued throughout 2002. On 30 July 2002 Rwanda and the DRC signed a peace deal. The deal centred on issues of the withdrawal of the Rwandan soldiers from territory of DRC and the dismantling of the Hutu militia. Signed on 6 September, the Luanda Agreement formalized peace between Congo and Uganda. By the end of 2002 Rwanda and Uganda claimed full withdrawal from the DRC though their claim remains disputed. On December 17, 2002 all Congolese rebels and political groups signed the Global and All-Inclusive Agreement. In April 2003 the Pretoria Peace agreement was signed by all of the parties to the inter-Congolese dialogue in South Africa. The agreement paved the way for installation of a transitional government in the DRC aiming at reunification, pacification, and reconstruction of the country, the restoration of territorial integrity and the re-establishment of the authority of the state throughout the national territory. [9]

On July 18, 2003, the Transitional Government came into being in which Kabila shared power with four vice-presidents. [10] A new constitution, introducing power-sharing and a two-term limit for the presidency was adopted 13 May 2005. Elections were held in July 2006 (first round of presidential election and parliamentary elections) and October 2006 (second round of presidential elections and local elections). Joseph Kabila was elected as president, and in February 2007 a new government was formed. However, throughout these periods, the Eastern provinces, specifically the Ituri, North Kivu, South Kivu, and Katanga provinces have remained unstable. Rebel groups, Rwandan-backed Tutsi rebels and Hutu militias (with Democratic Forces for the Liberation of Rwanda (FDLR)) continued to fight the government and rival groups. [11]

The Cost

Since independence in 1960, Congo has been ravaged by continuous inter-ethnic and civil strife, authoritarian rule etc. claiming numerous lives, plunging the country into chaos and poverty. The onset of the conflict brought further miseries with people getting displaced or killed, many losing their income-generating activities, and 'life becoming literally impossible in some parts of the country.' A glimpse of the huge humane cost of the conflict in the DRC can be gauged by the following facts: "On August 27, 1998, just a few days after the beginning of the civil war, the British Broadcasting Corporation (BBC) World Service reported that rebels and their Rwandan and Ugandan allies killed 200 civilians in Kassika in South Kivu. This was one of the first mass killings, called 'the massacre of Kassika.'

Later, 818 other civilians were killed in Makobola, known called 'the massacre of Makobola.' Their houses were burnt and almost at the same time fifteen women were buried alive in Kamituga. As early as February 1999, thirty people were killed at Kilambo in North Kivu by the Rassemblement des

Congolais pour la Démocratie (RCD), backed by the Rwandan army. RCD rebels and Rwandan soldiers and militias tied up men, raped women in front of their sons and husbands, and killed them. In May the same year, the RCD with its Rwandan allies killed at least thirty villagers in Katogota, south Kivu (Human Rights Watch 2001). In late 1999, the RCD with their allies sexually tortured and buried many women alive in Mwenga (Association Africaine de Défenses des Droits de l'Homme, ASADHO 2000)." [12]

United Nations human rights activists reported in 2003 that armed groups had carried out acts of cannibalism, inhumanity crossing all the limits. To quote Iyenda, "In mid-November 2002, rebels from the Mouvement de Libération du Congo (MLC) arrived in Mambassa and Mandima in the Eastern province of Congo. Mainly pygmies, people who are currently a protected race because of their potential disappearance, occupied these villages. As villagers fled into the bush, rebels systematically looted all their belongings. Rebels raped women and their daughters lying on the same bed, while their husbands, fathers, sons and brothers were watching. Under the command of Ramazani II, the so called 'Roi des Imbeciles' (King of Imbeciles), rebels killed, cooked and consumed pygmy meat in villages of Some, Mekimo, Makodu, Tobola, Malutu and Badisende surrounding Mambassa and Beni. Some of the killed people were grilled, and in most cases, rebels forced the victims' wives and other prisoners to cook the bodies of their killed relatives and to consume them." [13]

The forces from neighbouring Uganda and Rwanda and their allies have been accused of committing grave human rights abuses in the DRC. To quote Human Rights Watch report on DRC, "while Ugandan commanders were plundering gold, looting timber, exporting coffee, and controlling illicit trade monopolies in the Ituri district, their troops were killing and otherwise abusing the local population. Without international pressure, the situation can only get worse." [14]

The Congolese security forces with their allies too have been accused of killing, looting, arbitrarily arresting, torturing and raping women.

The conflict related deaths increased manifold with the destruction of livelihoods. Consequently, the destruction of livelihood led to food insecurity, malnutrition, lack of health facilities, high mortality rates, etc. An estimated 4 million people died in the conflict between 1998 and 2004, mostly from war-related diseases and starvation. The sustained level of violence throughout 2004 and internal displacements led the United Nations in March 2005 to describe Eastern Congo as 'world's worst humanitarian crisis.' Since 2000, the International Rescue Committee (IRC) has documented the humanitarian impact of war and conflict in the DRC through five mortality surveys. The first four studies, conducted between 2000 and 2004, estimated that 3.9 million people had died since 1998. Less than 10 per cent of all deaths were due to violence. Most of the deaths occurred due to curable diseases like malaria, diarrhea, pneumonia and malnutrition. Lack of a proper health system dramatically increased the death toll making it the world's deadliest documented conflict since World War II.

The fifth survey, covering the period from January 2006 to April 2007, concluded that 5.4 million deaths have occurred between August 1998 and April 2007, with as many as 45,000 people dying every month. An estimated 2.1 million of deaths occurred since the formal end of war in 2002. Only 0.4 per cent of all deaths were attributed directly to violence. As with previous IRC studies in the DRC, the majority of deaths have been due to infectious diseases, malnutrition and maternity related problems. The survey of IRC also found that more than four years after the signing of a formal peace agreement, national Crude Mortality Rate (CMR) of 2.2 deaths per 1,000 per month is 57 per cent higher than the average rate for sub-Saharan Africa. This rate being unchanged since the previous IRC survey in 2004 clearly indicates the country still remains in the midst of a major humanitarian crisis. [15] According to a Human Rights Watch report of 2003 by the middle of 2000, 2.3 million Congolese were displaced throughout the country. In June 2007 the United Nations Office for the Coordination of Humanitarian Affairs put the figures of internally displaced at 1.16 million. UNHCR in October 2007 put the figures of Congolese refugees in neighbouring countries of Burundi, Rwanda, Tanzania and Uganda at 310,000. The uprooted were deprived access to humanitarian services due to the overall insecure environment.

The neglect and deterioration of existing infrastructure, corruption, mismanagement etc. played havoc with the economy of DRC. Infrastructure suffered due to lack of maintenance. Public and private properties worth millions of dollars were destroyed. The conflicts have dramatically reduced national output and government revenue, and increased external debt. Foreign business houses have curtailed operations due to uncertainty atmosphere, lack of infrastructure, and the difficult operating environment. There has been increase in unemployment as owners have shifted their factories to the neighbouring countries of DRC. A country rich in natural resources has become one of the least developed countries in the world due to a combination of factors, conflict being the prime one. The country is the world's largest producer of cobalt, and a major producer of copper, diamond and tantalum. The GDP per capita in DRC has decreased significantly, dropping from US$ 380 in 1960 to US$ 224 in 1990 and to US$ 139 in 2006. [16] The wildlife of the country too could not escape the devastating effects. A survey by World Wide Fund in September 2005 put forward the population of hippopotamus in Virunga National Park at 900 from an estimated 29,000 thirty years ago, the main reason being illegal ivory production.

As already mentioned, one of the main reasons for the continuation of the conflict in DRC is economic, i.e. all the parties attempt to bring in their control the enormous natural resources. A United Nations report published in April 2001 clearly pointed the governments of Uganda, Rwanda, and Burundi were profiting from the conflict by looting resources of DRC. The report also accused the allies of the Congolese government- Angola, Namibia and Zimbabwe- of profiting from the conflict. Similarly, in 2005, the International Court of Justice found the Ugandan army guilty of grave human rights abuses and the illegal exploitation of Congolese natural resources. In the field of health, state expenditures in quite low in DRC. According to 1996 survey of the United Nations Children's Fund (UNICEF), only 26 per cent of people had access to health service.

The dismal situation further deteriorated with the onset of the violent conflict. A report published in 2001 showed that the percentage of non-enrolled children was 33 per cent in cities and 54 per cent in rural areas. The fragmentation of the social fabric, breaking up of families and other traditional solidarity networks along with the overall dismal scenario has put tremendous psychological pressure on the common people. The overall situation hence remains fragile and poverty is all pervasive. Life expectancy in DRC was 46 years in the year 2006. The under-5 mortality was 129 per thousand. Country's Human Development Index too has declined by more than 10 percent in the last ten years at 167 out of 177 countries. [17] The words of Jan Egeland, then United Nations Under-Secretary General for humanitarian affairs are worth quoting: "there are few places on earth where the gap between humanitarian needs and available resources is as large - or as lethal - as in Congo." [18]

The troubled situation in DRC has made the life of women more precarious. Besides getting killed and injured, hundreds of thousands of women and girls have been raped in the country. There are at least 40,000 survivors of sexual and gender-based violence in the DRC according to a report of World Health Organization published in 2005. According to the United Nations Special Rapporteur on Violence, Yakin

Ertürk, who toured eastern Congo in July 2007, violence against women in North and South Kivu included 'unimaginable brutality.'

According to another report published in October 2007 by the United Nations secretary-general, in the first six months of that year 4,500 cases of sexual violence were reported in South Kivu region alone. The report also conceded that for every rape that is reported as many as 10 or 20 cases may go unreported. The widespread rape led to the saying, 'eastern Congo is suffering from an epidemic of rape.' Alongside the physical suffering, women suffer long term psychological trauma of sexually transmitted diseases mainly HIV or unwanted pregnancy, the psychological disorder and social ostracizing due to the stigma attached with rape. [19] All armed forces involved in the conflict are guilty of rape. [20]

As in other conflicts rape in Congo conflict is not merely seen as a sex crime but a weapon of war, to humiliate the rival group or even, says the United Nations, a 'deliberate attempt to dehumanize and destroy entire communities.' The pervading lawlessness proved advantageous for anti-social elements, which may not be related to any warring faction. Cases of making women sexual slaves and thereafter the inhuman behaviour of the captivators too were reported from the country. To quote, "Most victims, as ever, are women and girls, some no more than toddlers, though men and boys have sometimes been targeted too. Local aid workers and UN reports tell of gang rapes, leaving victims with appalling physical and psychological injuries; rapes committed in front of families or whole communities; male relatives forced at gunpoint to rape their own daughters, mothers or sisters; women used as sex slaves forced to eat excrement or the flesh of murdered relatives. Some women victims have themselves been murdered by bullets fired from a gun barrel shoved into their vagina." [21]

Peace Keepers: Adding to the Cost

The peace keeping under MONUC was constituted in

1999 by a United Nations Security Council resolution to contain the crisis in the DRC. It can be mentioned here that MONUC is the largest and most expensive of all the peacekeeping operations. It has more than 16,000 troops from 18 nations, with India and Pakistan the leading troop contributors. The peacekeepers in the country have been accused of accentuating the cost of the conflict and thereby adding to the woes of the people. The United Nations operation in the DRC is the costliest in the world, costing over a billion dollars every year. The huge cost of the operation in a sensitive zone has also occasionally given rise to corruption charges against the peacekeepers. A significant amount of the money goes to the local United Nations procurement unit, which is at the centre of one of its most serious corruption scandals. An internal United Nations report - obtained by the BBC - reveals 'widespread and inherent corruption' pervading the procurement department in Kinshasa, the capital of DRC. The report concludes that just one of the officials under investigation had caused the United Nations losses that could 'be conservatively estimated to be in the hundreds of thousands of United States dollars.'

Besides charges of corruption, the peacekeeping forces in Congo have also been accused of sexual violence. According to a 2007 report of Human Rights Watch from December 2004 to August 2006, around 140 allegations of sexual exploitation involving United Nations personnel were recorded in Congo. The Indian contingent in the United Nations Peace-Keeping Force (UNPKF) in DRC has been subject to accusations of 'thirst for gold', 'arms for ivory' in a BBC news programme titled Panorama in the last week of April 2008. It is for the first time that such accusations were levelled against the Indian army contingent. The 18-month long BBC study into the conduct of the 17,000 strong peacekeepers allegedly found that United Nations troops have been involved in arming militia groups and smuggling gold and ivory. This revelation comes just three years after it emerged that the peacekeepers had perpetrated widespread abuse of refugees in the war-torn country.

The analysis of the BBC report generated controversy points that there are mainly five accusations involving Indian troops in the UNPKF in Congo. They are: the illegal purchase of gold from rebels of the FDLR—the former Rwandan army that fled to Congo following their involvement in the Rwanda genocide of 1994; the use of a United Nations helicopter to fly into the Virunga national park to exchange ammunition for ivory with the rebels; the exchanging with the rebels of rations for gold; the buying of drugs from the rebels and the failure to support the disarmament of this rebel group.

Reportedly, the BBC spoke to several eyewitnesses in Mongbwalu who said they had seen the Front Nationalist and Integrationist (FNI) re-armed. The FNI leaders known as 'Kung-fu' and 'Dragon', who are jailed in Kinshasa, have corroborated the BBC reports. Kung Fu, whose real name is General Mateso Ninga said: "Yes, it's true, they did give us arms. They said it was for the security of the country. So they said to us that we would help them take care of the zone… The FNI commanders took a vehicle to meet and negotiate with one of the Pakistani officers." He further said "They went in and came back with seven boxes of ammunition. After receiving these boxes, all the militia—including my young brothers—took their arms to go and attack the Congolese army." [22] The controversy acquired wider dimension in view of the fact that Uganda on April 29, 2008 has accused the peacekeepers in DRC of supplying arms to a dormant rebel group that is re-grouping in the troubled central African state. Kampala accuses the Allied Democratic Front of Uganda (ADF)—a dormant rebel movement hiding in eastern Congo—of recruiting and re-arming to destabilize Yoweri Museveni's government. ADF emerged as a localized movement in western Uganda's Ruwenzori mountain range in 1996, but finally defeated and chased across the border in 2004. "They (ADF members) come quietly and take people from the eastern

DRC and western Uganda to go and train in the eastern Congo. They are building forces there and we are very much aware," observed the Ugandan Defence Minister, Kiyonga.

The BBC had reported corrupt practices by Pakistani peacekeepers in DRC in 2007. The BBC alleged that the trafficking began in 2005 and cited witnesses who described secret negotiations between Pakistani blue helmets and FNI militia commanders in Mongwalu. In May 2007 the military spokesman of Pakistan, Maj Gen Waheed Arshad, said the reports were 'not only malicious but misleading and distorted' and without evidence. He also argued that the BBC was wrong to rely on the evidence of Mateso Ninga, a 'criminal in the prison.' The United Nations' own report, on 2 July 2007 concludes that the Pakistani contingent in Mongbwalu did indeed trade in gold with a group of Indian traders based in East Africa. The United Nations went on to hold just one Pakistani army officer responsible for what took place. It is hard to believe, the BBC argues, that one single officer, based in an isolated Congolese village, could organize a trade involving an estimated US$ 7 million in gold passing through four countries.

The United Nations officials said there was no evidence for many of the allegations aired on BBC's Panorama programme. They pointed out that the United Nations' Office of Internal Oversight Services (OIOS) had followed up every allegation against peacekeepers but had been unable to substantiate most of them. The only substantiated case was that of the three peace keepers from India who had brought wrought gold from a dealer at fire-sale prices. When the gold later turned out to be fake they traced down the dealer and detained him at their battalion headquarters. The purveyor of wrought gold later turned out to be having links with the rebels. The United Nations has promised action against the three. Its deputy spokesperson, Marie Okabe, stated, "much of the new information presented by the BBC report is either hearsay or comes from sources, such as the militia leaders, whose integrity and motivation are highly questionable as they themselves were arrested and put in prison by the peacekeepers." [23] Earlier in May 2007, MONUC announced an investigation into possible trafficking in gold and arms by peacekeepers deployed in 2005 in Ituri. After the internal probe the UN demanded Pakistani authorities punish the soldiers implicated in the case, including the commander, according to a 15 April 2008 letter to the BBC from Jean-Marie Guehenno, Chief of UN operations. The hugely embarrassing allegations against the United Nations peace keepers are a matter of grave global concern.

Current Scenario

Optimism for permanent peace in North Kivu came after the Goma agreement was signed on January 23, 2008 following negotiations between the Kinshasa government, Laurent Nkunda and Mai Mai militias. The deal aimed at ending the fighting that had resumed between the insurgents of Laurent Nkunda and the national army in December 2006. The deal included a ceasefire, the withdrawal of troops from key areas, the creation of a 'buffer zone' and amnesty for acts of war to militias. The fresh break out of fighting had led to renewed violence against civilians and displacement of over 370,000 civilians in the North Kivu province. However, the non-inclusion of the FDLR in the January 2008 talks and the government's pledge to forcibly disarm the rebels if they remain active has cast doubt over the prospects of permanent peace. An ICG report published in May 2008 sums up the current situation in DRC. It says that in Ituri, the risk of renewed violence is limited by the presence of the MONUC, the dismantling of the majority of armed groups and the local population's war weariness. However, the success of Congo's reconstruction would depend on effective ways to address the persisting root causes of the conflict –unequal access to land and unfair sharing of revenues from natural resource exploitation. [24]

Conclusion

DRC's five-year war officially ended in 2003, but the country is regularly listed as the site of one of the world's worst humanitarian crises. The country now has a democratic government though insecurity continues. The world's largest peacekeeping mission struggles to prevent violence there with itself occasionally engaging in the illegal activities. Since the beginning of the conflict in 1996, millions of people have been killed, unaccounted injured and millions of others have been displaced. The conflict had shattered the economy and virtually destroyed infrastructure with decades of mismanagement and authoritarian and corrupt rule. Health and educational services too have been severely affected. The persistent conditions provide enough evidence that recovery from conflict in DRC can take many years. The continuation of intermittent violence is a serious problem that the DRC government has to deal with. Without an integrated approach involving national and international institutions, the return to chaos is likely to occur as the imposed peace may gradually lose its grandeur.

To avoid the return of the conflict the reconstruction process has to accompany initiatives to contain violence. DRC needs global assistance in making speedy economic recovery and in ensuring that the fruits of the development are distributed equitably. There is an urgent need to address the disparities among different communities inhabiting the country, besides promoting democracy and rule of law, which can combat corruption and promote good governance. To ensure permanent peace it is also important to rehabilitate the displaced and provide people with alternate sources of livelihood. DRC is facing complex challenges currently. It is only the sustained and genuine efforts by local, national and international actors, working in tandem, can help people experience genuine democracy. The then United Nations Secretary-General, Kofi Annan, had stated in the year 2001, "One of the biggest challenges currently facing Africa and the

United Nations is the challenge of bringing peace and stability to the DRC." The challenge continues.

Notes

1. "Mortality in the Democratic Republic of Congo: An Ongoing Crisis," International Rescue Committee, New York, 2008.
2. R Lemarchand, *Political Awakening in the Belgian Congo* (Berkeley: University of California Press, 1964), p. 158.
3. M. MacNulty, "The Collapse of Zaire: Implosion, Revolution or External Sabotage?," *Journal of Modern African Studies*, vol. 37, no. 1, 1999, p. 57.
4. J. MacGaffey, *The Real Economy of Zaire: The Contribution of Smuggling and Other Unofficial Activities to National Wealth* (London: James Currey, 1991), p. 27.
5. J. Stremlav, "Ending Africa's Wars," *Foreign Affairs*, vol. 79, no. 4, 2000, p. 118.
6. Thomas Turner, "War in the Congo," *Foreign Policy in Focus*, vol. 5, no. 10, April 2000, p. 1.
7. Sagaren Naidoo, "The Role of Track Two Diplomacy in the DRC Conflict," *African Journal on Conflict Resolution*, vol. 1, no. 2, 2000, pp. 91-92.
8. F. Reyntjens, "Briefing: The Democratic Republic of Congo, from Kabila to Kabila," *African Affairs*, vol. 100, no. 399, April 2001, p. 312.
9. Shelly Whitman, "Women and Peace-building in the Democratic Republic of the Congo," *African Journal on Conflict Resolution*, vol. 6, no. 1, 2006, p. 38.
10. For details see, Dieudonné Tshiyoyo, "The Constitutional Referendum in the Democratic Republic of the Congo", *Conflict Trends*, no. 2, 2006, pp. 24-28.
11. "Congo: Bringing Peace to North Kivu," *International Crisis Group*, Africa Report no. 133, 31 October 2007.
12. Guillaume Iyenda, Civil Wars and Lootings in the Congo: How the Poor Pay the Bill, *African Journal on Conflict Resolution*, vol. 6, no. 2, 2005, pp. 13-14.
13. Ibid, pp. 14-15.
14. *Human Rights Watch World Report 2001: DRC*, New York, April 2001.
15. n. 1.
16. "DRC: Country Brief."

http://web.worldbank.org/WBSITE/EXTERNAL/COUNTRIES/AFRICAEXT/CONGODEMOCRATICEXTN/0,,menuPK:349476~pagePK:141132~piPK:141107~theSitePK:349466,00.html. (A. O. 10 May 2008).

17. Ibid.
18. "Congo (DR) conflict." http://www.alertnet.org/db/crisisprofiles/ZR_CON.htm. (A. O. 2 May 2008).
19. Anna Husarska, "Congo's Sex Crimes Rage On," *The Guardian Weekly*, 26 March 2008.
20. "The War within the War: Sexual Violence against Women and Girls in Eastern Congo," *Human Rights Watch*, June 2002.
21. "Atrocities Beyond Words," *The Economist*, 1 May 2008.
22. Martin Plaut, "Congo Gold: Is the UN Blocking an Enquiry?." http://www.bbc.co.uk/worldservice/documentaries/2008/04/080424_panorama_un.shtml (A. O. 20 April 2008).
23. *The Hindu*, 30 April 2008.
24. See "Congo: Four Priorities for Sustainable Peace in Ituri," *International Crisis Group,* Africa Report No. 140, 13 May 2008.

12

Kenya in Crisis: Causes and Consequences of the Post-December 2007 Election Conflict

Kennedy Agade Mkutu

This chapter [1] aims to shed a different light on the recent Kenya crisis, showing how the matter is not simply ethnic, but has at its root, problems of land grabbing and marginalization. It will look at struggles over land with particular reference to Laikipia as it is the area of interest for the author, and is a hot spot of violence over the past months. The issues of Laikipia however are pertinent all over Kenya.

Electoral Crisis and Costs

Kenya is a country of nearly 36 million people. For years, it was one of the most stable countries in the entire Greater Horn of Africa. However, Kenya's reputation was shattered on 29 December 2007 when the controversial presidential results led to rioting from coast to coast. The turmoil cost Kenya nearly 260 billion shillings (US$ 3.8 billion) in the first half of the year according to a 28 February dated report by the Kenya Association of Manufacturers. It noted that 100 billion shillings were lost in January alone, compared to the government's estimated of 60 billion. It was virtually impossible to transport goods, especially farm produce to the major markets in Nairobi. [2] Airline services were also not spared by the post conflict violence. Elections in Kenya have often been punctuated by clashes. Underlying discontent over land and other natural resources has fuelled violence that has at times in the last two decades left hundreds of people killed, thousands displaced and much property destroyed. The worst affected areas include Rift Valley, Western Coast, Nyanza and North Eastern provinces.

From 1969 when Kenya People's Union (KPU) party was abolished, Kenya functioned as a one party state. In 1982 Kenya was turned into a de jure one-party state with KANU as the sole party, moving in 1992 to a multiparty system. In the 1992 elections Kenyans voted in large numbers. Before the elections, most of the Western parts of Kenya and Rift Valley experienced land clashes. President Moi then defeated the opposition with a small margin. The second multiparty elections in which Moi was closely re-elected in 1997, was again highlighted by tension and clashes in parts of Kenya. The National Rainbow Coalition, led by Kibaki came to power in 2002. It was a unity of several parties that promised to unite Kenyans, stamp out corruption, address land issues and marginalization and provide a new constitution, such that many thought the skirmishes would be outdated. Indeed the 2002 elections were very peaceful and this was a hopeful time for Kenya. However, by 2005 the coalition had split and there was widespread disunity and discontent due to broken promises and the fact that Kenya's economic growth had not benefited most Kenyans.

On December 27, 2007 millions of Kenyans went to the polls in Kenya's fourth multi-party elections, with the hope of change and strengthening the institutions of democracy. During the author's visit and talk with people in Kisumu, Nairobi and Mombasa, all that was being spoken of was 'change.' Nearly 14.2 million (82 per cent of the total eligible voters) Kenyans were registered to vote, while 2,547 Parliamentary candidates were qualified to run in 210 constituencies. Nine candidates competed in the presidential election. The opposition made significant gains in the parliamentary elections. The Electoral Commission of Kenya, however, hastily declared President Kibaki as the winner of the presidential elections. He was quickly sworn in as president, while international and domestic election observers declared the elections as deeply flawed. The stand off between Kibaki and Raila Odinga who claimed the poll was rigged sparked off protests and spontaneous riots from Coast to Coast and from North to South. [3]

As of mid-February, more than 1,000 people had been killed and an estimated 500,000 reportedly became internal displaced. In addition to the recently displaced people, there remain thousands of people displaced from their farms since the 1990s, who are yet to return, as they fear fresh attacks. Once considered an oasis of peace in a region faced with conflicts, Kenya could now be classified with the other failed states. The conflict was costing Kenya more than 31 billion shillings a day. In early February, the opposition and the government began negotiations under the leadership of former United Nations Secretary General Kofi Annan. A coalition government was agreed and a mixed cabinet agreed in April 2008, with Odinga as Prime Minister. Violence has tentatively died down in most places and Kenya holds its breath to see how the coalition will fare.

The Road to the Conflict

Media reporting painted a picture of 'tribal warfare' linked to election anger. This explanation was justifiable in the worst instances of ethnic cleansing as in Eldoret, where Kikuyu women and children were burned alive in a church. A common explanation for the violence has been that members of the Kikuyu community are facing retaliation from others for their long-time 'dominance.' Like Kenya's first President, Jomo Kenyatta, President Mwai Kibaki is Kikuyu; opposition leader Raila Odinga is Luo. However, this paper argues that the underlying issues for the disunity in Kenya are not chiefly tribal, but elitism, marginalization and land.

Governance in East Africa is dominated by manipulation of ethnicity, patronage and a political culture of exclusion. This has continued, in large part, from the period prior to independence. Much ethnicized violence is linked to organized efforts by political strongmen who have experience in playing divide-and-rule. Brutal militias such as the Mungiki are well known to be closely linked to governing elites. In 1992 the Moi administration came under pressure to accept multipartism, which was a threat to its own survival. The politicians took advantage of the existing discontent to stir up racial tensions in the Rift Valley area to win votes. The result was the 1992 ethnic clashes in the Western Kenya and the Rift Valley. Kisumu, Raila Odinga's home region experienced conflict. But the epicentre of the conflict was in the Rift Valley where churches and people inside were burnt and even the former president's house was torched down. The same could be said for the 1992 and 1997 clashes. The fuel of the Rift Valley conflicts and the conflict of many other areas like the coast province was mainly historical, and mainly to do with land grabbing and marginalization. To simplify it as ethnic is a mis-representation.

Land Grabbing

Arid and semi arid lands (ASALs) occupy 467,200 square kilometers or about 80 per cent of Kenya's total land mass. According to the 1999 population census, nearly 10 million people (34.36 per cent) of the country were living in ASAL regions; they comprise pastoralists and a few agro-pastoralists. According to the Kenya Land Alliance, more than 65 per cent of all arable land is in the hands of only 20 per cent of the 35 million Kenyans. Most of the holders of the huge parcels of land are concentrated within the 17.2 per cent part of the country that is arable. [4] That has left millions landless while 67 per cent own on average less than an acre per person.

Since the colonial era, land has played a significant role in the political economy of Kenya. It remains a sensitive issue and its loss or acquisition has generated explosive political reactions. Exponential population growth has exerted palpable pressure on land resources, for farming and commercial activities. In the Rift Valley (read North Rift), this situation has created much bitterness among communities, with those who claim ancestral rights to the region feeling that 'migrant' communities, particularly those from central Kenya, are directly responsible for land scarcity. Since independence, until now, poor governance, and political campaigns that tend to promote negative views of ethnicity and regional economic imbalances, have further exacerbated the tensions in this region.

The Background

The colonial regime grabbed land from the 'natives' and distributed it to English settlers. However for most of the colonial period, land in the native reserve continued to be vested in tribes, clans, and kinship groups and the birth right of access to land was guaranteed. The introduction of land tenure under the Swynnerton plan in 1954 provided land grants to African individuals. As was anticipated in the Swynnerton Plan, rich Africans were able to acquire more land and poor farmers acquired less, creating a landowner and a landless class. [5] With the departure of the colonial regime from Kenya, the British government and the World Bank under the Settlement Transfer Fund Scheme Loan (STFSL) gave the Kenyatta regime the money intended to settle the landless, amongst them were the Mau Mau fighters.

Most of the power brokers in the Kenyatta regime formed land-buying companies and established huge farms in the Rift Valley, either jointly or on their own using the Settlement Transfer Fund Loan (STFL). [6] Kenyatta himself, during his 15-year rule, used the STFL to obtain large tracts of land under his family name. This is now widely distributed between the numerous family members all over Kenya. The extended Kenyatta family owns an estimated 500,000 acres, approximately the size of Nyanza Province, as estimated by independent surveyors and Ministry of Lands officials. [7] Among the best-known parcels of land are the 24, 000 acres in Taveta sub-district adjacent to the 74, 000 acres owned by former MP Basil Criticos.

The Kenyatta family also owns almost 15 per cent of the prime resort land on the Kenyan coast province, and a huge sisal plantation spanning both Taita and Taveta districts. The argument of the Kalenjin and other indigenous pastoralists who live in the Rift Valley is that the community's ancestral land was lost first to British settlers and later to migrant communities, courtesy of these land-buying companies who were supported by President Kenyatta's regime. Some, including the former Tinderet MP, Jean Marie Seroney, who was mysteriously murdered, raised this concern with Kenyatta. Bildad Kaggi, a Kikuyu of Mau Mau loyalty also found himself politically locked out due to raising these concerns and the famous Laikipia MP J.M. Kariuki was assassinated for speaking out. Thus even Kikuyus lost out as Kenyatta's cronies benefited at this time. This historic resentment underlies the recent violence in Kenya.

Current Scenario and Conflict

Land grabbing continues in the 21st century as the population grow and the rule of law is perverted. Land once designated as government land for preservation is now being grabbed by political elites, the current Mount Elgon dispute being a case in point. The sons of the Mau Mau (many of whom are operating as part of the brutal Mungiki sect) are demanding their share of land in various parts of Kenya. [8] Meanwhile in the Rift Valley, with population growth, land is in increasing demand. Agriculturalists are pushing their boundaries, and some moving to legitimately acquire pastoral lands, but the droughts of this decade have also pushed pastoralists to invade lands occupied by some of the land buying companies, in search of pasture and water. The scenario is made more ominous owing to the fact that the Rift Valley is one of the most militarized and weaponized region in the current Kenya particularly amongst the marginalized pastoral communities. Until now, pastoralists have mainly fought enemy pastoral groups, but there have been instances of armed attacks on settled groups in Trans Nzoia, Laikipia and Narok which can only be expected to increase.

Addressing Land Disputes

The land crisis in the country will be difficult to solve because the most powerful people in the country are also among its biggest landowners. Addressing land issues is also complex because in addition to the large tracts of land grabbed by the political elite; there are also genuine buyers. Some of them have bought land on a willing-buyer-willing-seller basis, while others have bought land that they did not realize was grabbed. This is a challenge for the rule of law as regards property rights. In Kenya courts do not function well when processing land disputes. The main reason is that such disputes have a complex cultural context, which cannot be resolved in normal adversarial procedures. In many parts of the country, traditional models of governance continue which often contradict the statute law. Most of the pastoral lands are communally managed under traditional governance systems. This means that it is difficult to resolve resource-based conflict through the statute laws alone since the people have, for centuries, been applying traditional approaches to land and resource management. The series of land acts, implemented on top of surviving customary tenure, has had the effect of creating confusion for the land allocating authority. This confusion enables proper procedures, if not justice, to be subverted. This tension between the two regimes is now leading to violent conflict among communities.

The Laikipia Case

Laikipia is made up of three districts out of the 71 districts in the Rift Valley Province. [9] It lies in the east of the province. It provides an opportunity to understand the dynamics of land and population growth, drought, armed violence and the agriculturalist/pastoralist interface. Laikipia is a multi-ethnic region comprising Kikuyu (60 per cent), Meru,

Samburu, Masai, Kalenjin, Borana, Turkana and Europeans. The Kikuyu and Meru occupy the urban and arable parts of the District and the Europeans mainly live in the ranches. The other groups of which most are pastoralists occupy the arid and semi-arid parts. The north is predominantly Maasai. There are four major economic activities in Laikipia: commercial farming, traditional cultivation, pastoralism and ranching. These activities require land and water and there is competition for these scarce resources. The ranches were established in 1904 by Sir Charles Elliot, the commissioner of the Protectorate who displaced the Maasai in the area. The total population of Laikipia District was estimated to be 345,460 (1999) and projected to rise to 378,477 in the 2001. Over the last ten years the population of Laikipia has increased by 60.8 per cent reflecting a 4.5 per cent growth rate per annum. [10]

The three new districts were created to manipulate the outcome of the 2007 elections. In a recent communication, an elderly man from Dol Dol noted: "Laikipia district was essentially one district with its headquarters in Nanyuki town. Due to political instigation it first became necessary to divide it into two, as constituencies, East and West. Laikipia West was carved from Laikipia East. However, the predominant population of the inhabitants was one ethnic community and that is the Kikuyus. The original owners of the land, the Maasai of Laikipia clan who mainly occupied the northern part of Laikipia, also agitated for their district since the other two were predominantly Kikuyu. Therefore the 'Government' decided to offer us a district purely on the basis that the Maasai of Dol Dol have for too long had outstanding issues of representation and marginalization." [11]

Several conflicts exist in Laikipia. Firstly, there are conflicts over grazing lands in all the three districts, between pastoralists and agriculturalists, and amongst pastoral groups. Secondly, there are armed cattle raids between Samburu and Maasai and between Samburu and Pokot with the Turkana on either side. The cattle raids are often followed with revenge raids. Thirdly, there are human and wildlife conflicts, which can be a serious threat to livelihood. Fourthly, we have state versus pastoralist conflicts, where the state attempts to subdue pastoral conflicts and this is strongly resisted. The recent conflict is distinct in that there is unity between two pastoral communities against agriculturalists, who are mainly Kikuyu. [12] The situation is made lethal by the use of arms, which the pastoralists now possess in plenty. Thus, there are now calls for the Kikuyu to be given armed home guards for protection.

Population Increase and Conflict

Over the last 40 years, grazing land in Laikipia has reduced substantially as foreign settlers, local investors and ranchers have bought large tracts of land. Land has been transformed from communal to individual land ownership through the acquisition of title deeds through corruption by elites. Land grabbing by the ruling class in Kenya has reached such proportions that it is hardly considered illegal. [13] Agriculturalists from the densely populated areas are now buying land in pastoral areas made available by the liberalization of the land market. The influx of a farming population translates into increased demand for food. In Laikipia [14] nearly 44 commercial ranchers and commercial farmers own 70 per cent of the land. [15] This forces pastoralists to graze their livestock on an ever-shrinking range of inferior quality land resulting in tension and conflict, despite the historical reality that this was the Maasai original ancestral land before being alienated by 1904 and 1911 British agreements to create some of the white highlands (Kenya Land Commission, 1933). Maasai elders are now calling for the large ranches and farms to revert to the pastoralists.

Drought since 2001 to date has led to massive loss of livestock in Laikipia and surrounding pastoral areas, forcing the Maasai and other pastoralists to migrate into private ranches and amongst agriculturalists in search of pasture and water. Ewaso Nyiro River (the river of God) and its tributaries are vital to the pastoralists in the Isiolo, Laikipia, Samburu and Garrissa districts. The river originates from the Aberdares in the Nyeri district, while its tributaries emerge from Mt. Kenya. However much of water is now being diverted by agriculturalists, leaving those downstream vulnerable to climatic variability. There is a high risk of conflict over these scarce resources unless special arrangements are made to ensure emergency access during droughts. Given the predicted climate change and now that most of the communities are armed, tension should be expected to increase.

During March and April 2008, nearly 8,000 people have been displaced and 25 killed in conflicts between farmers and Tugen and Turkana pastoralists in Laikipia West Districts. [16] The weapons of attack have been arrows or guns. [17] On 14 March 2008 a landowner Miano Gakuya was shot dead at his home in Rumuruti. The raiders were armed with rifles and when they sensed danger, they just sprayed him with bullets. [18] With climatic changes in early 2008, driven by the need for pasture and water, the Maasai have also invaded the white ranches, which are further increasing tension. [19] The situation in Laikipia has settled down after a peace initiative by the elders and a temporary presence of security personnel. A local Maasai ranch owner, whose father bought land in the early years of independence, noted that the conflict is over historical injustices that need to be addressed to give a sustainable solution that will be embraced with the warring communities. [20]

Conflict in Laikipia is not a new phenomenon. The interests of the pastoralists and agriculturalists have always been closely related to election outcomes. Clashes in 1992 had left large amounts of land unoccupied, and pastoralists used this. In 2002 when the NARC government began their first term, there was hope amongst pastoralists that they would be represented. However, instead, the state protected the interests of the agriculturalists who wished to reclaim the land they once occupied. These agriculturalists were mainly Kikuyu and Meru. Thus by 2007 the stakes were high for the outcome of the election, and land issues fuelled the ensuing conflicts.

Marginalization and Deprivation

Several groups have been marginalized in Kenya in various ways. Most well known is the marginalization of pastoralists. The powerful, wealthy, prestigious 'free pastoralists' of the early 18th century appears a story of the past, as they have been restricted or displaced from their land. Sedenterization is often preferred to pastoralism by states as it is easier to maintain law and order and collect taxes. The Minister for Heritage and Culture William Ole Ntimama has reportedly argued: "If you look at the example of Kenya today, the people of central Province lost only small areas of land like Thika, Kabete, Kikuyu and they have already recovered them and they are settling on them. So I don't know what compensation they would be looking for. The Kambas have got part of the east Athi River for example and most of them are occupying those areas. But we (Maasai) haven't got anything back. Nobody has considered us and I think this is because we have always been in the periphery and not near power like everybody else."

The government of Kenya has made some efforts to include pastoralists in the civil service, cabinet ministries, and the army, but they are still not adequately represented in political life and in decision-making organs. Additionally, those who are representing pastoralists in government do not always fulfil their responsibility. States always viewed pastoralism as a marginal economic way of life. When communities encounter injustice and the involvement of government officials in supporting criminals, tension is created and hence conflict. This prejudice is further reflected when the government sends security forces, who are already biased and take actions that do not meet the reported insecurity situation, to these areas. [21] It has been argued that pastoral conflict is the communities' response to what is perceived as the inability or failure to guarantee their security.

Youth and Conflict

Kenya has a population of approximately 37 million of which 65 per cent comprise of youth between the ages of 15-25 years. According to a recent World Bank Report, the youth population in Kenya is projected to be over seven times its 1950 level in 2010, and over 12 times its 1950 level in 2050. [22] Understanding some of the characteristics of the different generations is helpful in understanding the conflict. The author has used the following classification:

'Old guards' some of whom have enriched themselves from corruption and land grabbing and have become adept at manipulating issues of ethnicity and tribalism to their advantage to retain power and wealth.

'Nyayo milk' generation (So named because the president decreed free milk to children of that generation when at school! Also called the 7,4,2 generation because of the ordering of their years of education). Many still speak or understand their local languages, but also speak Swahili/English.

'Sheng' generation, who are Swahili/English speaking youths or 8-4-4 generation (also from education). Of this generation many are urbanized; they have little identification with their particular ethnic group and some are products of ethnically mixed marriages. They often cannot speak their ethnic mother tongue. They are usually educated, but jobless.

In rural areas, especially pastoral areas of the Rift Valley, with increase in droughts, many are finding the herding livelihood impossible due to diminishing cattle. This is the result of increasingly commercialized cattle raiding, aided by the influx of modern weaponry into marginal pastoral areas. Some of them are now being employed by wealthy cattle owners to guard cattle or to raid. Their lives are often in danger and they are unable to accumulate any assets for themselves, which has implications for their ability to marry. Marginalization of the pastoral areas as described has meant that little in the way of alternative livelihood options exist.

The urban youth are also marginalized and unemployed but often they are also educated. Even having good grades no longer guarantees a job as elites hold on to their positions and continue to have their contracts renewed past retirement age. [23] Many have turned to crime or are being recruited into militia groups like the Mungiki, Taliban, Jesi la Mzee, Sungu Sungu, Chinkororo, Baghdad Boys, Sabaot Land Defence Force (SLDF), Kaya Bombo. They are all similar, except perhaps in the degree of brutality.

In the recent crisis, many of the people, seen holding machetes, bows and arrows, were disillusioned youths determined to hit back at the society with whatever means they can find. They are the new faces of the marginalized in Kenya, young people who are unable to improve their lot, in a nation where the minority are too rich and the majority too poor. They feel that they have been enticed by politicians to do their dirty work, but the latter have not kept the deal to represent them. Security forces may be sent to flush out gangs and raiders in far-flung areas like Mt Elgon and Pokot, but urban areas are not safe either. If the trend continues, organized crime will become a way of life among the youth, and the more police try to crush them, the more determined they will get. In terms of security, the training of Kenya's security forces is inappropriate for these conflicts. Disarmament and the use of force are unlikely to defeat the Mungiki, the SLDF and the well-armed warriors of the North rift.

Conclusion

In conclusion, the Kenyan crisis was not primarily a tribal issue. It is a historical problem of inequality and marginalization, which repeatedly erupted through Kenya's political history but has never been resolved. The main barrier to resolution is simple, that it is not in the interests of many of the political elite. Another problem is that grabbed land has now been sold on to genuine buyers. Laikipia illustrates how the pressure on the land by agriculturalists and marginalized pastoralists can easily erupt into violence. Furthermore the pastoralists are heavily armed which does not bode well for the future. A former minister for internal security, G.G. Kariuki suggests that the Government should provide home guards, as is the case for groups in other North Rift Valley districts, to enable the Kikuyu to protect themselves against the armed pastoralists, since they are now vulnerable. Arming groups against the other is a short-term solution, but a long-term problem as it leads to more proliferation of arms in civilian hands. [24]

One way forward that has been suggested is the formation of a truth commission for settling longstanding disputes. However, there are inherent weaknesses that predispose truth commissions to myriad challenges. One such problem is the weakness of the rule of law and the lack of prosecutorial powers common with truth commissions the world over may make the exercise unsatisfying, as exemplified by several commissions that have taken place in Kenya in the past. To address the post-election violence, the Government has begun construction of police stations in the Rift Valley. This is a timely step, but it is also necessary to address the root cause of the conflict, particularly as the communities are now militarized. In the long term, the way to mitigate land conflict and marginalization is to develop and strengthen the institutions of governance, security and rule of law. This will give people confidence that their differences can be resolved through peaceful means. What is needed is a representative legislative process, a legal system that delivers justice without marginalization of any tribe, responsive local government and the honest and efficient delivery of social services.

In Kenya, for years many laws are made by executive decree and the executive has many tribunals and quasi-courts settling disputes and imposing penalties. These should be functions of a truly independent judiciary working strictly in accordance with the jurisprudential principles of 'due process.' It is this separation that will ensure that property rights and land issues are addressed; this will also ensure that institutions are protecting the governed from those who govern. The rule of law must be ensured. It must be objective and not discretionary, so that any person who leads cannot engage in patronage, nepotism or favouritism. People's rights are a function of law, not the whim of politicians and officials granting licences, protection, subsidies and government contracts. Secondly, there must be a separation of powers so that only the legislature legislates (makes laws), the executive executes (implements laws), and the judiciary adjudicates. This strict demarcation exists in theory but not in practice in many developing nations.

The key lesson for the international community to learn from recent violence is that a new government alone, especially if it welcomes perpetrators of violence into its core, cannot fix this deep problem of strongmen politics. Kenya will have to confront and address the problem of class which has ignored the mass poverty in its midst. This is directly related to the violence. The elites and middle classes must realize that so long as they have poverty amongst them, they are not safe in their gated homes. Finally, Kahli Gibran notes, "A leader will bring destruction into his nation if he can neither weave a garment, nor sow a seed nor lay a stone, but makes politics his occupation."

Notes

1. This work was originally presented at University of Oxford, African Studies Centre, St. Atoney College on 24 April 2008. Thanks for all the comments that have enriched it. Thanks also to Tessa Mkutu for editing the work.
2. *Daily Nation*, 11 January 2008.
3. *Daily Nation*, 1 January 2008.
4. See *East African Standard*, 1 October 2004. http://www.eastandard.net/archives/cl/hm_news/news.php?articl

eid=1916. (A. O. 23 October 2006).

5. Y. W. Bradshaw, "Perpetuating Underdevelopment in Kenya: The Link between Agriculture Rights in Land Undermined Tradition," *African Studies Review*, vol. 33 no.1, April 1990, p. 5.
6. They included Njenga Karume, the then Chairman of Gema Holdings, who acquired 20,000 acres in Molo where he is growing tea, coffee, pyrethrum and potatoes and 16,000 acres in Naivasha. GG Kariuki acquired his 5,000 acres at Rumuruti, Laikipia Division, while former Attoney-General Charles Njonjo bought the 100,000 acre Solio Ranch. Senior Chief Munyinge from Muiga took 400 acres. Initially, Senior Chief Munyinge was allocated only 70 acres but with time he managed to acquire 330 more acres. Mwai Kibaki acquired 20,000 acres in Nanyuki. Former MP Munene Kairu has 32,000 acres at Rumuruti. Isaiah Mathenge, the former powerful Provincial Commissioner under Kenyatta and an MP under Moi, is arguably the largest land owner in Nyeri municipality. He owns Seremwai Estate, which is 10,000 acres. Kibaki's friend, Kim Ngatende, a former government engineer, has 500 acres too. Mathenge also owns—jointly with former Provincial Commissioner Lukas Daudi Galgalo—the 10, 000-acre Manyagalo Ranch in Meru. D. S. Njoroge also owns the extensive Kelelwa Ranch in Koibatek.
7. *East African Standard*, n. 4.
8. *Daily Nation*, 27 April 2008.
9. Laikipia East (the capital in Nanyuki); Laikipia West (Nyahururu) and Laikipia North (Dol Dol).
10. *Government of Kenya, The District Statistics: Nanyuki* (Nairobi: Government Printers 1996). Also sec *Government of Kenya, Laikipia District Development Plan 1997-2001* (Nairobi: Government Printers, 1997).
11. Email communication, name withheld, 13 May 2008.
12. http://www.irinnews.org/report.aspx?ReportId=77532. (A. O. 20 April 2008).
13. J. Markakis, "Pastoralists and Politicians in Kenya," *Review of African Political Economy*, vol. 26, no. 80, 1999, pp. 293-296.
14. Dole Dole (Mukogodo division) occupies just 1,100 sq.km of Lakipia district (app. 10,000 sq. Km) in the Rift Valley of Kenya.
15. Muriithi, District Livestock Research Officer, Interview,

Nanyuki, 4 September 2002.
16. *East African Standard*, 15 March 2008.
17. *East African Standard*, 9 March 2008.
18. http://www.irinnews.org/report.aspx?ReportId=77532., n. 12.
19. Text message from Maasai elderly man in Dol Dol, Laikipia, name withheld, 17 May 2008.
20. Telephonic Interview, name withheld, 2 February 2008.
21. David Ethuro, Member of Parliament from Kenya, Speech given at the International conference on small arms, Jinja, Uganda, 8-13 November 2001.
22. "The Demography of Youth in Developing Countries and its Economic Implications," *World Bank Policy Research Working Paper*, no. 4022, 2006.
23. *Daily Nation*, 23 April 2008.
24. *Daily Nation*, 17 March 2008.

13

Sierra Leone Conflict: Liberation or Incarceration?

Zinurine Alghali

The Sierra Leone conflict was initiated by the Revolutionary United Front (RUF), under the leadership of deceased Corporal Foday Saybana Sankoh on 23 March 1991. The armed campaign started in the eastern part of Sierra Leone and later spread to the southern and central regions of the country. In their manifesto, *Footpaths to Democracy*, the RUF stated that they were "fighting for a new Sierra Leone. A new Sierra Leone of freedom, justice and equal opportunity for all ….and for democracy… equal opportunity and access to power to create wealth through free trade, commerce, agriculture, industry, science and technology." [1] The root causes of the conflict can be traced to the systematic long-term neglect of the rural areas of the country. Local governance was deliberately weakened for a centralized system; the judiciary became unreliable, infrastructure decayed and the provision of social services deteriorated consistently over a period of twenty-four years. State apparatus, including the security system were mere skeletons and made it easy for the 1992 National Provisional Ruling Council (NPRC) mutiny to end up as a coup and the establishment of a military government.

The escalation of hostilities during the NPRC rule with the RUF's expanded armed campaign resulted to a breakdown of civil authority in large areas of the country. An estimated 1.5 million civilians fled war-affected areas to towns and cities in search of refuge. Important mining operations such as Sierra Rutile, the Sieromco bauxite mine and key diamond fields, were taken over by the RUF twice in early 1995. This escalation of hostilities resulted in reduction of gross foreign exchange earnings by 50 per cent, disrupted agricultural production and curtailed the activities of development agencies and the private sector. The Armed Forces Revolutionary Council (AFRC)'s ouster of the Sierra Leone Peoples Party (SLPP) government of Ahmed Tejan Kabbah that assumed office through democratic elections in 1996 worsened both the humanitarian and economic situation in Sierra Leone. Their eight months stay in Freetown and control of the state was characterized by rampant looting and erosion of state resources and funds, violence and human rights abuses. The Economic Community of West African States (ECOWAS) supported Nigerian-led Economic Community of West African States Monitoring Group (ECOMOG) intervention that reinstated President Ahmad Tejan Kabbah also resulted in deaths of civilians and the destruction of basic infrastructure due to RUF's resistance.

The RUF/AFRC invasion of Freetown in January 1999 was terrible. The atrocities were unspeakably terrible: amputations, rape, massacres, and the destruction of infrastructure were the order of the day. The battle to evict the AFRC/RUF fighters from the city was equally disastrous because as AFRC/RUF fighters retreated, the more ruthless they became. The AFRC splinter group, the 'West Side Boys,' was no better than the RUF. With attributes of rag-tag bunch of armed thugs, they constantly terrorized civilians who inevitably had to pass through their roadblocks on the Freetown highway to the provinces. The distress faced by people in the surrounding villages of their base in the outskirt of Freetown was horrifying. Abducted teenage girls were turned into sex slaves and 'bush wives' and experienced unforgettable abuses. [2]

The Civil Defence Forces (CDF), a pro-government militia was also not exempted from the commission of atrocities and human rights abuses. Many civilians met death or were tortured for being perceived as RUF collaborators. Like the

RUF, they made extensive use of child soldiers who at present find it difficult to reconcile with their experiences during the conflict. The CDF's argument that they were fighting to protect the state and the people brought into the picture just and unjust war paradigm. However, this argument would have only been valid if they had strictly adhered to International Humanitarian Law, the law of armed conflict.

Costs and Consequences

The Sierra Leone conflict was characterized by systematic and widespread perpetration of all classes of gross human rights abuses against the civilian population. Civilians were shot in their houses, on the streets, thrown from the upper floors of buildings, used as human shields, and burned alive in cars and houses. They had their limbs hacked off with machetes, eyes gouged out with knives, hands smashed with hammers, and bodies burned with boiling water or hot oil. Women and girls were systematically sexually abused and raped, and children and young people were abducted in hundreds. [3]

Upon gaining control of villages and towns, RUF fighters usually embarked on systematic looting raids, in which families were hit by wave after wave of rebels demanding money and valuables. Those who didn't have what the rebels demanded were often murdered or maimed. RUF fighters also formed distinct units known for committing particular crimes, like the 'Burn House Squad,' 'Cut Hand Unit,' and 'Kill Man No Blood Gang,' etc. Some of these squads had a trademark way of killing. The Kill Man No Blood Gang's method was to beat people to death without shedding blood, the Born Naked Squad would strip their victims before killing them and the Cut Hand Unit routinely asked their captives whether they wanted 'long or short sleeve,' and on the basis of the answer cut their arms off at the wrist or the elbow. The closer ECOMOG or government forces got to rebel positions, the more these units were mobilized and sent on operation. While rape and abduction were widespread throughout RUF offensives, the pace of executions, amputations and burning of properties often picked up dramatically when fighters were forced to withdraw. The abuses committed during the last days of RUF occupation of any given village or town was of staggering proportion. [4]

A lot of the executioners of these atrocities were teenagers who were high on drugs. They committed atrocities as if they were executing commands from someone they were accountable to. The consistency displayed by RUF fighters in the commission of atrocities made it clear that massacre-style tactics was part of the RUF's modus operandi. A fifteen year old under the influence of drugs with a Kalashnikov (AK-47 rifle) in the midst of people (s)he regards as 'traitors' to their cause can only react in the way(s) he has been trained and used to behave. (S)he does not need a command to know what killing or maiming style to use or how to execute it. For a victim to expect anything less has less meaning than it otherwise would. Also, the irregular patterns of abuses and the playful ways in which atrocities were carried out speaks the fact that individual rebels on the ground were deciding at will who to kill, maim or kidnap.

By 1993 relief organizations estimated that about one million Sierra Leoneans of a total population of 4.5 million were displaced within the country or forced to take refuge in Guinea and Liberia. Civilian casualties continuously mounted with estimates ranging from thirty to seventy-five thousand war-related deaths, although these figures are impossible to confirm. The war also reportedly claimed the lives of over eight hundred regional peacekeepers by the end of May 1999. [5] Reliable, comprehensive figures on the numbers of people wounded or psychologically traumatized by the war do not exist. Atrocities such as the amputation of limbs, ears and lips with machetes, decapitation, branding and the gang rape of women and children have been common. In March 2000, the United Nations Humanitarian Co-ordination Unit reported that the number of survivors of amputation was approximately six hundred, rather than previous estimates ranging from three hundred to five thousand. It is assumed that the survivors represent only about a quarter of all amputees.

Social Effects: The social costs of the conflict have been equally high. Delivery of basic social services was dramatically curtailed in areas outside of the capital. Most of the rural displaced fled to urban areas. The population of Greater Freetown alone increased from seven hundred and thirty-one thousand in 1989 to more than 1.5 million by late 1995 thus exhausting the already overburdened social services. Many of the displaced persons were housed by extended families that barely had enough space and resources for themselves not to talk about the relatives joining them. According to the United Nations Office for the Coordination of Humanitarian Affairs (UNOCHA), there were still one hundred and fifty thousand registered IDPs in August 1999, and as many as one million people were at risk due to insecurity and the inability of humanitarian agencies to access large parts of the northern and eastern regions of the county. According to the United Nations High Commissioner for Refugees (UNHCR), many refugees still remain in neighbouring countries to date.

The costs of the Sierra Leone conflict have gone far beyond the conflict itself. Many people are now suffering from long-term injuries they suffered from combat, rape, and torture. It is extremely difficult for them to deal with the psychological effects they suffered from the trauma. They are still experiencing deep fear, distrust, depression, and a sense of hopelessness even though the conflict formally ended some six years ago. The psychological and social effects of the war on combatants and civilians are only beginning to be systematically assessed. A May 1999 sampling of civilians in Freetown carried out by Médecins Sans Frontiéres indicated that almost all of those surveyed had suffered from starvation, had witnessed people being wounded or killed, and half had lost someone close to them. Apart from psychological effects, violence during the conflict also led to the destruction of medical facilities and the disruption of drugs and medical supplies.

Effects on Women: The plight of women in the Sierra Leone situation confirms that the costs of conflict often fall disproportionately on women. According to a 2003 Human Rights Watch report, as many as two hundred and fifty seven women and girls may have been raped during the civil war. Another report released by Physicians for Human Rights found that half of those who came into contact with RUF forces experienced sexual violence. They were deliberately and systematically targeted and subjected to rape, sexual slavery and forced pregnancy. Once captured, women were frequently shared and divided among the combatants who took them as wives. These 'bush wives' were part of the household of the combatant or commander and were protected by him from other combatants. Her role was then to satisfy him sexually and also be responsible for his welfare. Women who were not lucky to get a commander or combatant as a 'bush husband' were constantly raped by more than one combatant and had no guaranteed protection. They also had to cook, do laundry, and fetch water at will of the combatants. [6]

Sexual violence was not a single event but a violation that is affecting survivors' lives in many ways. Many women and girls continue to suffer psychological, physical, social and economic effects up to date. Many victims decided not to share their experiences with anyone to avoid the shame and stigma associated with sexual violence. This is serving as an obstacle to their access to health care even though they are suffering physical side- effects of repeated sexual violence that includes damages to their reproductive organs, miscarriages, unwanted pregnancies, and sexually transmitted diseases. Many survivors felt too ashamed of their experiences to return to their own towns and villages, and were forced to build new lives away from their friends and families. Others are living in silence, unable to share their painful memories for fear of rejection by their families and community members.

Those known to be survivors of sexual violence tend to be confronted with blame and discrimination rather than support by those around them. The stigmatization and discrimination survivors face are huge obstacles to women and girls who are trying to rebuild their lives following traumatic experiences. Many want justice and reparations for their perpetrators to be held responsible for their actions and also for them to be economically independent. "The unimaginable brutality of violations committed against up to one third of Sierra Leone's women and girls, although well-documented, has still not been fully addressed by the government…the story is not over. They need appropriate healthcare and access to justice, work, economic opportunities and educational opportunities to help them to begin to re-build their lives," said Tania Bernath, Amnesty International's researcher on Sierra Leone. [7] What needs to be done now is a follow-up (by the new government) on the efforts that was made by the SLPP government in addressing gender and war-related concerns.

Economic Effects: In spite of the civil unrest that plagued the country during the 1990s, the government implemented successful series of stabilization and structural reform policies that yielded significant results up until the time of the May 1997 coup. From 1990/91 to 1996, annual inflation was reduced from over one hundred per cent to around 6 per cent, and the budget deficit was reduced from twelve per cent of GDP to 6.8 per cent in the period from 1989/90 to 1996. These gains were achieved while at the same time protecting social sector spending despite budgetary pressures related to the war. However, nine months of AFRC/RUF rule in 1997, and predominantly unstable economic and political conditions during 1998 and early 1999 reversed most of these advances. Real GDP was estimated to have contracted by over 20 per cent in 1997, the overall budget deficit stood at around eleven and a half per cent of GDP for 1998, and it was estimated that real output declined by approximately 9 per cent during the first half of 1999. Nonetheless, the economic situation during the second half of 1999 was expected to improve with the political stabilization resulting from the implementation of the Lomé Peace Agreement. Government revenue was projected to increase, and while budget outlays were also expected to increase in relation to emergency relief and rehabilitation expenditures, the primary budget deficit for the year as a whole was projected to be 7.8 per cent of GDP. The devastating consequences of the war and the deplorable situation afterwards however prevented these projections from materializing.

The civil war and coup-related unrest devastated the economy and led to large scale social disruption. Substantive damage was caused to the agriculture and mining sectors, thereby greatly reducing rural food security and revenue earning capacity of the country. A large percentage of public infrastructures were destroyed, and/or deteriorated. The loss of control over resources and diminished government revenues drastically reduced foreign exchange receipts and fiscal revenues. There was also a decline in export earnings from mineral resources, and a decline in agricultural productivity which led to increases in the importation of essential food items, such as rice. This exacerbated the already high levels of poverty in Sierra Leone.

With the withdrawal of foreign investment and the disruption of business, the private sector faced serious challenges which impacted on the country's economy greatly. Looting for food, cash crops and other material goods became a means of survival and often a source of profitable business for elements within both the RUF and the AFRC. Moreover, control over the illicit diamond mining and trade in the areas bordering Liberia became a way for the RUF to finance the procurement of arms and other supplies. These factors contributed significantly to the prolongation of the war and a huge loss of revenue to the government.

Peace Attempts

The Government of Sierra Leone signed the Abidjan Peace Accord, the Conakry Peace Plan, the Lomé Peace Agreement and the Abuja Ceasefire Agreement before the conflict finally came to an end. These agreements were signed at different stages in the conflict and were motivated by different actors and stakeholders from the local, regional and global levels. Before the international community's commitment to the attainment of peace in Sierra Leone, community leaders and a coalition of about sixty non-governmental and civil society groups that was referred to as the National Coordinating Committee for Peace (NCCP), made attempts to talk peace with the RUF. They succeeded in building a national peace constituency which advocated for peaceful resolution of the conflict. They galvanized international support with the then Ivorian President Henry Konan Bedié playing host to the peace talks that culminated in the signing of the Abidjan Peace Accord.

Signed on 30 November 1996, between the Government of Sierra Leone and the RUF, the Abidjan Peace Agreement, called for the following: [8]

1. Immediate cessation of hostilities
2. Amnesty for RUF members
3. The transformation of the RUF into a political movement
4. The withdrawal of Executive Outcomes (EO) within five weeks and regional forces within three months.
5. A process for the encampment, disarmament, demobilization and reintegration of RUF combatants
6. A reduction of the Sierra Leone army with RUF members forming part of the restructured armed forces.
7. Electoral, judicial and police reform, probity in government, protection for human rights, and a focus on rural areas and the urban poor in reconstruction and rehabilitation efforts.

A Commission for the Consolidation of Peace (CCP) was created to oversee the implementation of the agreement, along with a 'Neutral Monitoring Group from the international community.' The peace commission was to supervise and monitor a range of other bodies—a Socio-Economic Forum, annual Citizens' Consultative Conferences, a Multi-Partisan Council, a Trust Fund for the Consolidation of Peace, Demobilization and Resettlement Committee, and a National Budget and Debt Committee. Funding and other support was to be sought from the international community. Whilst peace talks were ongoing in Abidjan, the RUF was engaging the CDF and ECOMOG troops in intense battles to capture more territories to gain tactical advantage and a strong position for negotiations. The fact that hostilities continued even after the signing of the peace agreement revealed that Sankoh was not ready for peace. It became clear that he signed the peace deal to gain recognition, through which he was able to galvanize more support for his armed movement. All his actions were later understood as plans to strengthen his power base and he accused the government of waging all-out war against his movement. With EO out of the country, Sankoh refused to allow the United Nations to deploy peacekeepers and monitors.

The people of Sierra Leone also contributed immensely to the signing of the various peace agreements. They never stopped going to the streets to inform the world of the abuses they were subjected to. They stood their ground in registering their rejection of the RUF and AFRC even when they were fired at. The 2 June 1997 demonstrations in Freetown which resulted in an armed encounter between AFRC/RUF and the ECOMOG troops that were in Sierra Leone was one of such popular protests. This urged ECOWAS foreign ministers (the committee of five) to sign a peace plan with the AFRC in Conakry on 23 October 1997, calling for the restoration of power to the elected Kabbah government by 22 April 1998. The peace plan also called for an immediate cease-fire, disarmament and demobilization of combatants beginning on 1 December 1997, commencement of humanitarian assistance by

14 November 1997, return of refugees and displaced persons, amnesty for the May 1997 participants, and a broad-based government under President Kabbah.

Although the Conakry Peace Plan provided some hope for peace, the AFRC/RUF however did not comply with its implementation. They accused ECOWAS for non-compliance with the agreement and for inviting Alhaji Tejan Kabbah's representatives instead of the AFRC's at its meeting in Lome, Togo where future discussions should have been held. They also accused the SLPP government of training CDF fighters to pursue the war instead of cooperating with them (AFRC) to implement the six month plan. They then called for the immediate release of Foday Sankoh, the non-disarmament of the Sierra Leone Army and the reduction of the role played by the Nigerian contingent in ECOMOG as pre-cursors for a proper implementation of the peace plan. The AFRC expressed overwhelming commitment to the realization of the Peace Plan and suggested the formation of the following committees: Coordinating and General Purpose; Disarmament; Demobilization and Re-integration; Humanitarian Assistance Coordinating; and a Committee for the formation of the broad-based government of national unity.

Many conditions that were put forward by the AFRC/RUF made it evident that they were trying to buy time to extend their stay in power. Their non-compliance to the Conakry Peace Plan resulted in the ECOMOG intervention in February 1998 and the 6 January 1999 invasion of Freetown, were pointers to the fact that a more comprehensive approach and agreement was needed for a peaceful settlement of the Sierra Leone conflict. With over five thousand people dead, one thousand abducted and part of the capital city burnt down and destroyed in less than a month, the international community realized the seriousness of the Sierra Leone conflict. With the help of regional and international organizations (such as ECOWAS, then Organization of African Unity- OAU, the United Nations and the Commonwealth) and the governments of Nigeria, Guinea, Liberia, Burkina Faso, Libya, Togo, the United States and the United Kingdom, a temporary ceasefire was negotiated and this culminated in the signing of the Lomé Peace Agreement. Signed on 7 July 1999 between President Tejan Kabbah and Foday Sankoh of the RUF, and witnessed by the Chairman of ECOWAS, the UN Special Envoy of the Secretary General, and representatives of key regional governments, the Lomé Peace Agreement established the foundation for a lasting peace, return of security and initiation of reconstruction and development for Sierra Leone. Further more, it made provisions for the following:

1. Immediate end to the armed conflict between government forces and the RUF
2. Transformation of the RUF into a political party
3. Sankoh to assume the status of Vice President and become the Chairman of a Commission for Strategic Mineral Resources
4. RUF members to be allowed to hold public office and the formation of a broad-based government of national unity including RUF
5. Establishment of a Commission for the Consolidation of Peace
6. Pardon and amnesty for Sankoh, RUF, ex-AFRC, ex-SLA and CDF combatants
7. Establishment of a Constitutional Review Committee
8. Commitment to constitutional elections and the establishment National Electoral Commission
9. Replacement of ECOMOG by a UN peacekeeping force
10. Guaranteed safety, security and freedom of movement for peacekeeping personnel
11. All ex-combatants to be disarmed, demobilized and reintegrated
12. New national army to include ex-RUF, CDF and SLA combatants
13. Withdrawal of all mercenaries from Sierra Leone
14. Unconditional and immediate release of prisoners-of-war

and abductees

15. Voluntary repatriation and reintegration of refugees and internally displaced persons
16. The establishment of a Truth and Reconciliation Commission to deal with human rights violations since 1991
17. Programme of post-war resettlement, rehabilitation and reconstruction and the rehabilitation of war victims.

Among the numerous players involved in shaping the Lomé Peace Agreement, the Inter-Religious Council of Sierra Leone (IRCSL) stands out as the most highly visible and effective non-governmental bridge builder between the warring factions. They were part of NCCP and were very instrumental in all attempts to a negotiated settlement to free a population devastated and divided by violence. Despite these relatively favourable provisions in the agreement, and the powers given to Sankoh, he was still not satisfied and committed to the peace process. He refused to disarm his fighters, and ordered the abduction of over five hundred United Nations peacekeepers who ventured into RUF-held territories in their bid to deploy throughout the country to implement and monitor the peace agreement. It became evident that Sankoh wanted nothing less than total control of the country and was not ready for any peace deal, no matter what benefit it might offer him. This incident derailed the peace process and pointed to the fact that a reaffirmation of the commitment to the Lomé Peace Agreement was required.

With Sankoh in detention after ordering his RUF guards to shoot demonstrators in front of his house on 8 May 2000, the RUF and the government reaffirmed their commitment to the peace process. Organized by Parliamentarians and supported by civil society groups, the 8 May demonstration attracted citizens from all works of life who took to the streets demanding the release of the abducted United Nations peacekeepers. Although twenty one of the demonstrators were killed, they succeeded in registering their dissatisfaction of

Sankoh's refusal to disarm his combatants and demanded the RUF's commitment to the peace process. The signing of the Abuja Ceasefire Agreement between the Government of Sierra Leone and the RUF under its interim leader, Issa Sesay, was the agreement to this commitment. This agreement reaffirmed the determination of both the Government of Sierra Leone and the RUF to establish sustainable peace, stability and security in Sierra Leone and their commitment to the Lomé Peace Agreement of 7 July 1999 as the framework for the restoration of genuine and lasting peace to the country. It committed both Kabbah and Issa Sesay to the following: [9]

1. An observation of a cease-fire and to halt hostilities from 10 November 2000.
2. United Nations Mission in Sierra Leone's supervision and monitoring of the cease-fire, investigation and reporting of any acts of cease-fire violation.
3. United Nations Mission in Sierra Leone (UNAMSIL) deployment of its troops and other personnel throughout Sierra Leone including the diamond producing areas in the discharge of its responsibilities.
4. The restoration of civil authority throughout the entire territory of Sierra Leone, to ensure free movement of persons and goods, unimpeded movement of humanitarian agencies, and of refugees and displaced persons.
5. The immediate return of all weapons, ammunitions and other equipment seized by the RUF and the Disarmament, Demobilization and Reintegration Programme.
6. The Government of Sierra Leone's commitment to accelerate the process of restructuring and training of the Sierra Leone armed forces open to all Sierra Leoneans eligible to enroll.

Due to Sesay's cooperation and commitment to the process, the RUF disarmed with the SLA and CDF and went through the demobilization and reintegration phases of the DDR programme. This led to relative stability and peace amidst several hiccups. Normalcy was returned and access was granted to previously RUF-held territories. The government then speeded efforts to these areas in an effort to rebuild the country.

Current Scenario

The conflict officially ended over six years ago leaving the country in total ruins. The challenge was then on the rebuilding of the country and the reformation of its institutions. The recovery, rehabilitation and reconstruction processes were then aimed at effecting short, medium and long term changes in the country and its structures and systems. Although much was achieved with the United Nations mission being considered one of the United Nations' success stories, the country is still faced with numerous challenges in addressing the issues that caused the conflict. This can be attributed to the weak state institutions and structures to manage the change process and government-led projects and programmes aimed at restoring hope for ordinary citizens. However, the United Nations Integrated Office in Sierra Leone (UNIOSIL) which replaced the United Nations Mission in Sierra Leone (UNAMSIL) after the last batch of peacekeepers left in December 2005 is helping the government in peace-building and economic recovery. They are managing the US$ 35 million received in March 2007 from the United Nations Peace-building Fund, granted by the Peace-building Commission. They are coordinating efforts aimed at achieving sustainable peace and good governance.

The country is making slow but steady progress in addressing some pertinent issues linked to good governance and economic development. The peaceful handover of power by the incumbent SLPP government to the opposition APC party which won the 8 September 2007 Presidential Run Off elections points to the fact that Sierra Leone is strengthening its democratic values. At present, there is a diplomatic 'problem in the making' between Sierra Leone and Guinea over the eastern border town of Yenga. Guinea was supposed to have withdrawn its soldiers from the town after the end of the conflict but they are still there. A collaborative settlement of this issue is the best option to prevent a boarder crisis between the two countries.

The Special Court for Sierra Leone (SCSL) which was established to try those who bear the greatest responsibility for crimes committed during the conflict is yet to complete the sentencing of the remaining indictees. Citizens are also looking forward to the implementation of the recommendations of the TRC, the establishment of the Special Fund for War Victims and a full fledged reparations programme in line with the recommendations of the TRC. Their hope now is on the current President, Ernest Bai Koroma and the APC government after Kabbah's SLPP government failed to do so. These are meant to address victims' suffering as well as provide them with material benefits. To date the government's National Commission for Social Action (NaCSA) which was identified as the implementing agency had not utilized the initial funds that have been allocated for this programme from the UN Peace-building Fund. The late establishment of the National Human Rights Commission (HRC) has not helped the situation. However, citizens are hoping that, as a follow-up institution to the TRC, the HRC will facilitate the implementations of these important programmes aimed at addressing their concerns and restore their dignity.

It is an open-secret that the war and its consequences added many more problems and challenges to those who had plagued Sierra Leoneans since the 1970s. With seventy-two thousand four hundred and ninety ex-combatants disarmed, unemployment became worse than it has ever been. For the fifty-one thousand one hundred and twenty-two who received reintegration support, it became almost impossible for them to get jobs and opportunities to practice their skills even as apprentices. The problem is especially acute in urban areas and between the twenty to twenty-four years of age. Three of every ten young men are neither formally employed nor in school. Poverty is heavily concentrated in the rural and other urban areas outside Freetown. Roughly 70 per cent of the population lived below poverty line in 2004. The population below the poverty line in Freetown in 2003/04 was estimated at 15 per cent, compared to 79 per cent in the rural areas and 70 per cent in other urban areas. Sustained job creation will require more investments in infrastructure.

Amidst numerous challenges, there have been substantial economic growths propelled by remittances and investments from the Sierra Leone expatriate community, selected mining investments, notably in rutile and bauxite, debt relief and by foreign aid. Most fundamentally, in December 2006, Sierra Leone reached the Completion Point under the Enhanced Heavily Indebted Poor Countries (HIPC) initiative and, also gained additional relief under the Multilateral Debt Relief Initiative (MDRI). This total relief will amount to roughly US$ 1.6 billion spread over thirty years. According to World Bank estimates, real GDP grew by an estimated 6.8 per cent between 2000 -2007 despite rising oil prices. This allowed total exports to grow by 28 per cent in 2006 followed by a healthy 11 percent in 2007. The 10 per cent import growth in 2006 also contracted to 4 per cent in 2007 as the large mining rehabilitation projects were completed. The external current account deficit (including official transfers) therefore is estimated to have decreased to 2.4 per cent of GDP in 2007 from 5.7 percent of GDP in 2006.

Despite these increased growth levels, expectation of the international community and the people of Sierra Leone that post-war development policies, programmes and projects will improve Sierra Leone's health, education and economic standards have not been yet met. The causes of the conflict are still visible and many Sierra Leoneans, including ex-combatants continue to draw a balance between revenue from the country's natural resources, national revenues, aids donated and the standard of living of the average Sierra

Leonean. Citizens are not pleased and feel that they are not benefiting from the country's wealth and development programmes. There hope is on the APC government whom they expect to change the situation for the better. Whether the expectations of ordinary citizens will be met depends on the government's policies and their commitment to the development of the country.

Conclusion

The manner in which the RUF executed their campaign explains the fact that they did not focus on liberating the people of Sierra Leone or on the creation of the democratic state they had envisioned. It clearly showed that they were more interested in mobilizing a strong unified force through their construction of a common interest and identity among their fighters. This was what sustained their willingness to fight the war to its infinity. The notion that they had a 'common opponent' created new bonds and associations amongst them even though they were previously unrelated or had never met before. Identifying a 'common concern' allowed them not only to realize a common interest but also to reaffirm their shared identity that had some link to their situation before the war. This worked because most, if not all, RUF fighters were deprived and unemployed youths who, through their possession of arms and weapons, had an illusion of power and importance that generated both recognition and remuneration for them. The conflict then provided them 'employment' through their illegitimate income-generating activities they were involved in.

The economic costs caused a drop in GNP as resources and manpower were redirected away from productive endeavours. The workforce was scattered, either enlisted in the conflict or otherwise displaced as refugees and war and sabotage left infrastructures in ruins. Revenues from the natural resources were diverted from productive endeavours to purchase arms and pay troops. Other funds that could clearly have been spent on development activities were diverted to fight the war. If these funds that were spent in fighting the war as well as those spent on humanitarian assistance and efforts towards negotiated settlements, stability, recovery and peace-building were used in developing the different sectors of government, Sierra Leone's economic growth would have been astronomical.

The deliberate and arbitrary killings and the gross human rights abuses civilians suffered during the decade-long conflict was also too much for a population that had suffered injustices and deprivation from the various governments. With such experiences, the war may continue in people's minds for years, decades, or possibly generations. To address only the material restoration and physical needs of the population denies the shattered emotional worlds, ignores the destruction of basic human trust and benevolence, and leaves the moral and spiritual consequences of war unaddressed. Post-conflict recovery, rehabilitation and reconstruction processes should go beyond institutional, infrastructural and material focus to addressing issues aimed at rebuilding broken relationships, trusts, confidence, dignity and unity. A new construction of society, identities, concerns, and the creation of a new enemy-the challenge to build a new society, would reduce the risk of a return of old abuses.

Generally, conflict is viewed as a negative endeavour to make things right. This is based on the notion that conflict is often driven by a sense of grievance, be it scarcity, inequality, cultural or moral differences, or the distribution of power. Despite the humanitarian and material catastrophe caused by conflict, in its true sense, it has some benefits and positive elements and it was inevitable for the Sierra Leone conflict not to have some positive elements and outcomes. The conflict exposed the many problems that had plagued the country since the 1960s and provided a means of addressing these concerns. It was the engine of social teaching without which, attitudes, behaviours, and relationships would have stayed the same, regardless of whether they were fair or not. Although conflict helps to fight injustices and reshape institutions and systems, the challenge is then to realize its benefits in such a way that the huge costs associated with it are minimized. Disadvantaged or aggrieved groups should thus explore peaceful means for addressing their concerns as opposed to violent encounters. However, more research needs to be done to help explain the reason why some groups choose violent responses to deal with injustices and inequalities instead of embarking on peaceful struggles to make things right.

Notes

1. www.fas.org/irp/world/para/docs/footpaths.htm. (A. O. 12 April 2008).
2. www.wluml.org/english/newsfulltxt.shtml?cmd%5B157%5D=x-157-555117. (A. O. 15 April 2008).
3. www.hrw.org/backgrounder/africa/sl-bck0226.htm. (A. O. 18 April 2008).
4. majorityrights.com/index.php/weblog/comments/freetown_massacre_of_the_ruf/. (A. O. 12 April 2008).
5. See, Alan Bones, "Case Study: Peacekeeping in Sierra Leone," in Rob McRae and Don Hubert, eds., *Human Security and the New Diplomacy: Protecting People, Promoting Peace* (Montreal: McGill-Queen's University Press, 2001), pp. 55-64
6. http://www.brentstirton.com/projects/bushwives/body.html. (A. O. 12 April 2008).
7. Amnesty International. Sierra Leone 1998—A Year of Atrocities against Civilians. November 1998.
8. www.sc-sl.org/abidjanaccord.html. (A. O. 14 April 2008).
9. www.sierra-leone.org/lomeaccord.html. (A. O. 12 April 2008).

14

Darfur Conflict: Costs and Politics

Seema Shekhawat

The conflict that began in Sudan in February of 2003 is confined to the Darfur (an Arabic word literally meaning realm of the Fur) region of western part of this African country with local, regional as well as global implications. The region has been in a state of humanitarian emergency since 2003. This chapter attempts to study the conflict from a humanitarian perspective. It analyses the roots of the conflict, and then proceeds to highlight its costs and finally makes a brief study of the attempts by the international bodies to address the conflict and difficulties in the process. Like some of other African conflicts, it can be noted, the Darfur conflict too has ethnic, economic as well as international dimensions. It is one of the most recent conflicts, or to put in a different way, it is one of the first conflicts in 21st century with its roots deeply embedded in 20th century or further past.

History of the Conflict

Darfur was an independent sultanate for several hundred years before it was incorporated into Sudan by Anglo-Egyptian forces. The long tradition of independence has been a continuing source of tension between Darfur and the rest of Sudan. Within Anglo-Egyptian Sudan, Darfur was neglected and bulk of resources was devoted toward Khartoum and Blue Nile Province. The trend almost continued after Sudan got independence in 1956, leading to a rising sense of deprivation and negligence among the natives of Darfur. However, the economic marginalization of the region took a dangerous political turn in 1968 elections. The factionalism within the ruling Umma Party led candidates to use the theory of 'divide and rule' to gain political leverage over the adversaries. The political leaders divided the people by blaming nomadic Arabs for underdevelopment on the one side and appealing to the Arab nomads of Darfur region to support their fellow Nile Arabs on the other. The hitherto non-existing 'Arab-African dichotomy' was exacerbated with involvement of foreign powers.

The attempts of President Muammar al-Gaddafi of Libya to establish an Arab belt across the Sahel by propagating the ideology of Arab supremacy also added fuel to the fire. [1] To quote a report, "The deep causes of the rebellion lie in the feeling of superiority and cultural elitism of the 'Arabs' and of resentment and perceived oppression and neglect on the part of the 'Africans.' The 'African' rebels point out that in spite of being a loyal part of the Muslim north, Darfur is in fact badly off in terms of infrastructure, education and economic development as the Christian south." [2]

The conflict, thus, has many interwoven causes ranging from decades of economic marginalization to political complicity, from climate change to environmental degradation, from struggle for over increasingly scarce farmland and water resources to ethnic assertions. On 16 June 2007, United Nations Secretary General Ban Ki-Moon pointed, "amid the diverse social and political causes, the Darfur conflict began as an ecological crisis, arising at least in part from climate change.... derives, to some degree, from man-made global warming." [3] The decades of drought has brought about the desertification of the region. The 1983 and 1984 droughts in the region killed an estimated 95,000 people out of a population of 3.1 million. This accompanied by increase in population has led to scarcity of resources and consequent struggle to control the scarce resources.

A United Nations Environment Programme (UNEP) report has pointed that the scale of historical climate change, as recorded in Northern Darfur, is almost unprecedented and the reduction in rainfall has turned millions of hectares of already marginal semi-desert grazing land into desert. The impact of climate change is considered to be directly related to the conflict in the region, as desertification has added significantly to the stress on the livelihoods of pastoralist societies, forcing them to move south to find pasture. The study published in 2007 thus suggested the genesis of the conflict pre-dates 2003 and is to be found in failing rains and creeping desertification. [4]

The desertification of the areas compelled the Arab nomadic tribes of the region to stretch their area. Consequently, they moved further south to ensure continuous supply of water and grazing lands for their livestock, a place occupied by Black African farming tribes namely the Fur, Zaghawa and Masalit. There started a struggle to control the resources. With the nomadic Arab tribes getting the support of the government of Sudan, the conflict in Darfur assumed violent proportion in February 2003 when two groups, the Zaghawa-backed Justice and Equality Movement (JEM) and the Sudan Liberation Movement (SLM), mainly comprising Fur and Massaleit tribes, accused the government of oppression and exploitation. On one side of the conflict are the Janjaweed (literally means devils on horseback), an Arab militia group comprising largely of the Arab Abbala tribes. Though the government of Sudan denies its support to the Janjaweed, there are many reports of the official complicity in terms of providing not only the logistic and financial assistance but also the military support. On the other side, there are multiple rebel groups including the Fur, Zaghawa and Massaleit ethnic groups. The ongoing fight for over five years has turned the region into the site of one of the most violent conflicts.

The current conflict that started in early 2003 reached a critical point on 25 April when the SLM rebels attacked el-Fasher, the provincial capital and killed 72 troops of the garrison besides destroying four aircrafts and capturing

General Ibrahim Bushra, the garrison commander. The reaction of the government was a combination of panic, accusation (Israel, the United States, the Sudan People's Liberation Army and Eritrea were all held responsible for the crisis) and denial of the political reality. [5] During May and June 2003, the fighting grew in intensity and government forces reacted with violent attacks on civilian population. The Sudanese government besides using army to suppress the rebellion is also accused of arming the Janjaweed and organizing joint attacks against the Fur, Zaghawa, and Massaleit ethnic groups. The government mounted a campaign of aerial bombardment supporting ground attacks by the Janjaweed. Air power was used for indiscriminate bombing and machine-gunning of civilians. As part of its strategy, the government of Sudan also destroyed the means of livelihood of the natives-filled the wells, killed the livestock and destroyed foodstuff stores.

On 5 May 2006, Minni Minnawi's faction of the main rebel group, SLM signed a peace deal with the Sudanese government. Other rebel groups refused to sign the agreement called Darfur Peace Agreement. The situation, thus, was further complicated with the fragmentation in the rebel groups and consequent rise in the number of the rebel groups with different demands. Currently, there are around two dozen rebel groups. There were more than 30 armed groups by the end of 2007, including armed groups representing Arabs. The conflict has also spilled over Sudan's borders into Chad and Central African Republic.

As of now, the government of Sudan continues carrying out massive air strikes in the region. Government-backed militias also continue to carry out large-scale attacks across Darfur. The rebel groups too wage their fights. Amidst all these fights, the civilian population is the ultimate sufferer. To quote a report of International Crisis Group, "The NCP (National Congress Party) wants Darfur in chaos to limit the room for an opposition to emerge, while resettling key allies on cleared land and defying Security Council resolutions by integrating its Janjaweed irregulars into official security structures instead of disarming them. Rebel DPA signatories, particularly the Sudan Liberation Army faction of Minni Minawi (SLA/MM), have been responsible for attacks on civilians, humanitarians, the AU mission (AMIS) and some of the violence in the internally displaced person camps. Their leaders have been given government jobs and land and, as ardent supporters of the status quo and without a clearly defined role in the new negotiations, are potential spoilers. Rebel movements that did not sign have further splintered and only just begun tentative steps toward reunifying their ranks. Many have boycotted the talks and increased military action. As they divide along tribal lines, their messages become more fragmented and less representative of constituencies they claim to speak for." [6]

The Cost

The violent methods used by all parties involved in the conflict bring grim consequences for the millions of civilians. As part of its operations against the rebels, government forces waged a systematic campaign of 'ethnic cleansing' against civilians who are members of the same ethnic groups as the rebels. The Government forces and allied militia are accused of committing widespread and consistent war crimes and crimes against humanity including mass killing, torture, mass rape, loot, summary executions and arbitrary detention. Sudanese government forces and the Janjaweed militias burned and destroyed hundreds of villages, caused tens of thousands of civilian deaths, displaced millions of people, and raped and assaulted thousands of women and girls. [7]

According to Lydia Polgreen, "The battle in Darfur has long been a proxy, fought with villages and towns as battlefields and civilians as its primary victims. Rebel groups - at least half a dozen factions and splinter groups have surfaced since the conflict began- occupy villages, which the government attacks by air with Antonov bombers and gunships. The rumble of the aircraft gives the fighters plenty of time to escape, but the less-mobile civilians bear the brunt of the aerial attacks." [8] The rebel groups too have been reported to be guilty of human rights violations. The following quotation from a Human Rights Watch report lucidly summarizes the current situation in Darfur wherein all the parties involved are playing the game using civilians as pawns. The report said, "While the Darfur conflict is often characterized as a clash between 'Arab' and 'non-Arab' African people, this radically oversimplifies and mischaracterizes the conflict. Rather, the ways in which both the rebel movements and primarily the Sudanese government have manipulated ethnic tensions have served to polarize much of the Darfur population along ethnic lines.

These tensions create shifting alliances among the government, Arab and non- Arab tribes, and rebel groups as well as internecine conflicts among competing Arab groups and among rebel factions. Rebels and former rebels have directly targeted civilians from other non-Arab groups and attacked African Union (AU) peacekeepers and humanitarian workers trying to provide assistance to Darfurians. These subsidiary conflicts themselves contribute to the mass displacement and deaths of people. The government continues to stoke the chaos and, in some areas, exploit inter-communal tensions that escalate into open hostilities, apparently in an effort to 'divide and rule' and maintain military and political dominance over the region." [9]

The following estimates on deaths in Darfur conflict portray the horrendous character of the violence. The Sudanese government claims the figure of conflict related deaths is only 10,000, which appears to be gross under estimation. In its April 2005 report, the Coalition for International Justice (CIJ) estimated that 400,000 people in Darfur had died since the conflict began with on an average 500 people dying everyday. The Washington-based CIJ and experts from Northwestern and

Toronto Universities estimated Sudanese government forces and their proxy militia have killed 140,000 people and 250,000 Darfur civilians have died from disease, starvation or exposure. [10] In the same year, the United Nations Emergency Relief estimated 10,000 dying each month from disease and other preventable causes, excluding deaths due to ethnic violence. [11]

In September 2004, the World Health Organization estimated there had been 50,000 deaths in Darfur since the beginning of the conflict mostly due to hunger. An updated estimate the following month put the number of deaths for the 6-month period from March to October 2004 due to starvation and disease at 70,000. In May 2005, the Centre for Research on the Epidemiology of Disasters (CRED) stated approximately 134,000 total deaths in Darfur and Eastern Chad over the 17 months from September 2003 to January 2005. Of these deaths, 120,000 were excess deaths directly attributable to the conflict, 35,000 of which were violent deaths. The US State Department estimated a possible range of 98,000-181,000 total deaths over 23 months - from March 2003 to January 2005. Estimates of excess deaths due to the conflict ranged from 63,000-146,000 over the same period. [12] The United Nations puts the death toll at roughly 300,000. "The conflict in Darfur is deteriorating, with full deployment of a new peacekeeping force delayed until 2009 and no prospect of a political settlement for a war that has killed perhaps 300,000 people in five years," U.N. officials said on 22 April 2008. However, Egeland, the former U.N. humanitarian chief, estimated in 2006 that 200,000 people had lost their lives because of the conflict, from violence, disease and malnutrition. He puts the current figures to be around 400,000. [13] Humanitarian assistance in Darfur continues to be at risk of collapse due to continuing violence.

Displacement is one of the major contributions of conflict situations, and Darfur is no exception to this phenomenon. As per a United Nations report of 2005, there were about 1.6

million internally displaced persons and about 200,000 persons took refuge in neighbouring Chad. As of April 2008, some 2.5 million displaced people-- mostly farmers and villagers from non-Arab groups - live in camps in Darfur and more than 200,000 are living as refugees in Chad. The displaced are entirely dependent on international humanitarian assistance. In many areas they cannot go far from the camps due to fear of the attacks. Displaced women are frequently raped and assaulted. To quote a report of Amnesty International, "Rape continued to be widespread, especially of displaced women and girls collecting firewood outside their camps. Sometimes women were beaten, or attacked but managed to escape. They rarely reported what happened to the police. Men continued to leave the task of collecting firewood to women because the men feared being killed if they ventured outside the camps. Several internally displaced women, including teenage girls, were raped as they went outside IDP camps in Zalingei to collect firewood in the second half of 2007." [14]

The displaced also cannot return to their homes due to the continuing presence of militias in their native places. Because of the widespread displacement of farmers and disruption of trade, the economy of Darfur has been severely disrupted. Around 2 million people are 'conflict-affected' and in dire need of assistance because the conflict has damaged the local economy. There have also been many incidents of government forces and Janjaweed destroying and looting mosques, killing imams and others seeking refuge inside mosques and desecrating the Koran while attacking civilian villages. For example, Human Rights Watch documented in just one small area of West Darfur Sudanese government forces and the militia destroyed 62 mosques in late 2003 and early 2004. [15]

The government of Sudan is accused of gagging independent media and in Khartoum and Darfur journalists and lawyers are targeted for revealing the details and extent of human rights violations. The government adopted a policy of killing or imprisoning the witnesses to its atrocities on the non

Arab groups. The Sudan security forces have been blamed of carrying out summary executions in the region. The government is also accused of using every possible excuse to stop any humanitarian aid reaching Darfur. For example, on 16 November 2003, it refused to unload the US food aid bound for Darfur on the pretext that the cereals were genetically modified.

Again, in early January 2004 a humanitarian conference in Geneva was organized to collect relief for Darfur. Despite promising access to the needy in Darfur, the government refused at the last moment with the plea to prevent internationalization of the conflict. [16] The government has also been accused of tampering with evidence such as mass graves to eliminate their forensic values. In March 2007, the United Nations accused the government of orchestrating and taking part in 'gross violations.' The United Nations peacekeepers too have been targeted. Recently seven peacekeepers were killed by 'unidentified culprits' but many do not rule out the possibility of the government complicity in targeting the peacekeepers.

Role of the United Nations and Global Powers

The United Nations has since the inception of the 'world's greatest humanitarian crisis' has taken several steps to address the conflict and the humanitarian issues related to it but the political games played by national and international players have further complicated the situation. Though many refer to the crisis in Darfur as a case of genocide, the United Nations did not recognize the killings as genocide on technical grounds but declared the happenings there as highly inhuman. In a report published in January 2005, the United Nations accepted the fact of massive violations of human rights and humanitarian law in Darfur but did not call it genocide on the ground 'genocidal intent appears to be missing.' In a recent report it described attacks by Sudanese forces on Darfur villagers in early 2008 as 'violations of international humanitarian and human rights law.'

In early 2007, a High Level Mission led by Nobel Prize Winner Jody Williams was set up to analyze the situation and work out modalities for working with the government of Sudan to put an end to the critical humanitarian situation. However, the Mission was not allowed to enter the Sudanese territory by the government. In its report of March 2007 based on the facts collected from Ethiopia and Chad, the Mission noted the failure of government of Sudan to fulfill its responsibility. Later, the United Nations Human Rights Council appointed seven human rights special rapporteurs to form a group of experts on Darfur.

This group included: the special rapporteur on the situation of human rights, the special rapporteur on extrajudicial, summary or arbitrary executions; the special representative of the Secretary-General for children and armed conflict; the special rapporteur on violence against women, its causes and consequences; the special representative of the Secretary General on the situation of human rights defenders; the representative of the Secretary General on the human rights of internally displaced persons and the special rapporteur on the question of torture and other cruel, inhuman or degrading treatment or punishment. In June 2007, the group of experts issued a list of recommendations for the government of Sudan and urged for implementation. On 11 December 2007, the group of experts in its final report concluded that the Government's implementation of human rights recommendations has been largely inadequate. [17]

Sudanese government has shown reluctance in allowing the United Nations peacekeeping troops to the country. It has more than once failed to provide needed support to the African Union and the United Nations in their efforts to restore peace on the pretext of securing its sovereignty. On 31 August 2006, the United Nations Security Council approved Resolution 1706 that called for a new peacekeeping force called United Nations-African Union Mission in Darfur (UNAMID). Sudan strongly objected and proclaimed that it would consider the peacekeepers as foreign invaders. Recently under intense international pressure, the government allowed a joint United Nations-African Union Mission of 26,000 people to help protect civilians. This has been considered an important step towards the peace restoration in the region. The mission has replaced the African Union Mission in Sudan (AMIS) that was itself in trouble due to a variety of factors ranging from lack of logistics to meager finance and from clear mandate to insufficient staff. The expectations from UNAMID are high from a peace perspective however it remains to be seen if it can deliver accordingly owing to many obstacles that it may have to confront.

To quote a Human Rights Watch report, "Expectations are high for what UNAMID could accomplish, but it will face many challenges. It is therefore imperative that alongside the peacekeeping operation, the international community maintains continual pressure on the Government of Sudan, as well as other parties to the conflict, to reverse abusive policies and practices that contribute to civilian insecurity. These policies include deliberate and indiscriminate attacks on civilians, continuing support for abusive militia/Janjaweed and the failure to disarm them, obstructing the deployment and work of AMIS peacekeepers and humanitarian workers, failing to address the culture of impunity (including by failing to abolish laws providing immunity or otherwise strengthen the justice system) and refusing to cooperate with the International Criminal Court, and allowing the consolidation of ethnic cleansing through land use and occupation." [18]

The United Nations has also set up a sanctions committee and a panel of experts to investigate individuals who violate the arms embargo, commit human rights abuses, or impede the peace process. The move however has not been very successful owing to the fact that despite the widespread continuation of the violence sanctions have been imposed only on four individuals and none of them was senior government official. However, referring the situation to the International Criminal Court (ICC) is considered an important step. On 14 July 2008, the ICC's chief prosecutor on Darfur, Luis Moreno-Ocampo, filed ten criminal charges against Sudan's President Omar al-Bashir for sponsoring war crimes and crimes against humanity. The ICC's prosecutors have claimed that al-Bashir 'masterminded and implemented a plan to destroy in substantial part' three tribal groups the Fur, Masalit and Zaghawa in Darfur. Al-Bashir is not likely to face trial in The Hague at least in the near future, as Sudan rejects the jurisdiction of ICC.

Despite passing an array of resolutions on Darfur over a period of five years the situation in the region continues to be critical. In a report of 2006, Minority Rights Group pointed out the United Nations and other international bodies have fallen short of their duty in preventing the Darfur crisis, adding few lessons appear to have been drawn from their ineptitude during the Rwandan Genocide. To quote Mark Lattimer, the executive director of the Group, "Darfur would just not be in this situation had the UN systems got its act together after Rwanda: their action was too little too late....this level of crisis, the killings, rape and displacement could have been foreseen and avoided... The warning signs that the conflict was worsening went ignored and the information that trickled in was not effectively used by the international community to prevent the catastrophe." [19]

Besides the Minority Rights Group allegations, the non-cooperative attitude of some of the major powers is a main reason for the failure of United Nations to bring back the peace in the region. There is lack of unanimity over Sudan issue in the Security Council. Russia and China have often supported the Sudanese government because of their ideological commitments and economic interests. The Sudanese government buys and receives military supplies from several countries, including China and Russia. The oil resources in the country have also prompted countries like China to support the government of Sudan. China imports around 47 per cent of its oil from Sudan. It is argued by the advocates of human rights that the government of Sudan uses the oil revenues in buying arms to commit atrocities against the civilians in the Darfur region. The oil politics in itself has also contributed to large-scale human rights violation in Sudan since the natives are removed from the oil rich areas for exploration. There has been evidence of the Sudanese government's murder of civilians to facilitate the extraction of oil. The Civilian Protection Monitoring Team, which investigates attacks in southern Sudan, has pointed, "As the Government of Sudan (GoS) sought to clear the way for oil exploration and to create a cordon sanitaire around the oil fields, vast tracts of the Western Upper Nile Region in southern Sudan became the focus of extensive military operations." [20]

In early 2008 an NGO, Human Rights First, has claimed that over 90 per cent of the light weapons currently being imported by Sudan and used in the conflict are from China. [21] But, according to Stockholm International Peace Research Institute, between 2003 and 2007 Sudan received 87 per cent of its major conventional weapons from Russia and 8 per cent from China. [22] Though China has cited the Stockholm report many times to deny its role in fueling the Darfur conflict, the charges against the Asian power are only increasing. A BBC investigative documentary telecast in July 2008 titled 'China Fueling War in Darfur,' shows Chinese Dongfeng trucks in western Darfur, and alleges that their markings indicate they were exported to Sudan in 2005 after the UN arms embargo had been imposed. It also cites unnamed sources that China was training pilots for jet fighters exported to Sudan. [23] The training of pilots is a shocking revelation from two points. First, the terms of the arms embargo imposed on Sudan cover not only the supply of weapons, military vehicles, paramilitary equipment. It also covers training any technical assistance, so the training of pilots falls within the scope of the embargo. Second, as already mentioned the government of Sudan has used its air power heavily to counter the rebels in the Darfur region. Training of its pilots is likely to be used for combating the rebels.

According to some reports, China has promised Sudan of using veto in the UN Security Council to protect Khartoum from sanctions. China has so far remained successful to thwart every stern United Nations move on Darfur to protect its interests in Sudan. An international campaign has already started to pressure China to refrain from becoming a catalyst in the Darfur conflict. Many international renowned people have called for pressurizing China to relook its Sudan policy. Recently, the noted US film director Steven Spielberg has withdrawn from the assignment of artistic adviser for the opening and closing ceremonies of the 2008 Olympic Games in Beijing. In a statement, he accused China of not doing enough to pressure Sudan to end the 'continuing human suffering' in the troubled western Darfur region. Rebel groups in Darfur said this was exactly the kind of pressure that was needed to get Beijing to change its policy towards the Sudanese government. [24] But, the pressure has not been able to deliver expected results. Recently, Russia and China are seeking delay in any action against Sudanese President on charges of genocide on the pretext it could have an adverse impact on the peace process in the region. The situation remains fluid with adverse impact on peace attempts, thus lingering the fragile scenario and torment for the common people in Darfur.

The Darfur conflict is relatively a recent conflict in the post-cold war world order. Its disastrous effects on civilians in particular and on broader aspects of African as well global peace and development are far reaching. Despite the United Nations attempts to bring the violent elements in Sudan to justice, the complex power politics at the apex international body has repeatedly thwarted such moves. The horrendous crimes and its enormous costs both orchestrated by the government as well as rebels is one of the crude realities of the emerging world order in which the African nations due to their very socio-economic conditions and ethnic composition have borne the brunt more ferociously. However, in this dim background of things, it appears tragic while the ICC attempts to bring the Sudan dictator to book for his crimes, some of the major powers would support him for their interests. It appears the crude realism motivated these countries to support the Sudanese government at the cost of human security and global peace and development. Ultimately, the people of Darfur are the sufferers, and their suffering in coming years would likely continue or further aggravated if international players fail in their responsibility.

Notes

1. Gérard Prunier, *Darfur: The Ambiguous Genocide* (New York: Cornell University Press, 2005), p. 52-53.
2. "The Darfur Conflict: Crimes against Humanity in Sudan." http://www.crimesofwar.org/africa-mag/afr_02_darfur.html. (A. O. 2 March 2008).
3. Ban Ki Moon, "A Climate Culprit in Darfur," *Washington Post*, 16 June 2007.
4. "Environmental Degradation Triggering Tensions and Conflict in Sudan." http://www.unep.org/Documents.Multilingual/Default.asp?DocumentID=512&ArticleID=5621&l=en. (A. O. 23 April 2008).
5. "The Darfur Conflict, Crimes against Humanity in Sudan," n. 2.
6. "Crisis in Darfur," *International Crisis Group*, http://www.crisisgroup.org/home/index.cfm?id=3060. (A. O. 6 July 2008).
7. "Q & A: Crisis in Darfur." http://www.hrw.org/english/docs/2004/05/05/darfur8536.htm (A. O. 12 February 2008).
8. Lydia Polgreen, "Grim New Turn Likely to Harden Darfur Conflict," *New York Times*, 23 October 2003.
9. "Darfur 2007 Chaos by Design, Peacekeeping Challenges for AMIS and UNAMID," *Human Rights Watch*, vol. 19, no. 15(A), pp. 5-6.

10. "New Analysis Claims Darfur Deaths Near 400,000." http://coalitionfordarfur.blogspot.com/2005/04/new-analysis-claims-darfur-deaths-near.html. (A. O. 4 April 2008).
11. "UN's Darfur Death Estimate Soars," *BBC News*, 14 March 2005.
12. Debarati Guha-Sapir, Olivier Degomme and Mark Phelan, "Darfur: Counting the Deaths: Mortality Estimates from Multiple Survey Data," *Centre for Research on the Epidemiology of Disasters*, Brussels, 26 May 2005, p. 6.
13. "U.N. Says Darfur Conflict Getting Worse with Perhaps 300,000," 22 April 2008. http://www.foxnews.com/story/0,2933,352205,00.html. (A. O. 24 April 2008).
14. *Sudan-Amnesty International Report 2008.* http://thereport.amnesty.org/eng/regions/africa/sudan. (A. O. 23 May 2008).
15. "Q & A: Crisis in Darfur," n. 7.
16. "The Darfur Conflict: Crimes against Humanity in Sudan," n. 2.
17. "Human Rights Situations that Require the Council's Attention." http://www2.ohchr.org/english/bodies/hrcouncil/docs/6session/A.HRC.6.19AEV_en.pdf. (A. O. 22 March 2008).
18. "Darfur 2007…," n. 9.
19. "UN could have Averted Darfur Crisis – MRG." http://www.iol.co.za/index.php?set_id=1&click_id=136&art_id=iol1160956523318B235 (A. O. 22 March 2008).
20. "Final Report of Investigation: Violence Against Civilians Along the Bentiu-Leer-Adok Road," *Civilian Protection Monitoring Team.* http://www.ecosonline.org/back/pdf_reports/%2F2003%2Foilroadfinal%2Edoc. (A. O. 12 May 2008).
21. "90% of the Weapons for Darfur Come from China." http://www.asianews.it/index.php?l=en&art=11773. (A. O. 12 April 2008).
22. "SIPRI Arms Transfers Data for 2007." http://www.sipri.org/contents/armstrad/PR_AT_data_2007.html/view?searchterm=darfur. (A. O. 23 May 2008).
23. Hilary Andersson, "China is Fuelling War in Darfur,'" *BBC News*, 13 July 2008.
24. "Spielberg in Darfur Snub to China," *BBC News*, 13 February 2008.

Index

Index

A

ABAKO (Alliance des Bakongo), 218
Abdurajak Janjalani, 182
Abidjan Peace Agreement, 260
Abuja Ceasefire Agreement, 260, 265
Abu Sayyaf, 182, 183
Afghanistan, 14, 73, 76, 77, 150, 157, 182
Africa Growth and Opportunities Act (AGOA), 212
African Union Mission in Sudan (AMIS), 282
Agung Network, 181
Akbar Bugti, 68, 71, 72
Akhnoor, 16, 149
Alex Boncayo Brigades, 167
Alhaji Tejan Kabbah, 262
Alienation, 6, 44, 70, 74
All Party Hurriyat Conference (APHC), 161
Allied Democratic Front of Uganda (ADF), 229
Anglo-Egyptian Sudan, 272
Angola, 13, 14, 217, 220, 226
Al Qaida, 182
Arab-African dichotomy, 273
Arab Bank for Economic Development in Africa (BADEA), 212
Arabian Sea, 73
Arid and semi-arid lands (ASALs), 238
Armed Forces of the Philippines (AFP), 164
Armed Forces Revolutionary Council (AFRC), 253
Atal Behari Vajpayee, 160
Asymmetric Conflict, 30, 33

B

Balay Mindanaw Foundation, 186
Baloch, 63, 64, 67, 68, 70, 71, 72, 73, 75, 76, 77
Balochistan, 63, 65, 67, 70, 71, 73, 74, 76, 77
Baloch Students Organization (BSO), 70
Bangladesh, 157
Ban Ki-Moon, 273
Basil Criticos, 240
Bay of Bengal, 5
Belfast Agreement, 47
Belgian Congo, 217
Belgium, 28, 197, 215, 218
Bildad Kaggi, 240
Bill Clinton, 151
Bishops-Ulama Forum, 181
Blue Nile Province, 272
Britain, 37, 40, 218
British Broadcasting Corporation (BBC), 222
Buddhism, 128, 129
Burn House Squad, 254
Burundi, 13, 14, 28, 33, 200, 201, 215, 217, 220, 225, 226

C
Cambodia, 14, 101, 103, 104, 105, 106, 107, 108, 109, 110, 111, 112, 113, 114, 115, 116, 117, 119, 120, 122, 123, 124, 125, 126, 127
Carnegie Commission Report, 13
Cease Fire Agreement (CFA), 138
Center for Social Development (CSD), 121
Central African Republic, 217
Centre for Research on the Epidemiology of Disasters (CRED), 278
Chandrika Bandaranaike Kumaratunga, 134
Charles Taylor, 6
China, 24, 73, 78, 90, 105, 143, 283, 284, 285, 287
Chinkororo, 247
Citizens' Consultative Conferences, 261
Civil Defence Forces (CDF), 253
Civilian Protection Monitoring Team, 284
Coalition for International Justice (CIJ), 277
Commission for the Consolidation of Peace (CCP), 260
Common Market for Eastern and Southern Africa (COMESA), 212
Communist Party of Nepal: United Marxists Leninist (CPN-UML), 86
Communist Party of Philippines, 167
Comprehensive Agrarian Reform Law, 164
Comprehensive Peace Agreement (CPA), 96
Conakry Peace Plan, 260, 262
Congo Free State, 217
Congo-Kinshasa, 217
Congolais pour la Démocratie (RCD), 223
Congo-Léopoldville, 217
Consortium of Bangsamoro Civil Society, 181
Constitutional Review Committee, 263
Convention for the Protection of Cultural Property, 12
Convention on the Prevention and Punishment of the Crime of Genocide (1948), 12
Convention on the Rights of the Child (1989), 12
Convention on the Status of Refugees (1951), 12
Coronel Ferrer and Raquiza Report, 168
Corporal Foday Saybana Sankoh, 252
Corporate-led globalization, 172
Cory Aquino, 168, 170
Cotabato City, 184
Criminal Tribunal in Rwanda (ICTR), 118
Crude Mortality Rate (CMR), 224
Cut Hand Unit, 254

D
Dalits, 82
Demobilization and Resettlement Committee, 261
Democratic Forces for the Liberation of Rwanda (FDLR), 222
Democratic Republic of Congo (DRC), 6, 217
Democratic Socialist Republic of Sri Lanka, 128
Democratic Unionist Party, 45, 50
Dera Bugti, 68, 69, 72, 76
Destruction of Rwanda's Economy, 206
Doda, 157
Durfur, 272, 273, 274, 275, 276, 277, 278, 279, 280, 281, 283, 284, 285, 286, 287

E
East India Company, 78
Economic Community of West African States (ECOWAS), 253
Economic Community of West African States Monitoring Group (ECOMOG), 253
Economic Survey 2007-08, 151
Education Commission-International Peace Research Association (PEC-IPRA), 184
Electoral Commission of Kenya, 236
Electoral Crisis and Costs, 233
Enhanced Heavily Indebted Poor Countries (HIPC), 268
Ernest Bai Koroma, 267
EU Support Programmes, 45
Europeon Union, 41, 45, 58, 145
Ewaso Nyiro River, 244
Extraordinary Chambers in the Courts of Cambodia (ECCC), 112

F
Fidayeen, 150
First World War, 217
Foday Sankoh, 262, 263
Footpaths to Democracy, 252
France, 24, 28, 103, 218
Free Media Movement (FMM), 140
Front Nationalist and Integrationist (FNI), 229

G
Gaelic Athletic Association (GAA), 53
Gender Empowerment Measure (GEM), 107
Geneva Conventions (1949), 12
Global and All-Inclusive Agreement, 221
Global Terrorism and Local Extremism, 182
Greater Freetown, 256
Gross National Income

(GNI), 108

H

Hague Convention, 4
Heavily Indebted Poor Countries (HIPC), 268
Henry Konan Bedié, 260
High Security Zone (HSZ), 132
HIV/AIDS, 95, 202, 203, 206
Horn of Africa, 235
House of Representatives (HOR), 88
Hukbalahap or HUK, 166
Human Development Index (HDI), 107, 226
Human Rights Commission, 49
Human Rights First, 284
Human Rights Watch Report of 2003, 225
Hun Sen and Norodom Ranariddh, 112
Hutu militia, 221
Hutu Social Movement, 200

I

Ibrahim Bushra, 275
Impunity and the Khmer Rouge Tribunal, 110
India, 5, 11, 14, 60, 64, 73, 75, 77, 78, 90, 91, 93, 99, 128, 139, 143, 146, 147, 148, 149, 150, 151, 152, 153, 155, 160, 161, 162, 228, 230
Institute of Research and Dialogue for Peace (IRDP), 209
Inter-Congolese dialogue, 221
Interim Self-Governance Authority (ISGA), 133
Internally Displaced Persons (IDPs), 7
International Covenant on Civil and Political Rights (1966), 12, 135
International Criminal Court (ICC), 118, 283
International Human Rights Organizations, 134
International Humanitarian Law, 254
International Institute on Peace Education (IIPE), 184
International Peace Bureau (IPB), 30
International Peace Research Association, 184
International Rescue Committee (IRC), 224
Inter-Religious Council of Sierra Leone (IRCSL), 264
Irish Free State, 38
Issa Sesay, 265

J

J.M. Kariuki, 240
Jabidah Massacre, 177
Jan Egeland, 226
Janatha Vimukthi Pearamuna (JVP), 133
Jathika Hela Urumaya (JHU), 133
Jean Baker Miller Training Institute (JBMTI), 26

Jean Marie Seroney, 240
Jean-Marie Guehenno, 231
Jemiyah Islamiyah, 182
Jesi la Mzee, 247
Jody Williams, 281
Joint United Nations-African Union Mission, 282
Jomo Kenyatta, 237
Joseph Kabila, 221
Joseph Kasavubu, 218
Joseph-Désiré Mobutu, 219
Joseph Estrada, 164

K
Kargil, 16, 149
Kashmir, 9, 12, 14, 16, 73, 147, 148, 149, 150, 151, 153, 154, 156, 157, 158, 159, 160, 161, 162, 163
Kaya Bombo 247
Kenya, 28, 235, 236, 237, 238, 239, 240, 241, 243, 245, 246, 247, 248, 249, 250
Kenya People's Union (KPU) Party, 236
Khmer Rouge Tribunal (KRT), 102
Khmer Rouge's rule, 103
Kigali Institute of Health (KIH), 211
Kill Man No Blood Gang, 254
King Birendra, 78, 89
King Leopold II of Belgium, 218
Kofi Annan, 232, 237
Kung-fu and Dragon, 229

L
Ladakh, 154
Lake Tanganyika, 217
Laurent Kabila, 220
Laurent Nkunda, 231
Laurent-Désiré Kabila, 221
Least Developed Country (LDC), 92
Lewis A. Coser, 4
Liberation of the Congo (Alliance des Forces Démocratiques pour la Libération du Congo-Zaire, AFDL), 220
Liberation Tigers of Tamil Eelam (LTTE), 129
Line of Control (LoC), 149
Lomé Peace Agreement 259, 260, 263
Luanda Agreement, 221
Luis Moreno-Ocampo, 283
Lydia Polgreen, 276

M
Maharaja Hari Singh, 148
Mai Mai militias, 231
Mangala Samaraweera, 129
Mark Lattimer, 283
Market and Opinion Research International (MORI), 155
Marxist New People's Army (NPA), 164
Massacre of Kassika, 222
Massacre of Makobola, 222
Mateso Ninga, 229, 230
Mau Mau fighters, 239
Médecins Sans Frontiéres, 256
Memorandum of

Understanding (MoU), 129
Miano Gakuya, 244
Millennium Development Goals, 31
Mindanao Independence Movement (MIM), 176
Mindanao Peace Advocates Conference, 181
Mindanao Peoples' Caucus, 181
Mindanao Peoples' Peace Movement, 181
Mindanao Solidarity Network, 181
Minni Minnawi, 275
Minority Rights Group, 283
Model for Peace-building, 55
Moise Tshombe, 219
Moro Islamic Liberation Front (MILF), 164
Moro National Liberation Front (MNLF), 166
Mount Elgon, 240
Mouvement de Libération du Congo (MLC), 223
Mouvement National Congolais (MNC), 218
Mozambique, 157
Mt Elgon and Pokot, 247
Mt. Apo, 184
Mt. Kenya, 244
Muammar al-Gaddafi, 273
Multi Barrel Rocket Launchers (MBRL), 141
Multilateral Debt Relief Initiative (MDRI), 268
Multi-Partisan Council, 261
Mujahideens, 150
Mungiki, 247
Mwai Kibaki, 237
Myanmar, 14, 107

N

National Budget and Debt Committee, 261
National Commission for Social Action (NaCSA), 267
National Coordinating Committee for Peace (NCCP), 260
National Democratic Alliance, 160
National Democratic Front, 167
National Human Rights Commission (HRC), 267
National Peace Council (NPC), 139
National Peace Council Report, 135
National Provisional Ruling Council (NPRC), 252
National Rainbow Coalition, 236
National Unity and Reconciliation Commission (NURC), 210
Negotiation and Agreement, 45
Nepal, 5, 78, 79, 80, 81, 82, 84, 85, 86, 87, 88, 89, 90, 91, 92, 93, 94, 95, 97, 98, 99, 100
Nepal Human Development Report 2001, 89
Neutral Monitoring Group from the International

Community, 261
New People's Army (NPA), 164
New Realpolitik: Self-interest Identical with Common Interest, 24
Northern Ireland Civil Rights Movement, 39
North-South Ministerial Council, 48
Notre Dame University, 184
Nur Misuari, 177
Nyanza Province, 239

O

Office of Internal Oversight Services (OIOS), 230
Official Development Assistance (ODA), 108
Old Realpolitik: Self-interest Defined by Borders and Honour, 22
Olympic Games in Beijing, 285
Omar al-Bashir, 283
Organization of African Unity- OAU, 262
Organization of Islamic Conference (OIC), 178
Orange Order, 52
Overseas Filipino Workers (OFWs), 172

P

Pakistan, 14, 63, 64, 65, 67, 70, 71, 73, 75, 76, 77, 143, 147, 148, 149, 150, 160, 161, 162, 228, 230
Patrice Lumumba, 218
Peace Advocates Zamboanga, 181
Peace Education Commission, 184
Peace Process and Human Rights Violations, 132
Pervez Musharraf, 160
Philippines, 14, 15, 45, 164, 165, 166, 167, 169, 170, 173, 175, 180, 181, 183, 184, 186, 187, 188, 189
Philippine Overseas Employment Administration (POEA), 172
Pol Pot, 103, 104, 106, 111, 126
Poonch, 157
Post-Marcos Comprehensive Agrarian Reform Law, 164
Post-Tsunami Operational Management Structure (P-TOMS), 133
Press Emblem Campaign Report, 140
Pretoria Peace Agreement, 221
Prevention of Terrorism Act (PTA), 131
Problems of Embedding the Peace, 50
Psychosocial Consultations Service, 204

R

Raila Odinga, 237
Rajouri, 157
Rassemblement des Congolais pour la

Démocratie (RCD), 223
Rastriya Prajatantra Party (RPP), 87
Reform the Armed Forces Movement (RAM), 170
Relational-Cultural Theory (RCT), 26
Republic of Congo, 14, 217
Revolutionary United Front (RUF), 252
Rift Valley, 239
Roi des Imbeciles (King of Imbeciles), 223
Royal Nepal Army, 80
Rwanda, 13, 14, 24, 28, 29, 33, 41, 118, 122, 126, 193, 194, 196, 197, 200, 201, 203, 206, 207, 209, 210, 211, 212, 213, 214, 215, 216, 217, 220, 221, 222, 223, 225, 226, 229, 283
Rwandan Genocide, 283

S

Sabaot Land Defence Force (SLDF), 247
Salman Rushdie, 150
Satanic Verses, 150
Second World War, 157
Somalia, 157
Second Congo War, 220
Senator Benigno Aquino, 168
Settlement Transfer Fund Loan (STFL), 239
Settlement Transfer Fund Scheme Loan (STFSL), 239
Seven Political Parties Alliance, 80
Shimla Agreement, 149
Siachen Glacier, 149
Sierra Leone, 14, 157, 252, 253, 254, 256, 257, 258, 259, 260, 261, 262, 263, 265, 266, 268, 269, 270, 271
Sierra Leone Peoples Party (SLPP), 253
Sir Charles Elliot, 242
Social and Cultural Rights (1966), 12
Social Conflict and the Massacres of 1959, 199
Social Democratic and Labour Party (SDLP), 46
Social Democratic and Unionist Party and Sinn Féin, 45
Socio-Economic Forum, 261
Sovereignty versus Federal Democracy, 64
Soviet Union, 219
Soviet-brokered Tashkent Agreement, 149
Special Court for Sierra Leone (SCSL), 267
Sri Lanka, 14, 15, 73, 75, 128, 129, 130, 131, 133, 134, 135, 136, 137, 139, 140, 141, 142, 143, 144, 145, 146
Sri Lanka Air Force (SLAF), 137
Sri Lanka Freedom Party (M), 129
Sri Lanka Monitoring Mission (SLMM) report, 133
Steven Spielberg, 285

Stockholm International Peace Research Institute (SIPRI), 31, 284
Sudan Liberation Movement (SLM), 274
Sudan People's Liberation Army, 275
Sudan, 217
Sungu Sungu, 247
Swynnerton Plan, 239

T

Taliban, 247
Tamil New Tigers (TNT), 130
Tanzania, 217
Tejan Kabbah, 263
Trust Fund for the Consolidation of Peace, 261

U

Udhampur, 157
Uganda, 8, 14, 16, 199, 217, 220, 221, 223, 225, 226, 229, 230, 251
Ulster Unionist Party and Democratic Unionist Party, 45
Umma Party, 273
United National Front (UNF), 132
United Nations, 4, 12, 16, 20, 73, 87, 99, 105, 112, 116, 123, 124, 125, 134, 135, 136, 140, 144, 149, 175, 193, 199, 223, 224, 225, 226, 227, 228, 229, 230, 231, 232, 233, 237, 255, 256, 264, 265, 261, 262, 266, 273, 278, 280, 281, 282, 283, 285
United Nations Children's Fund (UNICEF), 226
United Nations Development Programme (UNDP), 4
United Nations Group of Experts Report, 119
United Nations High Commissioner for Refugees (UNHCR), 256
United Nations Human Rights Council, 281
United Nations Humanitarian Co-ordination Unit, 255
United Nations Integrated Office in Sierra Leone (UNIOSIL), 266
United Nations Mission in Sierra Leone (UNAMSIL), 265
United Nations Office for the Coordination of Humanitarian Affairs (UNOCHA), 256
United Nations Peace-building Fund, 266
United Nations Peace-keeping Force (UNPKF), 228
United Nations Security Council, 281
United Nations Special Rapporteur on Violence, 226
United Nations Transitional Authority in Cambodia (UNTAC), 105
United Nations' Millennium

Project (2005), 31
United Nations-African Union Mission in Durfur (UNAMID), 281
Universal Declaration of Human Rights, 25
Uppasala Conflict Data Project, 4

V

Vienna Declaration and Programme of Action (1993), 9
Vietnam, 157
Village Development Committee (VDC), 93
Virunga National Park, 225

W

Waheed Arshad, 230
Western Upper Nile Region, 284
World Bank, 16, 100, 106, 107, 239, 246, 251, 268
World Conference on Human Rights, 9
World Council for Curriculum and Instruction (WCCI), 184
World Health Organization, 226
World Wide Fund, 225

Y

Yugoslavia, 157

Z

Zaghawa-backed Justice and Equality Movement (JEM), 274
Zaire, 217, 220, 233
Zambia, 217
Zia-ul-Haq, 71